THE ULTIMATE COOK'S MANUAL

For Jérôme

MARIANNE MAGNIER-MORENO
COOKING AND INSTRUCTIONS

THE ULTIMATE COOK'S MANUAL

BECOME THE CHEF YOU HAVE ALWAYS WANTED TO BE

A STEP-BY-STEP GUIDE TO MASTERING THE FUNDAMENTALS OF GOOD COOKING

PHOTOGRAPHY BY PIERRE JAVELLE
ILLUSTRATIONS BY YANNIS VAROUTSIKOS
SCIENTIFIC EXPLANATIONS BY ANNE CAZOR

hardie grant books

CONTENTS

HOW TO USE THIS BOOK

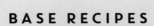

BASE RECIPES

Discover the basic recipes needed for good cooking,
categorised into stocks, sauces, emulsions, mixtures, pastries, ingredients
and cooking methods. For each base recipe there is a diagram and
explanation of the specific preparation techniques required.

RECIPES

Put the base recipes to work to make entrées, main dishes and side dishes. Each
recipe includes cross-references to the base recipes, a diagram for understanding
the concept of the dish and step-by-step photos to achieve each stage of the recipe.

ILLUSTRATED GLOSSARY

Learn and enrich your knowledge with further information on the
use of products and illustrations of the main techniques.

CHAPTER 1
BASE RECIPES

WHITE
POULTRY STOCK

Understand

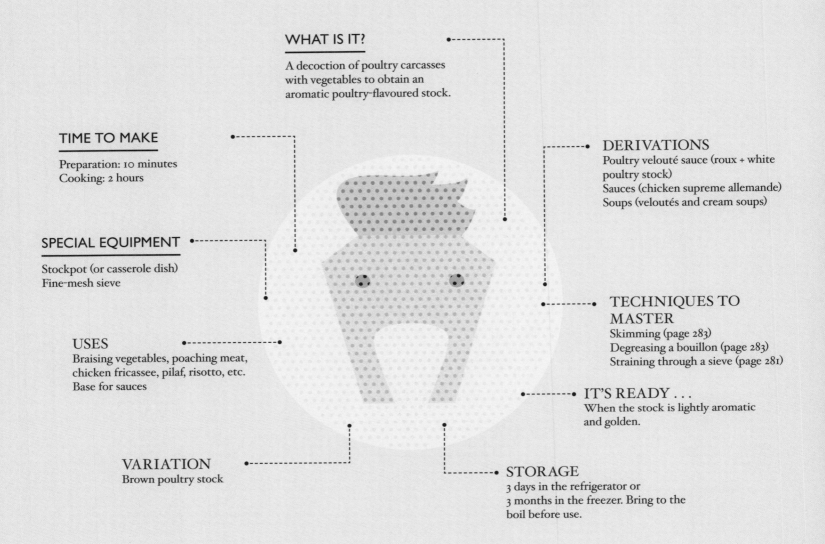

WHAT IS IT?

A decoction of poultry carcasses
with vegetables to obtain an
aromatic poultry-flavoured stock.

TIME TO MAKE

Preparation: 10 minutes
Cooking: 2 hours

SPECIAL EQUIPMENT

Stockpot (or casserole dish)
Fine-mesh sieve

USES

Braising vegetables, poaching meat,
chicken fricassee, pilaf, risotto, etc.
Base for sauces

VARIATION

Brown poultry stock

DERIVATIONS

Poultry velouté sauce (roux + white
poultry stock)
Sauces (chicken supreme allemande)
Soups (veloutés and cream soups)

**TECHNIQUES TO
MASTER**

Skimming (page 283)
Degreasing a bouillon (page 283)
Straining through a sieve (page 281)

IT'S READY . . .

When the stock is lightly aromatic
and golden.

STORAGE

3 days in the refrigerator or
3 months in the freezer. Bring to the
boil before use.

WHY 'WHITE' STOCK?

*Unlike 'brown' stock, the bones aren't
browned before being covered with water.
The brown molecules that result from the
Maillard reactions (page 282) are therefore
absent and the stock isn't dark.*

WHAT IS DECOCTION?

*A method to extract the components of the
ingredients through boiling. The product is
poached in cold water then brought to the
boil, resulting in aromatic broths.*

**WHAT GIVES A STOCK ITS
FLAVOUR?**

*During cooking, the proteins are broken
down in the water into amino acids, which
provide flavour. The fat extracted from
the meat also captures and enriches the
aromatic notes that form during cooking.*

MAKES 2 LITRES (8 CUPS)

1.5 kg poultry carcasses or chicken wings
½ onion
1 carrot
1 celery stalk
1 leek
1 thyme sprig
1 bay leaf
½ teaspoon black peppercorns

1 Remove any fatty or bloody parts from the poultry carcasses. Peel, trim and wash the vegetables.

2 Put the carcasses in a stockpot and cover with 2.5 litres (10 cups) cold water. Bring to the boil, then skim off any foam.

3 Add the vegetables, thyme, bay leaf and peppercorns. Cook at a gentle simmer for 2 hours, skimming off any foam and degreasing from time to time.

4 Strain the stock through a fine-mesh sieve.

BROWN
VEAL STOCK

Understand

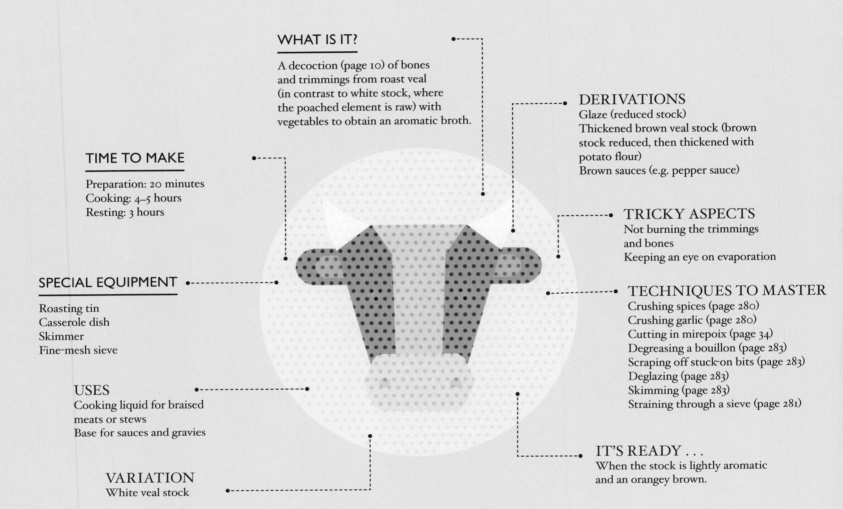

WHAT IS IT?

A decoction (page 10) of bones and trimmings from roast veal (in contrast to white stock, where the poached element is raw) with vegetables to obtain an aromatic broth.

DERIVATIONS

Glaze (reduced stock)
Thickened brown veal stock (brown stock reduced, then thickened with potato flour)
Brown sauces (e.g. pepper sauce)

TIME TO MAKE

Preparation: 20 minutes
Cooking: 4–5 hours
Resting: 3 hours

TRICKY ASPECTS

Not burning the trimmings and bones
Keeping an eye on evaporation

SPECIAL EQUIPMENT

Roasting tin
Casserole dish
Skimmer
Fine-mesh sieve

TECHNIQUES TO MASTER

Crushing spices (page 280)
Crushing garlic (page 280)
Cutting in mirepoix (page 34)
Degreasing a bouillon (page 283)
Scraping off stuck-on bits (page 283)
Deglazing (page 283)
Skimming (page 283)
Straining through a sieve (page 281)

USES

Cooking liquid for braised meats or stews
Base for sauces and gravies

IT'S READY . . .

When the stock is lightly aromatic and an orangey brown.

VARIATION

White veal stock

WHY 'BROWN' STOCK?

The stock is brown due to the colouring of the meat at the beginning of cooking, before adding water.

WHY BROWN THE MEAT?

In order to provide aromatic notes. The browning results from the chemical process called the Maillard reactions (page 282).

WHY CHOP THE VEGETABLES IN MIREPOIX?

The bigger the pieces, the longer it takes to extract the aromatic elements from the

vegetables. Because the stock is cooked for a long time, it's fine for the vegetables to be chopped in larger chunks.

WHY MUST THE BONES BE COVERED WITH WATER THROUGHOUT COOKING?

The extraction of the components of the bones (mainly collagen) occurs only in water. The extracted collagen is transformed into gelatine, which gives cold stock its jellyish consistency.

TIP

Quick brown veal stock: brown the trimmings in the stockpot in a little butter, then remove from the pot and sweat the vegetables in the same pot. Add the tomato paste, cook for 1–2 minutes, then deglaze with a little water, scraping any stuck-on bits off the bottom, return the trimmings to the pot and cover with water. Reduce to a very low simmer until you obtain the desired quantity of liquid (30 minutes to 1 hour). Strain through a sieve.

STORAGE

3 days in the refrigerator, 3 months in the freezer. Bring to the boil before use.

MAKES 1.5 LITRES (6 CUPS)

1.5 kg veal trimmings and bones (veal brisket with cut bones), cut into 10 cm pieces
2 garlic cloves
3 carrots
1 large onion
60 g (¼ cup) tomato paste (concentrated purée)
1 teaspoon black peppercorns
2 bay leaves

1 Preheat the oven to 220°C. Arrange the pieces of veal in a roasting tin so that they don't overlap. Roast for about 45 minutes, or until well browned. Peel and crush the garlic cloves. Peel and chop the carrots and onion in mirepoix. Crack the peppercorns under the base of a saucepan.

2 Add the tomato paste to the roasting tin and mix. Add the carrot, onion and garlic but don't mix. Roast for 10 minutes then remove the tin from the oven. Reduce the oven temperature to 100°C.

3 Using a skimmer or slotted spoon, transfer the veal pieces and vegetables to a casserole dish, so that they are touching, in two layers.

4 Degrease the tin. Deglaze the tin with 200 ml boiling water. Scrape any stuck-on bits off the bottom and pour it all into the casserole dish.

5 Pour in enough water to cover the meat by 5–10 cm. Heat to a simmer, then carefully skim and degrease. Add the pepper and the bay leaves. Transfer to the oven, with the lid off, for 3–4 hours. Check halfway through cooking that the bones are still covered with water, adding more water if necessary.

6 Skim off any fat. Strain through a fine-mesh sieve, without pushing. Allow to cool, then degrease.

FISH STOCK

Understand

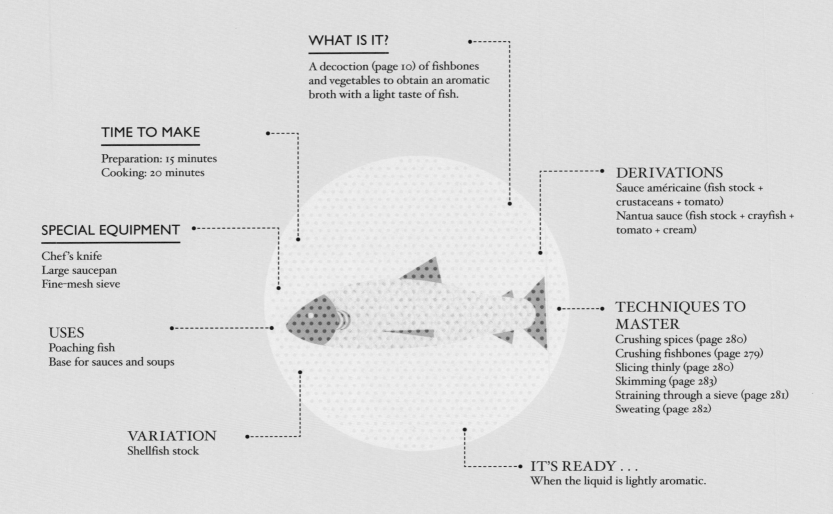

WHAT IS IT?

A decoction (page 10) of fishbones and vegetables to obtain an aromatic broth with a light taste of fish.

TIME TO MAKE

Preparation: 15 minutes
Cooking: 20 minutes

SPECIAL EQUIPMENT

Chef's knife
Large saucepan
Fine-mesh sieve

USES

Poaching fish
Base for sauces and soups

VARIATION

Shellfish stock

DERIVATIONS

Sauce américaine (fish stock + crustaceans + tomato)
Nantua sauce (fish stock + crayfish + tomato + cream)

TECHNIQUES TO MASTER

Crushing spices (page 280)
Crushing fishbones (page 279)
Slicing thinly (page 280)
Skimming (page 283)
Straining through a sieve (page 281)
Sweating (page 282)

IT'S READY . . .

When the liquid is lightly aromatic.

WHY A SHORT COOKING TIME (LESS THAN 20 MINUTES)?

Lengthening the cooking time causes chemical reactions that lead to the formation of compounds which are detrimental to the flavour of the stock.

TIPS

Reducing the quantity of liquid intensifies the stock (but make sure the bones and vegetables are constantly covered).
Don't use more than 1.1 litres of liquid, or the stock will take too long to reduce and won't taste as good.

STORAGE

2 days in the refrigerator
or 1 month in the freezer.

MAKES 1 LITRE (4 CUPS)

1 French shallot
1 small onion
600 g fishbones from a thin fish (sole, whiting, john dory, hake, etc.)
40 g butter
100 ml white wine or Noilly Prat (dry vermouth)
1 thyme sprig
1 bay leaf
5 black peppercorns

1 Crush the peppercorns. Peel and thinly slice the shallot and onion. Remove any remaining pieces of blood from the fishbones and crush the bones roughly using a chef's knife.

2 Melt the butter in a large saucepan over medium heat. Sweat the shallot and onion for 1–2 minutes.

3 Add the fishbones and allow them to sweat without colouring. Pour in 1 litre (4 cups) water and the wine. Add the thyme and bay leaf. Bring to the boil, then simmer for 20 minutes. Skim off any foam. Add the crushed peppercorns 5 minutes before the end of the cooking time.

4 Strain through a sieve without pressing.

COURT BOUILLON

Understand

WATER +
VINEGAR

CARROT

AROMATIC
HERBS

ONION

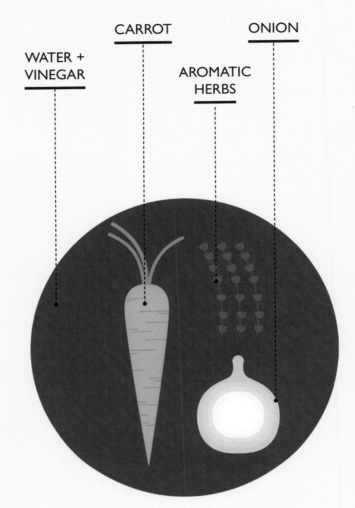

WHAT IS IT?
An aromatic broth with vinegar, used for poaching large ingredients in a reduced volume of liquid (*court* in French means 'short').

TIME TO MAKE
Preparation: 15 minutes
Cooking: 20 minutes
Resting: 1 hour

USES
Poaching fish (whole or in pieces) and large crustaceans

DERIVATION
Nage: court bouillon in which the vegetables are carefully cut; sometimes reduced then butter whisked in.

TRICKY ASPECT
Cutting the vegetables: not too large, so they still flavour the court bouillon, but not too fine, so they don't dominate

TECHNIQUE TO MASTER
Skimming (page 283)

TIP
Don't add vinegar when poaching salmon or trout: it discolours the flesh.

IT'S READY . . .
When the court bouillon is cold, aromatic and slightly acidic.

STORAGE
2 days in the refrigerator.

WHY FINELY CHOP THE VEGETABLES?

The more finely the vegetables are chopped, the greater the surface area they have. Extraction of the aromatic components is therefore greater when the pieces are small. Finely chopping the vegetables for a court bouillon gives it a stronger taste.

WHAT DOES THE VINEGAR DO?

The vinegar (or the wine) acidifies the court bouillon. This acidity improves the coagulation of the proteins and thus the texture of the fish poached in it.

WHY MUST COURT BOUILLON BE USED COLD?

The ingredients are first submerged, then the liquid is heated. Starting from cold in this way allows the fish to firm up first due to the acidity, then more with the elevation in temperature. These two phases of firming up improve the texture of the fish and prevent overcooking.

MAKES 1 LITRE (4 CUPS)

1 carrot
2½ tablespoons vinegar or 100 ml white wine
20 g flat-leaf (Italian) parsley
3 thyme sprigs
1 bay leaf
½ teaspoon black peppercorns
15 g coarse salt
1 onion

1 Peel, wash and cut the carrot into 3–4 mm thick slices.

2 Bring 1 litre water and the vinegar or wine to the boil in a saucepan with the carrot, parsley, thyme, bay leaf, peppercorns and salt. Skim off any foam, then simmer for 15 minutes.

3 Peel, wash and cut the onion into 3–4 mm thick slices. Add to the pan and cook for a further 5 minutes.

4 Allow the court bouillon to cool for 1 hour (without straining).

ROUX

Understand

WHITE ROUX BROWN ROUX BLOND ROUX

WHAT IS IT?

A one-to-one mixture of flour and butter, cooked for a short or longer time (white to blond to brown roux) to obtain a smooth preparation used for thickening.

TIME TO MAKE

Preparation: 5 minutes
Cooking: 5 minutes

SPECIAL EQUIPMENT

Whisk
Saucepan large enough to contain the liquid to be thickened

USES

Thickening a soup or sauce in simmered dishes. Gradually pour the liquid to be thickened into the roux, whisking constantly. Bring to the boil, then let it cook for 1–2 minutes while whisking.

DERIVATIONS

Béchamel sauce (page 22)
Velouté sauce (page 20)

TRICKY ASPECT

Cooking: stop cooking as soon as you achieve the desired colour; for a white roux, don't stop cooking too soon or the taste of the flour will remain in the final dish

IT'S READY . . .

When the mixture is frothy and off-white.

WHY MUST THE ROUX BE COOKED LONG ENOUGH?

To break down the amylose molecules contained in the starch grains of the flour. This removes their floury taste.

HOW DOES THE ROUX COLOUR?

The flour contains proteins and sugars. With heat, the proteins and the sugars go through a process known as the Maillard reactions (page 282). These reactions provide both colouration and aromatic components.

TIP

For a very white roux, add the flour as soon as the butter has melted, otherwise the butter will colour.

MAKING ROUX WITH MEAT JUICES

For some recipes that contain meat in a sauce, sprinkle flour over the meat and roast it in the oven for a few minutes to colour; the cooking fats and the flour are then mixed to make a blond roux (or a brown roux, depending on the roasting time).

THICKENS 1 LITRE (4 CUPS) LIQUID

40–70 g butter
40–70 g plain (all-purpose) flour

The one-to-one mixture is varied depending on the desired thickness of the final liquid: use 40 g of each for a soup and 70 g for béchamel sauce.

1 WHITE ROUX

Cut the butter into pieces and melt them in a saucepan over low heat.

Add the flour as soon as the butter has melted.

Whisk until the mixture is smooth.

Allow to cook over low heat, whisking constantly, until the mixture becomes frothy.

2 BLOND ROUX

Continue cooking over low heat until the mixture becomes lightly golden.

3 BROWN ROUX

Continue cooking until the preparation browns slightly.

VELOUTÉ SAUCE

Understand

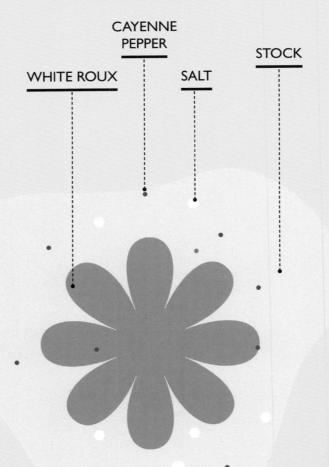

WHITE ROUX

CAYENNE PEPPER

SALT

STOCK

WHAT IS IT?

A sauce obtained by mixing a white roux with a white stock or fish stock.

TIME TO MAKE

Preparation: 5 minutes
Cooking: 10 minutes

SPECIAL EQUIPMENT

Whisk
Large saucepan

USES

Base for sauces or soups
It provides cohesion to reduced sauces

DERIVATIONS

Supreme sauce (velouté sauce + cream)
Ivoire sauce (velouté sauce + cream + reduced veal stock)
Cream of asparagus soup, creamy cauliflower soup, etc. (velouté sauce + cream + vegetables)
Sauce for blanquette of veal (velouté sauce + cream + egg yolk)

WHY DO LUMPS FORM SOMETIMES?

The starch in flour absorbs water and swells up in the heat; in other words it gelatinises. When we add water to flour, the flour clumps into 'packets'. The starch at the periphery of these packets absorbs the water and swells up. The water doesn't reach far enough to hydrate the centre of the packet, and these form partially gelatinised lumps.

TIP

Whisk vigorously as soon as you add the liquid, to avoid lumps forming.

TRICKY ASPECT

Avoiding lumps

TECHNIQUE TO MASTER

Reducing a sauce (page 283)

IT'S READY . . .

When the stock has thickened and its flavours are a little concentrated.

STORAGE

1 hour covered in a bain-marie or 3 days in the refrigerator.

MAKES I LITRE (4 CUPS)

WHITE ROUX

70 g butter
70 g plain (all-purpose) flour

WHITE STOCK OR FISH STOCK

1 litre (4 cups) white poultry stock
(page 10) or fish stock (page 14)

SEASONING

1 teaspoon salt
pinch of cayenne pepper

1 Prepare the white roux: cut the butter into pieces and melt in a large saucepan over low heat. Add the flour as soon as the butter has melted. Whisk until the mixture is smooth. Cook over low heat, whisking constantly, until the mixture turns pale and becomes frothy.

2 Pour the white stock or fish stock into the roux in one go and whisk immediately.

3 Bring to the boil and continue to whisk until the liquid thickens.

4 Reduce the sauce by simmering for about 10 minutes, whisking from time to time. Season with the salt and cayenne pepper.

BÉCHAMEL SAUCE

Understand

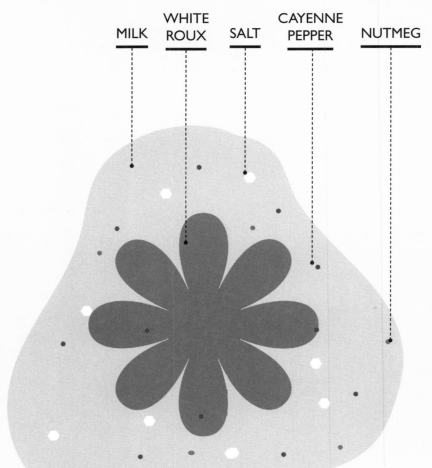

MILK   WHITE ROUX   SALT   CAYENNE PEPPER   NUTMEG

WHAT IS IT?

A thick sauce obtained by mixing a white roux with boiling milk.

TIME TO MAKE

Preparation: 5 minutes

SPECIAL EQUIPMENT

Whisk
Large saucepan

USES

Soufflés (page 120)
Vegetable gratins
Lasagnes

DERIVATIONS

Mornay sauce (béchamel sauce + egg yolk + gruyère)
Cream sauce (béchamel sauce made with a mixture of milk + cream + lemon juice)

TRICKY ASPECT

Cooking (avoiding lumps)

IT'S READY . . .

When the mixture has thickened well.

WHY DOES THE ROUX THICKEN THE MILK?

When the roux is heated with milk, the starch in the flour swells up, which triggers a first thickening phase. By continuing to heat the mixture, the starch molecules break down and release two constituent molecules – amylose and amylopectin – which bind the milk together and continue to thicken the mixture.

WHY NOT ADD THE MILK STRAIGHT AWAY?

Coating the flour in butter first helps to limit lumps because the butter separates the flour granules preventing them clumping together.

STORAGE

Cover with plastic wrap and set aside in a bain-marie.

TIPS

Whisk vigorously as soon as you add the liquid, to avoid lumps forming.
If the béchamel sauce is not perfectly smooth at the end of cooking, strain through a sieve.

MAKES 1 LITRE (4 CUPS)

WHITE ROUX

70 g butter
70 g plain (all-purpose) flour

LIQUID

1 litre (4 cups) milk

SEASONING

pinch of cayenne pepper
pinch of freshly grated nutmeg
1 teaspoon salt

1   Prepare the white roux: cut the butter into pieces and melt in a large saucepan over low heat. Add the flour as soon as the butter has melted. Whisk until the mixture is smooth. Cook over low heat, whisking constantly, until the mixture turns pale and becomes frothy.

2   Pour the milk into the roux in one go and whisk immediately.

3   Bring to the boil and continue to whisk until the liquid thickens.

4   Simmer while whisking continuously for 1–2 minutes. Season with the cayenne pepper, nutmeg and salt.

TOMATO SAUCE

Understand

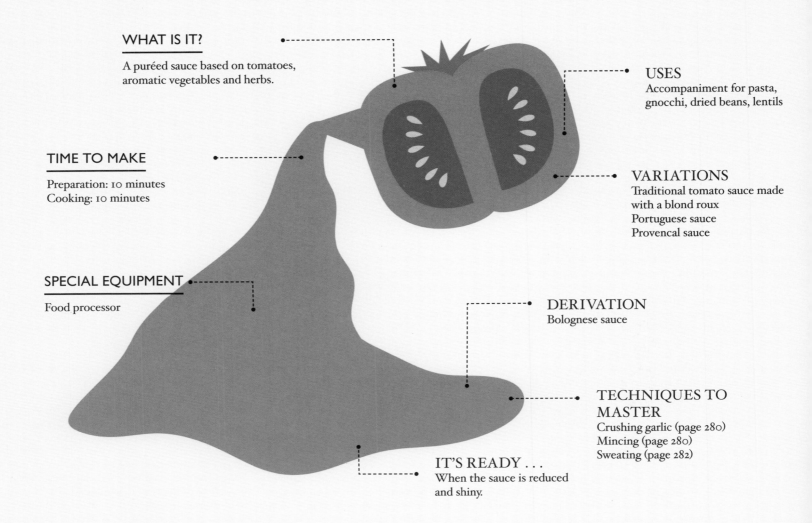

WHAT IS IT?

A puréed sauce based on tomatoes, aromatic vegetables and herbs.

TIME TO MAKE

Preparation: 10 minutes
Cooking: 10 minutes

SPECIAL EQUIPMENT

Food processor

USES
Accompaniment for pasta, gnocchi, dried beans, lentils

VARIATIONS
Traditional tomato sauce made with a blond roux
Portuguese sauce
Provencal sauce

DERIVATION
Bolognese sauce

TECHNIQUES TO MASTER
Crushing garlic (page 280)
Mincing (page 280)
Sweating (page 282)

IT'S READY . . .
When the sauce is reduced and shiny.

WHY DOES THE COOKED SAUCE TAKE ON A SWEET TASTE?
During cooking, the water evaporates enabling the sugars in the sauce to become concentrated.

STORAGE
2 days in the refrigerator or 3 months in the freezer.

MAKES 780 ML

1 garlic clove
1 onion
25 g butter
½ teaspoon dried oregano
½ teaspoon salt
800 g tin chopped tomatoes
1 teaspoon sugar
1½ tablespoons olive oil
freshly ground black pepper (3 grinds)

1   Peel and crush the garlic. Peel and mince the onion. Melt the butter in a medium saucepan over medium heat. Add the onion, salt and oregano crushed between your fingers. Sweat the onion until it colours.

2   Add the crushed garlic and cook for about 30 seconds, until it becomes aromatic. Add the tomatoes and sugar. Bring to the boil, then simmer for about 10 minutes or until thickened.

3   Remove from the heat and add the olive oil and pepper. Purée in a food processor, then adjust the seasoning.

MAYONNAISE

Understand

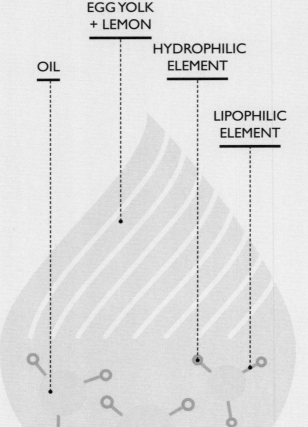

EGG YOLK
+ LEMON

HYDROPHILIC
ELEMENT

OIL

LIPOPHILIC
ELEMENT

WHAT IS IT?

A cold emulsion of oil in egg yolk and lemon juice.

TIME TO MAKE

Preparation: 10 minutes

SPECIAL EQUIPMENT

Whisk
Round- or flat-bottomed bowl

USES

Accompaniment for cold preparations (meat, fish, crustaceans, eggs, vegetables)
Dressing a salad

DERIVATIONS

Tartare sauce (mayonnaise + capers + cornichons + parsley + chervil + tarragon)
Cocktail sauce (mayonnaise + tomato sauce (ketchup) + cognac + Worcestershire sauce + Tabasco sauce)

TRICKY ASPECT
Incorporating the oil

TIP
Season the egg yolk first, to avoid traces of salt at the end.

IT'S READY . . .
When the mayonnaise is creamy and firm enough for the whisk to leave a trace.

STORAGE
No more than 1 day in the refrigerator, covered with plastic wrap.

WHAT IS AN EMULSION?

A mixture of two ingredients that are in principle non-miscible (do not mix). In mayonnaise, oil is combined with water (contained in the egg yolk and lemon juice).

HOW DOES AN EMULSION FORM?

The proteins in the egg yolk play the role of a surfactant, consisting of a hydrophilic part (attracted by the water in the egg yolk and lemon juice) and a lipophilic part (attracted by the fat content of the oil). They stabilise the oil in the water to form an emulsion.

WHY ADD THE OIL GRADUALLY?

The mayonnaise is an emulsion of oil in water. When oil is added gradually, it forms droplets which are incorporated into the water.

WHY DOES THE MAYONNAISE SOMETIMES SPLIT?

This happens when the water emulsifies in the oil rather than the other way around. This is usually because the oil has been added too quickly, the bowl is too big, or the whisking is ineffectual.

THE IMPORTANCE OF WHISKING

Whisking helps to form a stable mayonnaise by creating more droplets of oil that bind the mixture together.

SALVAGING MAYONNAISE
The mayonnaise is too firm (using an electric mixer at too high a speed): thin it down by mixing in a little water.
The ingredients are too cold: add a few drops of warm water.
There's too much oil compared to egg yolk: add another egg yolk.

Learn

MAKES 200 G

1 tablespoon lemon juice
½ teaspoon salt
¼ teaspoon freshly ground black pepper
1 egg yolk
180 ml (¾ cup) sunflower or peanut oil

1 Whisk 1 tablespoon water, the lemon juice, salt, pepper and egg yolk in a round- or flat-bottomed bowl for 1 minute.

2 Pour in a few drops of the oil, whisking constantly.

3 Continue to add the oil, in a thin stream, still whisking constantly. After you've added one-third of the oil, add the rest a little more quickly.

4 Whisk to thicken the mayonnaise. Cover the surface with plastic wrap and refrigerate.

WITH AN ELECTRIC MIXER

Follow step 1, then use a stand mixer with the whisk attachment, a hand-held blender or a food processor with the blade attachment to make the mayonnaise emulsion while adding the oil.

BEURRE BLANC

Understand

FRENCH
SHALLOT   VINEGAR

BUTTER   WHITE WINE

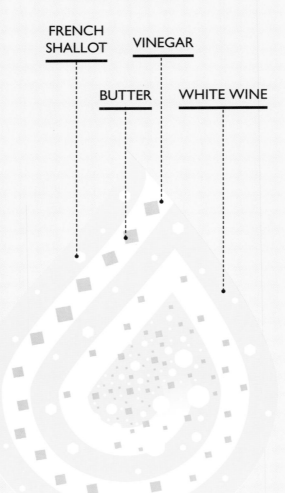

WHAT IS IT?

A hot emulsion of butter in a
reduction of vinegar and white
wine, flavoured with French shallot.

TIME TO MAKE

Preparation: 15 minutes
Cooking: 5 minutes

SPECIAL EQUIPMENT

Fine-mesh sieve

USES
Accompaniment for grilled or
poached fish

VARIATION
Beurre nantais: beurre blanc with
French shallots (not strained)

TRICKY ASPECTS
Incorporating the cold pieces of
butter
Cooking the butter gently

TECHNIQUES TO
MASTER
Pushing through a sieve (page 281)
Straining through a sieve (page 281)
Reducing a sauce (page 283)
Chopping finely (page 280)

WHAT HAPPENS WHEN THE
BUTTER IS INCORPORATED?

*Mixing fats into the vinegar and wine base
gives an oil-in-water emulsion: the butter
is incorporated into the vinegar and warm
wine in the form of droplets. This emulsion
has a different texture from a classic butter
sauce: beurre blanc is 'half-hard, half-
melted'.*

WHY MUST THE VINEGAR AND
WINE MIXTURE BE REDUCED?

*If the base is too liquid, the sauce will be
too thin.*

WHY ADD THE BUTTER
GRADUALLY?

*If the butter is added too quickly, the oil-in-
water emulsion risks becoming a water-in-
oil emulsion and the sauce may split.*

WHY MUST BEURRE BLANC BE
USED IMMEDIATELY?

*Beurre blanc is an unstable emulsion. If it
is reheated, it may debstabilise and split.*

TIP
To help form the emulsion, add 1 tablespoon
crème fraîche after reducing the white wine
and vinegar, then reduce once more.

IT'S READY . . .
When the sauce is smooth and thick but
fluid.

STORAGE
Use quickly. Cover and keep warm (over very
low heat, at no more than 50°C).

Learn

MAKES 270 G

20 g French shallots
2½ tablespoons white wine
(preferably a Muscadet)
2½ tablespoons white wine vinegar
(or sherry vinegar)
250 g cold butter, cut into large dice

1 Peel and mince the French shallots. Put them in a medium saucepan with the white wine and vinegar.

2 Reduce, uncovered, for 2–3 minutes, until only a tablespoon of the liquid remains.

3 Press the mixture through a fine-mesh sieve and return the liquid to the saucepan. Discard the shallot.

4 Over medium heat, add one or two pieces of the butter and swirl the saucepan to move the butter around, or whisk it, until the butter is almost melted.

5 Add another one or two pieces of butter and stir until melted. Continue in this way until all the butter has been incorporated.

HOLLANDAISE SAUCE

Understand

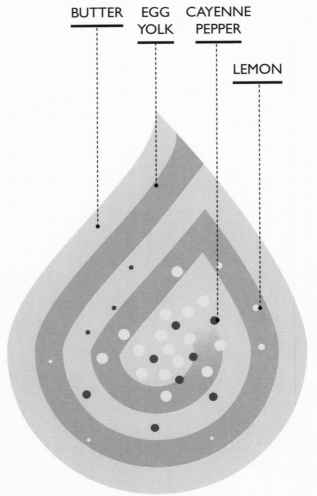

BUTTER   EGG YOLK   CAYENNE PEPPER

LEMON

WHAT IS IT?

Hot emulsion of butter in a sabayon (egg yolks + water), with lemon juice added.

TIME TO MAKE

Preparation: 15 minutes

SPECIAL EQUIPMENT

Sauteuse pan (saucepan with flared sides)
Whisk
Thermometer

USES

Accompaniment for fish, eggs (eggs benedict) and poached vegetables

DERIVATIONS

Mousseline sauce (hollandaise sauce + whipped cream)
Maltese sauce (hollandaise sauce + orange zest and juice)
Mustard sauce (hollandaise sauce + mustard)

TRICKY ASPECT

The sabayon

IT'S READY . . .

When the sauce resembles a runny mayonnaise.

STORAGE

No more than 1 hour, covered. Reheat over very low heat while whisking.

WHY ADD THE BUTTER GRADUALLY?

This helps small drops of fat to link easily and form a stable emulsion that doesn't split.

WHY MUST THE SABAYON NOT GO ABOVE 60°C?

The eggs contain proteins that coagulate above 60°C. Beyond this temperature, the sauce will take on a grainy texture.

WHY ADD THE CLARIFIED BUTTER WHEN LUKEWARM?

If the butter is cold, it can't be added gradually, and so the emulsion won't form easily. If the butter is too hot, the egg proteins will coagulate.

WHY DOES THE SAUCE SOMETIMES SPLIT?

Either through excessive coagulation of the egg yolks (cooking temperature too high) or through the water–fat emulsion breaking down.

SALVAGING THE SAUCE

The sauce is too thick: loosen with a little cold water.
The sauce splits from the beginning: remix it with a little warm water and incorporate the butter slowly.

MAKES 350 G

250 g clarified butter (page 51)
½ lemon
4 egg yolks
1 teaspoon salt
pinch of cayenne pepper

1 Keep the clarified butter lukewarm (about 40°C). Squeeze the lemon half.

2 In a saucepan, whisk the egg yolks with 25 ml water and the salt. Set over low heat and whisk constantly to make a sabayon. It is ready when the temperature reaches about 60°C and the mixture is creamy and thick.

3 Remove from the heat and let the mixture cool slightly. Gradually add the lukewarm clarified butter while whisking constantly (as for a mayonnaise).

4 Add the lemon juice and cayenne pepper while still whisking. Adjust the seasoning, to taste.

BÉARNAISE SAUCE

Understand

VINEGAR +
WHITE WINE

BUTTER +
EGG YOLK

TARRAGON

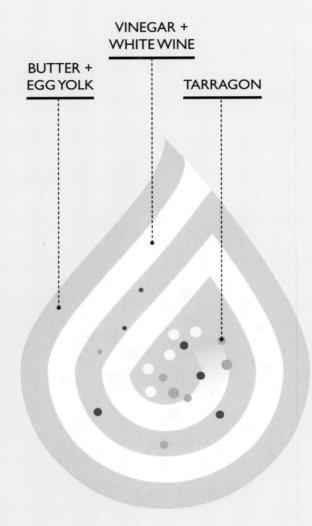

WHAT IS IT?

A hot emulsion of butter and egg yolks in a reduction of vinegar and white wine, flavoured with French shallots, chervil and tarragon.

TIME TO MAKE

Preparation: 25 minutes

SPECIAL EQUIPMENT

Whisk

USES
Accompaniment for meats and grilled (broiled) fish

VARIATIONS
Paloise sauce (replace the tarragon with mint)
Choron sauce (replace the tarragon and the chervil with a reduced puréed tomato sauce, page 24)

TRICKY ASPECT
Making the hot sabayon (adding the egg yolks to the reduction)

TECHNIQUES TO MASTER
Chopping finely (page 280)
Mincing (page 280)
Crushing spices (page 280)
Reducing a sauce (page 283)
Straining through a sieve (page 281)

IT'S READY . . .
When the sauce is creamy and light.

TIP
Use a small saucepan, otherwise the egg yolks will coagulate too quickly without gaining volume.

WHY ADD THE BUTTER GRADUALLY?
Béarnaise sauce resembles a mayonnaise made with butter rather than oil. By adding the butter and egg a little at a time and by whisking constantly, small fat bubbles form containing egg (the proteins that stabilise the emulsion) and mostly water (from the vinegar and wine). If butter is added too quickly, the fat bubbles won't form and the emulsion will be reversed – that is, bubbles of water will form in the butter.

SALVAGING THE SAUCE
The sauce is too thick: loosen it with a little cold water.
The sauce splits from the beginning: remix it with a little warm water and incorporate the butter slowly.

STORAGE
No more than 1 hour, covered. Reheat over very low heat while whisking.

Learn

MAKES 400 G

250 g clarified butter (page 51)
3 tarragon sprigs
4 chervil sprigs
2 French shallots
1 teaspoon black peppercorns
2 tablespoons white wine
2 tablespoons red wine vinegar
4 egg yolks
½ teaspoon salt

1 Keep the clarified butter lukewarm (about 40°C). Wash, dry, pick and finely chop the tarragon and chervil leaves. Peel and mince the shallots. Crack the peppercorns.

2 In a small saucepan, bring the white wine and vinegar to the boil with half the tarragon and chervil, the shallots and the crushed peppercorns. Reduce the mixture by simmering for 2–3 minutes, until only 4 tablespoons of liquid remain. Set aside to cool a little.

3 Add the egg yolks and salt and whisk to form an emulsion. Set over low heat and whisk constantly to make a sabayon. It is ready when the mixture is creamy and thick.

4 Remove from the heat and let the mixture cool slightly. Gradually add the lukewarm clarified butter while whisking constantly.

5 Stir in the remaining chopped herbs, then taste and adjust the seasoning if necessary.

AROMATIC
FLAVOURINGS

Understand

1 BOUQUET GARNI

WHAT IS IT?

A mixture of aromatics tied together, used to flavour a liquid preparation (broth, stew, etc.).

SPECIAL EQUIPMENT

Kitchen string

USES

Aromatic base for stocks, sauces, meats, offal and stuffed poultry
Cooking dried pulses

VARIATION

Bouquet garni for white stock: white part of a leek, thyme, bay leaf and parsley stems

INSTRUCTIONS

For 1.5–2 litres (6–8 cups) water
10 parsley stems
2 thyme sprigs
1 bay leaf

Wash all the ingredients. Group them into a bouquet and hold together firmly by winding string two or three times around the top (leaving about 20 cm of string free), then wind it around the bottom and finally around the middle. Tie in a knot (this technique stops the bouquet falling apart during cooking).

2 MIREPOIX

WHAT IS IT?

Aromatic base consisting of raw carrots and onions, cut into pieces of 1 cm (short cooking time) to 1.5 cm (long cooking time). The mirepoix is often retained as part of the dish.

USES

Sauce bases and sauces (such as for boeuf bourguignon)
Cooking dried pulses (for purées and soups)

VARIATIONS

Traditional mirepoix: add an equal weight of streaky bacon cut into 1–1.5 cm dice
Matignon (garniture of thinly sliced onions and carrots, strained before serving)

INSTRUCTIONS

Equal quantities of carrot and onion

Peel the carrot and the onion. Cut the carrot into 6 cm lengths and trim the ends. Cut into even lengthways slices, about 1 cm thick. Put the slices on top of each other then cut into even batons, 1 cm thick. Bring the batons together, then cut them into 1 cm cubes. Cut the onion in half lengthways. Lay the halves flat then slice them lengthways every 1 cm, stopping before the root (bottom) end. Slice crossways to obtain 1 cm dice.

1

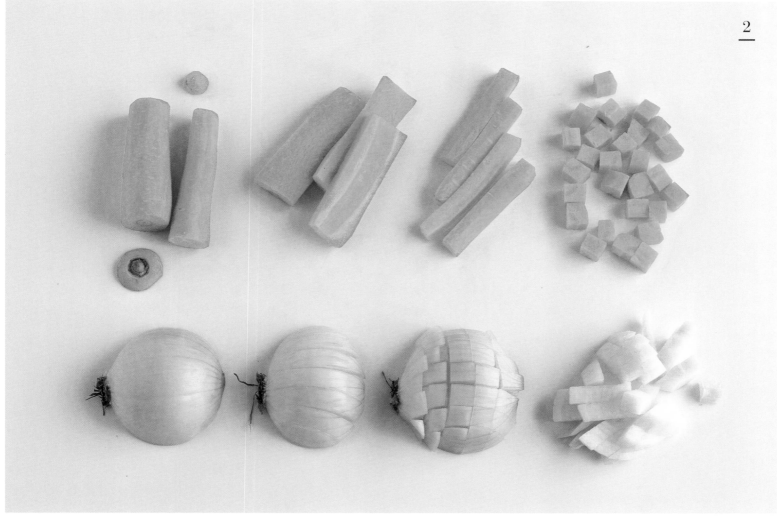

2

35

CUTTING
VEGETABLES

Understand

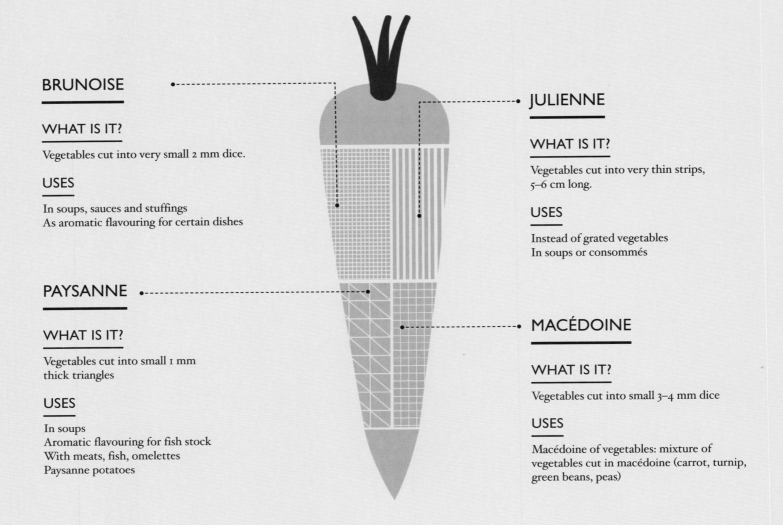

BRUNOISE

WHAT IS IT?

Vegetables cut into very small 2 mm dice.

USES

In soups, sauces and stuffings
As aromatic flavouring for certain dishes

PAYSANNE

WHAT IS IT?

Vegetables cut into small 1 mm
thick triangles

USES

In soups
Aromatic flavouring for fish stock
With meats, fish, omelettes
Paysanne potatoes

JULIENNE

WHAT IS IT?

Vegetables cut into very thin strips,
5–6 cm long.

USES

Instead of grated vegetables
In soups or consommés

MACÉDOINE

WHAT IS IT?

Vegetables cut into small 3–4 mm dice

USES

Macédoine of vegetables: mixture of
vegetables cut in macédoine (carrot, turnip,
green beans, peas)

WHICH CUT FOR WHICH USE?

*This depends on the type of dish to be cooked, and on the role the vegetable plays in its
preparation. The finer the vegetable is cut, the faster it will cook and diffuse its flavour, and
the quicker it will break down and thereby thicken the dish.*

SPECIAL EQUIPMENT

Utility knife
Mandoline (optional)

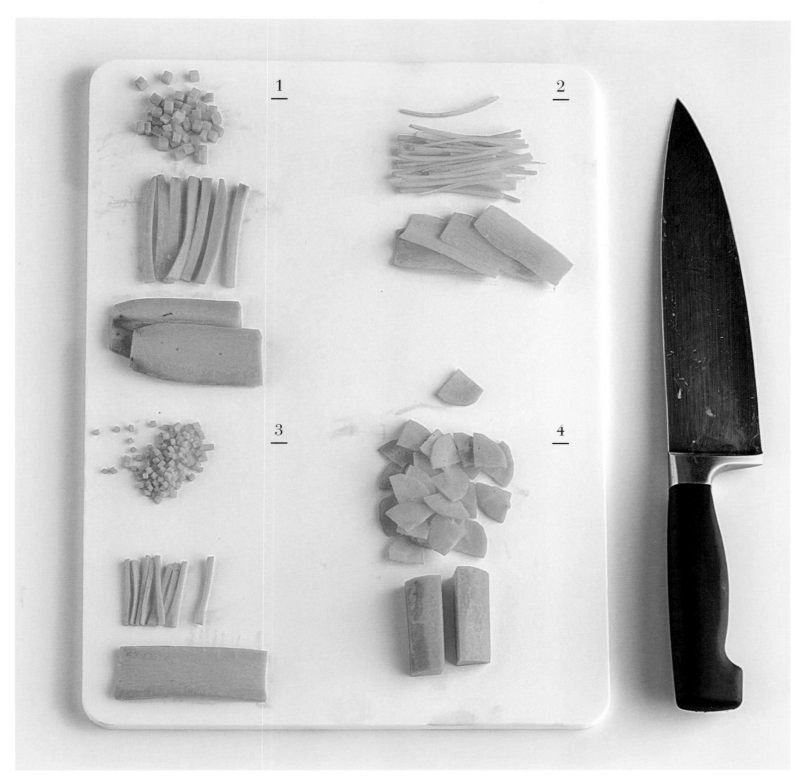

1 MACÉDOINE

Cut 6–7 cm lengths, then cut a thin lengthways slice off one side of each piece to stabilise them.

Cut the lengths into even 3–4 mm thick slices, then 3–4 mm batons, then 3–4 mm dice.

2 JULIENNE

Cut the vegetable into 5–6 cm lengths. Cut a thin lengthways slice off one side of each piece to stabilise them. Slice them thinly lengthways.

Put small groups of the slices on top of each other, then cut them lengthways into very thin strips.

3 BRUNOISE

Cut the vegetable into 6–7 cm lengths. Cut a thin lengthways slice off one side of each piece to stabilise them.

Cut the lengths into even 2 mm thick slices (or use a mandoline). Pile up a few slices then cut them into even 2 mm batons.

Bring together small groups of batons, piling them up, then cut them into even 2 mm dice.

4 PAYSANNE

Cut the vegetable in half lengthways, then in half lengthways again.

Cut into 1 mm thick slices.

TURNING
VEGETABLES

Understand

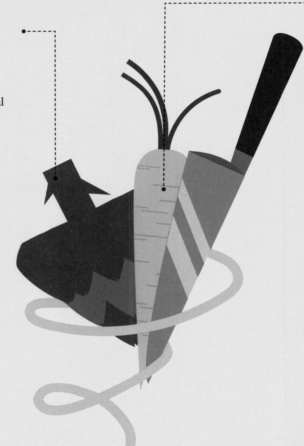

TURNED ARTICHOKE

WHAT IS IT?

An artichoke trimmed of its leaves to reveal the artichoke heart.

SPECIAL EQUIPMENT

Utility knife

USES

Stuffed artichoke (cooked first)

TIP

Remove the choke after cooking.

TURNED CARROT

WHAT IS IT?

Small, even lengths of carrot.

SPECIAL EQUIPMENT

Utility or peeling knife

USES

Turned carrots 2–2.5 cm and 3–4 cm long are accompaniments for meat and fish dishes, 4–5 cm long carrots may form part of a vegetable assortment in a side dish. Larger carrots of 5–6 cm in length are used for cooking in pot-au-feu and for poached chicken.

WHY MAKE TURNED VEGETABLES?

Turned carrots, turnips or potatoes have an aesthetic purpose: the vegetables are even and harmonious. In addition, they are easily coated in accompanying sauces.

TURNING POIVRADE ARTICHOKES

These are small purple Provencal artichokes. Remove the outermost leaves by hand. Lightly peel the parts exposed by removing the leaves. Rub with lemon. Retain 3–4 cm of the stalk. Lightly peel the stalk and rub it with lemon. Cut the leaves at the level of the heart, so that only the tender part remains.

Learn

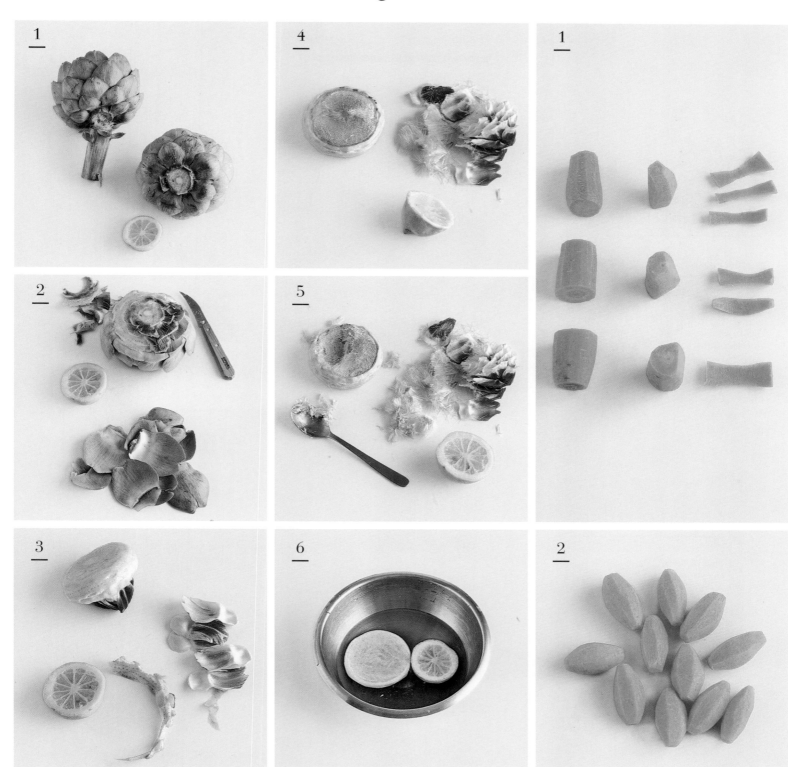

ARTICHOKE

1 Fill a bowl with cold water and the juice of half a lemon. Snap off the artichoke stalk.

2 Trim the exposed base until it is flat and smooth. Rub a lemon half over the cut part. Progressively remove the leaves at the base while rounding off the artichoke with a knife.

3 Squeeze lemon juice over the exposed parts of the artichoke as you go.

4 Continue to remove the leaves until you reach the choke. Trim the heart to give it a round and even shape.

5 Remove the choke with a spoon.

6 Keep the artichoke heart in the cold lemon water until cooking.

CARROT

1 Cut the carrot into even lengths. Depending on the diameter of the carrot, leave the lengths as they are or cut in two, three or four pieces lengthways.

2 Using a utility knife, trim each length to give it an even, rounded shape: hold the length in one hand with your thumb resting against the end of the carrot piece, and the other four fingers holding the knife. The carrot pieces should be thin at the top and bottom, and thick at the centre.

FLAVOURED BUTTERS

Understand

ESCARGOT BUTTER

WHAT IS IT?

A compound butter made by mixing cold butter with raw ingredients: garlic, flat-leaf (Italian) parsley, French shallot and white breadcrumbs.

USES

Served with snails, clams and mussels

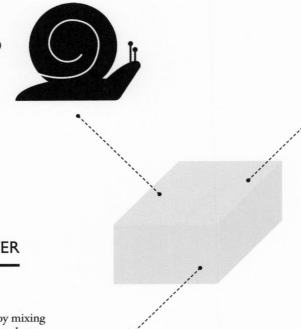

MAÎTRE D'HÔTEL BUTTER

WHAT IS IT?

A compound butter made by mixing cold butter with a mixture of raw ingredients: lemon juice and flat-leaf (Italian) parsley.

USES

Cold: accompaniment for meats and grilled fish
Hot: to finish off certain sauces

DERIVATIONS

Hôtelier butter: maître d'hôtel butter + stuffing (page 42)
Colbert butter: maître d'hôtel butter + meat glaze + tarragon

ANCHOVY BUTTER

WHAT IS IT?

A compound butter made by mixing cold butter with anchovies and raw French shallots.

USES

Accompaniment for fish
Served with appetisers

THE TEMPERATURE OF THE BUTTER

Butter has no melting point but a melting range, from −50°C to +40°C.
- At 4°C, 70 per cent of the fat content is in solid form.
- At 20°C, the butter is soft. It is at a good temperature for being mixed.
- At 30°C, 90 per cent of the fat content is in liquid form.

TECHNIQUES TO MASTER
Chopping finely (page 280)
Mincing (page 280)
Crushing garlic (page 280)

TIP
To prevent the roll of butter being squashed out of shape, plunge it into iced water until firm, before putting it in the fridge.

STORAGE
Softened butter: 2 hours at room temperature.
Rolled butter: 3 days in the refrigerator.

OTHER FLAVOURED BUTTERS
Cold composed butters with raw ingredients: smoked fish butter, cheese butter.
Cold composed butter with cooked ingredients: lobster butter.
Hot composed butter: beurre rouge (crustacean butter).

ESCARGOT BUTTER (180 G)

1 French shallot
20 g flat-leaf (Italian) parsley
2 garlic cloves
20 g day-old white bread (no crusts)
150 g softened butter
½ teaspoon salt
freshly ground black pepper (8 grinds)

1   Peel and mince the shallot. Wash, dry, pick and finely chop the parsley leaves. Peel and chop the garlic cloves. Crumble and push the bread through a wide flat-bottomed sieve, then combine with the shallot, parsley and garlic in a large round-bottomed bowl.

2   Add the butter and mix while crushing the ingredients into the butter using a stiff silicone spatula. Season and mix again. Make a roll of butter in the middle of a piece of plastic wrap, then roll it up and close the ends well. Refrigerate, then cut into slices for when required.

MAÎTRE D'HÔTEL BUTTER (130 G)

10 g flat-leaf (Italian) parsley
1 teaspoon lemon juice
115 g softened butter
½ teaspoon salt
freshly ground black pepper (8 grinds)

1   Wash, dry, pick and finely chop the parsley leaves. Combine the parsley and lemon juice in a large round-bottomed bowl.

2   Follow step 2 for escargot butter.

ANCHOVY BUTTER (370 G)

50 g French shallots
150 g anchovies in oil
1 tablespoon lemon juice
150 g softened butter, cut into pieces
20 g almond meal

1   Peel the shallots and cut them into quarters. Using a food processor with the blade attachment, combine the anchovies, shallot and lemon juice.

2   Pulse several times to obtain a purée. Add the butter. Continue to pulse until the mixture is creamy. Add the almond meal and pulse one last time.

DUXELLES

Understand

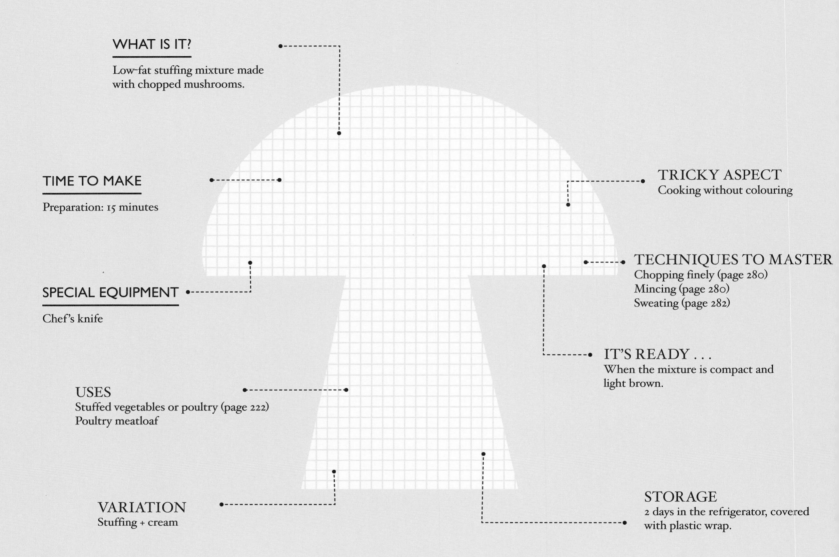

WHAT IS IT?
Low-fat stuffing mixture made with chopped mushrooms.

TIME TO MAKE
Preparation: 15 minutes

SPECIAL EQUIPMENT
Chef's knife

USES
Stuffed vegetables or poultry (page 222)
Poultry meatloaf

VARIATION
Stuffing + cream

TRICKY ASPECT
Cooking without colouring

TECHNIQUES TO MASTER
Chopping finely (page 280)
Mincing (page 280)
Sweating (page 282)

IT'S READY . . .
When the mixture is compact and light brown.

STORAGE
2 days in the refrigerator, covered with plastic wrap.

WHY DO CHOPPED MUSHROOMS GO BROWN?

Cutting mushrooms exposes and crushes their inner cells. The contents of these cells leak out and react with each other and with oxygen in the air, causing the mushrooms to brown. By using a very sharp chef's knife, the cuts are cleaner, which reduces the chance of the cells crushing and thus the leakage of contents susceptible to oxidation.

WHY MUST THE MIXTURE BE DRIED?

So that the mixture is not soggy and holds together.

TIPS

If you're not going to cook the chopped mushrooms straight away, cover them with paper towel that has been soaked in the juice of half a lemon, to prevent them oxidising – the paper should be touching the mushrooms.
Use a large saucepan so that any water evaporates quickly from the mushrooms.

MAKES 120 G

1 flat-leaf (Italian) parsley sprig
2 French shallots
20 g butter
200 g button mushrooms
¼ teaspoon salt
freshly ground black pepper (3 grinds)

1   Wash, dry, pick and finely chop the parsley leaves. Peel and finely chop the shallots. In a large frying pan, sweat the shallot in the butter over medium heat for 2 minutes, stirring from time to time. Remove from the heat.

2   Using a chef's knife, remove the mushroom stalks, and discard, then peel the caps and cut them into thin slices in one direction and then the other, to obtain a very small dice.

3   Add the mushrooms to the pan and cook for about 5 minutes over medium heat, stirring constantly until they are dry.

4   Add the parsley and stir well. Season with salt and pepper.

SHORTCRUST PASTRY

Understand

WHAT IS IT?

A dry lining pastry made with butter rubbed into flour.

TIME TO MAKE

Preparation: 15 minutes
Refrigeration: 20 minutes

USES

Base for tarts, quiches, or meat or fish pies
Cooked after filling, or baked blind

VARIATION

Sweet shortcrust pastry: 5 g sugar for each 100 g flour (pastry very lightly sweetened in comparison to the rich shortcrust pastry of patisserie)

DERIVATIONS

Rich shortcrust pastry (patisserie shortcrust pastry + sugar (40 g su for each 100 g flour).
Sablé pastry (patisserie): rich shortcrust (50 g sugar for each 1c flour) + whole eggs.

TRICKY ASPECTS

Rubbing in the butter without heating it up too much
Not overworking the pastry

TECHNIQUE TO MASTER

Rubbing in butter (page 281)

IT'S READY . . .

When the pastry ball has a smooth, uniform consistency, without being elastic, and is still cold.

WHY AVOID OVERWORKING THE PASTRY?

When you knead pastry, a network of proteins develops known as the gluten network. This lends elasticity to the pastry, which makes it difficult to roll out as it springs back like elastic.

WHY CHILL THE PASTRY?

To allow the butter to harden. During cooking, it will melt and lend softeness to the pastry, while minimising shrinkage.

TIP

Rub the butter in with your hands a little above the bowl, to prevent the pastry becoming too warm.

STORAGE

2 days in the refrigerator. Bring to room temperature for 15–45 minutes before rolling out.

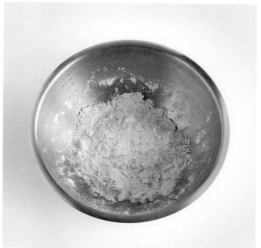

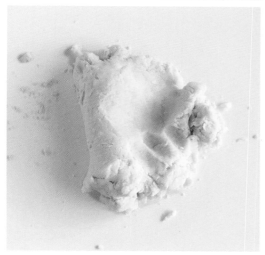

MAKES 300 G

170 g plain (all-purpose) flour, plus extra
for dusting
⅔ teaspoon salt
85 g cold butter, cut into small dice
1 egg yolk

1 Mix the flour and salt in a large bowl.

2 Add the diced butter and rub into the flour using
your fingertips.

3 Stop when the flour has taken on an ivory colour
and the butter resembles large breadcrumbs.

4 Make a small well in the centre of the mixture and
pour in the egg yolk and 60 ml (¼ cup) water. Bring
the mixture together using a fork until there is no
more dry flour.

5 Turn the pastry out onto a lightly floured
work surface. Knead briefly until supple and no
longer sticky.

SHAPING

Roll out the pastry straight away on a floured work
surface and line the dish you are using. Refrigerate
for at least 20 minutes, to minimise shrinkage
during cooking.

QUICK PUFF PASTRY

Understand

WHAT IS IT?

A fast variation of the classic recipe: dry pastry made with flour, water, salt and small pieces of butter, created by folding.

TIME TO MAKE

Preparation: 20 minutes
Resting: 1 hour

SPECIAL EQUIPMENT

Food processor with blade attachment
Rolling pin

USES

Hot hors-d'œuvres (cheese straws, small meat pies, vol-au-vents, etc.)
Koulibiac (Salmon in puff pastry, page 174)
Boeuf en croûte (page 232)

VARIATION

Classic puff pastry: the butter is layered in the pastry, which is then given successive foldings and rest periods

TRICKY ASPECT

The temperature of the room: it should be cool (no higher than 20°C)

THE PASTRY IS READY TO BE ROLLED AND FOLDED . . .

When it starts to pull together in the food processor.

HOW DOES THE FLAKINESS HAPPEN?

This recipe is a fast version of the more traditional puff pastry. The very cold butter doesn't have time to melt as the pastry is worked and stays in small pieces. These specks of butter as well as the final folding step give the pastry its flakiness.

NOTE

Some butters, particularly organic butters, aren't hard enough – even when cold – for success with this recipe.

TIPS

If the room is too warm (more than 20°C), refrigerate the flour before using.
When buying the butter, press on it to ensure it is very hard and not slightly soft.

STORAGE

2 days in the refrigerator or 3 months in the freezer, wrapped in plastic wrap. Defrost overnight in the refrigerator before using.

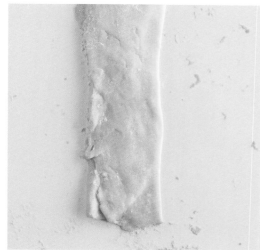

MAKES 660 G

290 g plain (all-purpose) flour plus extra
for dusting
280 g cold, very hard butter,
cut into 1–1.5 cm dice
2 teaspoons salt

1　In a food processor, pulse the flour with 60 g of
the butter for 1 second at a time, 12 times, until the
butter is absorbed. Add the rest of the butter, then
pulse once or twice to distribute the butter in the
flour; it should still be in big pieces.

2　Dissolve the salt in 90 ml cold water, then add to
the flour and butter. Pulse three or four times, until a
dough just starts to form.

3　Turn the dough out onto a work surface and press
it into a rectangle. Roll it out to about 45 cm × 30 cm.
Regularly dust the pastry, work surface and rolling pin
with flour.

4　Fold the upper third then the lower third
towards the middle to obtain a rectangle about
45 cm × 10 cm.

5　Starting from a short side, roll the pastry up in a
coil. Press the edges of this pastry packet to make a
square shape. Wrap in plastic wrap and refrigerate for
at least 1 hour, until the pastry is firm.

6　If you want to divide the pastry into pieces, cut it
perpendicular to the direction of the coil. Push each
piece into a 2–3 cm thick rectangle and use as required.

SALT

Understand

WHAT IS IT?

A mineral condiment basically composed of sodium chloride.

FINE SALT

Small crystals. Use hot (in cooking) and cold.
Without additives: has a fresh, delicate taste, reminiscent of the ocean.
Role: seasoning evenly, before, during and/or after cooking.

COARSE (COOKING) SALT

Grey (Atlantic) or white (Mediterranean), large crystals.
Role: seasoning cooking water, salt crusts, preserving.

FLEUR DE SEL

White crystals that form at the surface of salt marshes.
Role: partial seasoning of a plated dish to create contrasts in flavour and texture.

ROLES

Seasoning: salt accentuates the flavours of a dish, it's a natural flavour-enhancer.
Cooking in a salt crust: cooking a large item (fish, meat, vegetables) under an airtight layer of coarse salt in the oven (see opposite).
Cooking in 'half salt': used raw to deeply season a fish that has white, dense flesh (such as cod) and firm up the flesh before cooking.
Preserving: salt stops the bacteria responsible for the deterioration of foods and reduces microbial activity.

WHEN SHOULD YOU ADD SALT?

MEATS
Before cooking, to allow the formation of a 'crust' that will add taste and texture to the piece of meat.

SAUCES, SOUPS, STEWS
Throughout cooking. If the same quantity of salt is added at the end of cooking, the sauce will be less balanced and complex, because the salt won't have had the chance to flavour all the ingredients.

FISH
Just before cooking, to avoid 'burning' the delicate flesh. For the same reason, avoid using coarse salt.

WHEN SHOULD YOU ADD PEPPER?

In contrast to salt, pepper must be added at the end of cooking. If it is added at the beginning of cooking, it can lose its piquant flavour.

SALTING WATER AND FAT

SALTING COOKING WATER
For seasoning throughout: pasta and other starchy ingredients: 10 g per litre; green vegetables, potatoes: 20 g per litre.

SALTING FAT
Salt doesn't mix with fat. Dissolve it first in a water-based ingredient (water, vinegar, lemon juice, etc.).

Cooking in a salt crust

CELERIAC
IN A SALT CRUST

Celeriac steamed whole under an airtight layer of coarse salt, which makes it tasty and soft.

Preparation: 10 minutes
Cooking: 2 hours 30 minutes
Resting: 40 minutes
Special equipment: ovenproof saucepan or casserole dish

WHAT HAPPENS UNDER THE CRUST?

The salt forms a barrier that allows the celeriac to cook in its own juices and to be seasoned. At the same time, the salt absorbs the water on the surface of the celeriac. This mixture quickly reaches a higher temperature than boiling water, so the celeriac is well cooked on the surface and soft in the middle.

WITH OR WITHOUT EGG WHITE?

The addition of egg white can give the crust a better structure. The egg proteins coagulate, and stiffen the crust. If you cook in a container (such as a saucepan) and use a grey salt, which is wetter, the egg white isn't necessary.

SERVES 4

1 celeriac (about 900 g), unpeeled
2 kg coarse grey sea salt
60 g butter

1 Preheat the oven to 150°C. Wash the celeriac thoroughly, then dry with a clean tea towel (dish towel). Pour 2–3 cm of salt into the bottom of a saucepan. Rest the celeriac on the salt then cover with the remaining salt. Bake for 2 hours 30 minutes. Leave the celeriac to cool inside the crust for 40 minutes.

2 Melt the butter in a separate, small saucepan. Break the crust and extract the celeriac, then cut it into four portions. Put each portion on a serving plate, then pour over the melted butter.

FAT

Understand

WHAT IS IT?

Fatty foods: foods with a high fat content.

FORMS

Oils (olive, peanut, sunflower, canola, etc.): grease of plant origin, 100 per cent fat.
Butter (unsalted or lightly salted): grease of animal origin, 80 per cent fat.
Cream: grease of animal origin, 30 per cent fat.

ROLES

Butter
Cooking: sealing meat or fish; braising a vegetable.
Taste: depth, sweetness.
Basting food with grease during cooking: concentrates flavours, cooks and colours evenly, gives body to a sauce.

Oil
Cooking: frying, sautéing.
Seasoning: flavours and adds smoothness at the end of preparation (a drizzle of olive oil).

USES

Butter
Melting range (temperature at which it liquefies): between 30°C and 45°C.
Toxic point (point at which some fats start to degrade to toxic compounds): 130°C.
For use at moderate heat.

Oil
Smoke point of refined oils: 200°C on average. Use for frying (which demands high temperatures).
Smoke point of virgin oils (cold-pressed): 100–160°C.
Exception: extra-virgin olive oil has the smoke point of refined oils.

WHAT IS THE SMOKE POINT?

The temperature at which the oil releases smoke and starts to become toxic.

WHY COOK IN OIL?

To achieve a good Maillard reaction (page 282) on the food without burning any fat (because oil can withstand high temperatures). The fat itself doesn't pass its flavour onto the food (except in dishes cooked at low temperatures).

WHY COOK IN BUTTER?

Butter passes on its flavour to the food (such as the taste of roasted hazelnuts in beurre noisette).

WHY COOK IN BUTTER + OIL?

Start cooking in oil for a Maillard reaction, then finish in butter for its taste. In addition, mixing butter with oil modifies its melting behaviour. The oil allows the butter to reach a higher temperature without burning.

WHY DOES FAT MEAN FLAVOUR?

Many aromas are primarily fat-soluble. During chewing, fat gets dispersed and coats all components of the dish. This in turn enhances the flavour, as the aromas of fat-soluble compounds get intensified.

CLARIFIED BUTTER

Understand

IMPURITIES   CLARIFIED BUTTER   WHEY

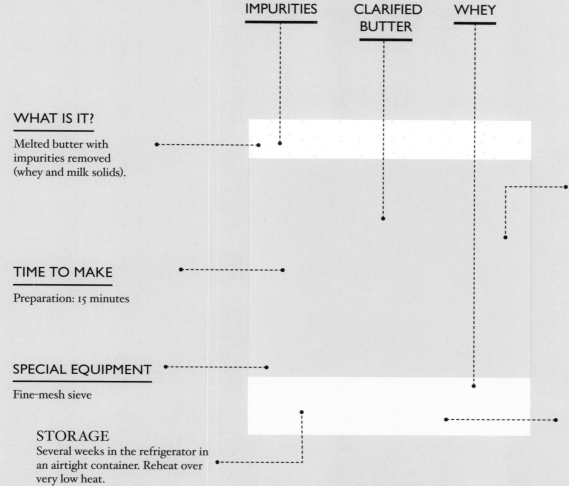

WHAT IS IT?

Melted butter with impurities removed (whey and milk solids).

TIME TO MAKE

Preparation: 15 minutes

SPECIAL EQUIPMENT

Fine-mesh sieve

STORAGE
Several weeks in the refrigerator in an airtight container. Reheat over very low heat.

WHAT HAPPENS WHEN THE BUTTER IS HEATED?

Butter is an emulsion with an 80 per cent fat content. The remaining 20 per cent is made up of water, proteins and lactose. When the butter is melted, the emulsion is destabilised: the fat content (clarified butter) rises to the top, while the water and proteins (the buttermilk) are separated from the fat.

WHAT'S THE POINT?

By removing the proteins in the butter, its smoke point increases to 170°C, as opposed to non-clarified butter, which has a smoke point of 130°C. Clarified butter can therefore be used for cooking at higher temperatures, and notably to replace oil for sautéing.

FROM 250 G BUTTER

1 Cut the butter into cubes. Melt them in a small saucepan over low heat without stirring.

2 After about 15 minutes, when the whey has separated to the bottom of the saucepan, remove all the white foam that has risen to the surface.

3 Strain the butter through a fine-mesh sieve taking care to leave behind all the whey at the bottom of the saucepan. You should have nothing but yellow fat. Use immediately or refrigerate until required.

FAST VARIATION
Melt the butter over medium heat. Pour it into a heatproof container and let it cool. Seal and refrigerate (or freeze) until the butter is set. Scrape the top to remove the foam. Push a little on the butter and let the whey underneath run out. Discard the whey. The clarified butter is all that remains.

NOTES
Butter loses 20–25 per cent of its weight during the clarification process.
Ghee: the Indian name for clarified butters.

BEURRE FONDU

Understand

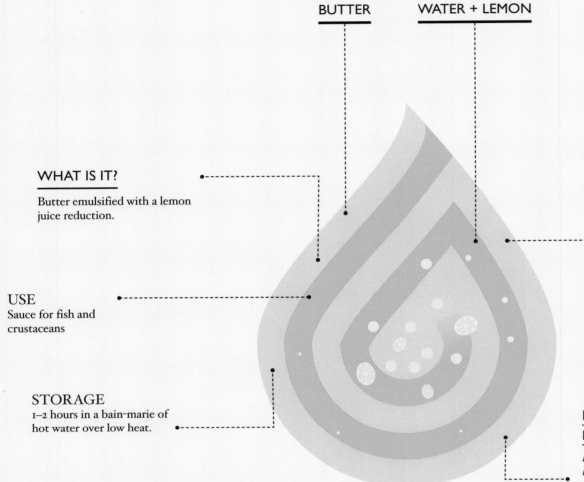

BUTTER

WATER + LEMON

WHAT IS IT?
Butter emulsified with a lemon juice reduction.

USE
Sauce for fish and crustaceans

STORAGE
1–2 hours in a bain-marie of hot water over low heat.

WHY START WITH A WATER + LEMON JUICE REDUCTION?
Water is added to the lemon juice to soften the lemon flavour. This mixture is then reduced to limit the amount of liquid added to the final preparation (and therefore to stabilise the emulsion).

HOW DOES IT DIFFER FROM PLAIN MELTED BUTTER?
Emulsifying the butter with the lemon juice flavours the butter and gives it a thicker texture.

MAKES 200 G

1 tablespoon lemon juice
200 g cold butter, cut into large dice
½ teaspoon salt
pinch of cayenne pepper

1 Bring one tablespoon water and the lemon juice to the boil in a saucepan. Let it reduce for 30 seconds to 1 minute, until it is one-quarter of its original volume.

2 Add a cube of butter over medium heat and swish the saucepan to move the butter around, or whisk until it is almost melted.

3 Add another one or two cubes of butter and let them melt while swirling the pan or whisking.

4 When the butter is almost melted, add the other cubes until all the butter has been incorporated. Season with salt and cayenne pepper.

BEURRE NOISETTE

Understand

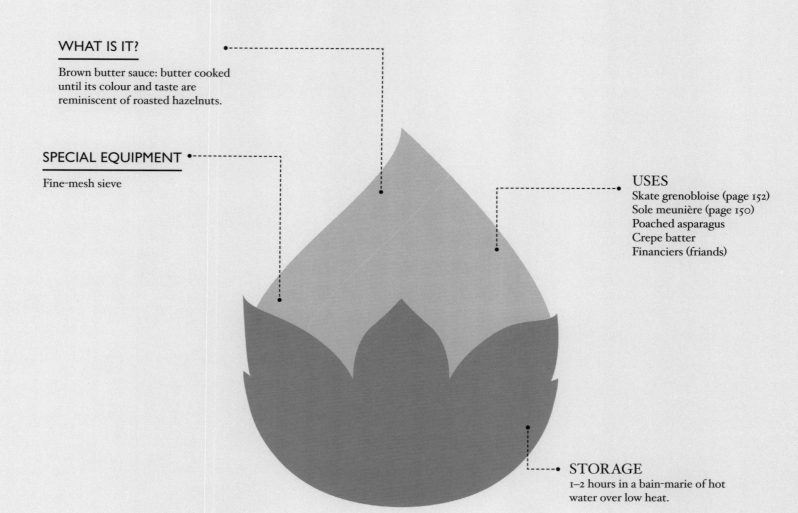

WHAT IS IT?

Brown butter sauce: butter cooked until its colour and taste are reminiscent of roasted hazelnuts.

SPECIAL EQUIPMENT

Fine-mesh sieve

USES
Skate grenobloise (page 152)
Sole meunière (page 150)
Poached asparagus
Crepe batter
Financiers (friands)

STORAGE
1–2 hours in a bain-marie of hot water over low heat.

WHAT HAPPENS WHEN THE BUTTER IS HEATED?

Molecules in the butter become brown and aromatic. Caramelisation reactions between the proteins and the lactose add caramel notes.

WHAT GIVES IT ITS 'HAZELNUT' FLAVOUR?

The proteins and the lactose in the butter react with each other, resulting in aromatic hazelnut notes.

MAKES 150 G

200 g butter

1   Cut the butter into large dice. Melt them in a small saucepan over medium heat.

2   Scrape the bottom of the pan with a spatula from time to time to remove the residue at the bottom of the saucepan and to watch its colour.

3   When the residue becomes brown, strain the butter through a fine-mesh sieve into a bowl to stop it cooking.

ACIDITY

Understand

WHAT IS IT?

An aromatic note that adds balance to a dish.

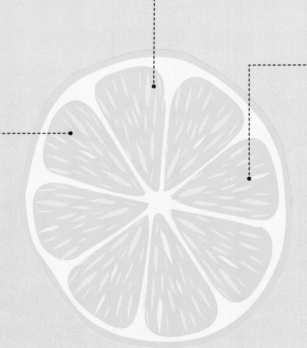

FORMS

Vinegar: red wine vinegar, sherry vinegar, apple cider vinegar, etc.
Lemon and lime juice
Other citrus fruits: grapefruit, orange, citron, kaffir lime, etc.
Wines
Acidic dairy products: yoghurt, crème fraîche, goat's cheese, etc.
Pickled vegetables: capers, cornichons, etc.
Mustards

ROLES

FRESHNESS
The taste of a dish seems fresher with an acidic note.

CONTRAST
It contrasts with the sugar of honey or the roundness of oil in a vinaigrette.

FLAVOUR ENHANCEMENT
Acidity (sourness) comes just after saltiness in the order we sense each of the five tastes.

'COOKING'
It promotes the coagulation or setting of proteins and thus the 'cooking' of a food (e.g. ceviche).

STORAGE
Pickling in acidic mixtures (e.g. pickled vegetables) reduces the development of bacteria. Acidity also prevents the oxidation of fruits and vegetables such as avocados, artichokes, bananas, witlof (chicory), apples, etc.

WHY DOES FISH SOAKED IN LEMON JUICE SEEM COOKED?

Lemon juice is acidic, promoting the coagulation or setting of the proteins contained in the fish, which 'cooks' it.

WHY DOES A LACK OF ACIDITY REDUCE THE QUALITY OF A DISH?

Just like salt, acidity helps to add balance and flavour to a dish.

WHEN SHOULD YOU ADD ACIDITY?

It can be incorporated at any time from the beginning to the end of preparation (like wine in a sauce, for example) but it is often added only at the end of cooking. For example: a drizzle of vinegar or squeeze of lemon juice added just before serving, to create contrast.

GASTRIQUE

Understand

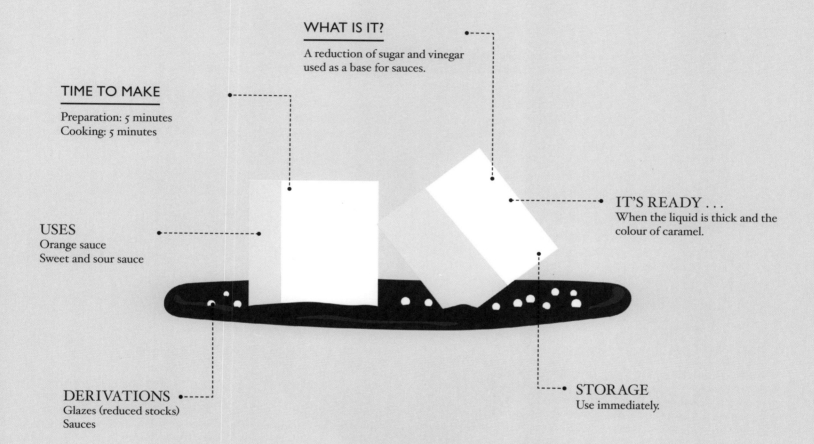

WHAT IS IT?
A reduction of sugar and vinegar used as a base for sauces.

TIME TO MAKE
Preparation: 5 minutes
Cooking: 5 minutes

IT'S READY . . .
When the liquid is thick and the colour of caramel.

USES
Orange sauce
Sweet and sour sauce

DERIVATIONS
Glazes (reduced stocks)
Sauces

STORAGE
Use immediately.

WHY DOES THE SUGAR CRYSTALLISE WHEN VINEGAR IS ADDED?

Adding the vinegar at room temperature reduces the temperature of the caramel which makes the sugar clump together and return to its crystal form. When the temperature of the mixture rises, the sugar dissolves once more.

MAKES 30 G

40 g sugar
2 tablespoons sherry vinegar

1   Make a dry caramel: heat the sugar in a frying pan over very high heat in a thin layer covering the base of the pan. When the sugar turns into a transparent syrup, stir until you have a golden caramel.

2   Remove from the heat and pour in the vinegar. It will crystallise.

3   Return to medium heat and cook until the sugar melts again.

ONIONS

Understand

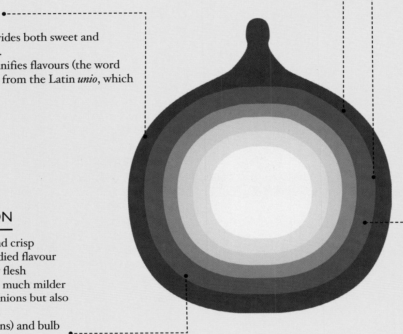

WHAT ARE THEY?

Plants whose bulbs are harvested for use as a vegetable and condiment.

ROLES

Taste: it provides both sweet and savoury notes.
Linkage: it unifies flavours (the word 'onion' comes from the Latin *unio*, which means 'one').

USES BY TYPE

White onion: raw (salads) or cooked (often for stuffings)
Brown onion: cooked (aromatic flavouring, caramelised, 'melted')
Red and pink onions: raw or cooked (French onion soup, hamburgers)
Spring onion (scallion) and bulb spring onion: raw or cooked (chicken consommé)
Baby or pearl onions: cooked, glazed (caramelised), pickled (with cornichons)

TYPES OF ONION

White onion: mild and crisp
Brown onion: full-bodied flavour from its slightly spicy flesh
Red and pink onions: much milder in taste than brown onions but also blander when cooked
Spring onions (scallions) and bulb spring onions: mild and delicate
Baby or pearl onions (miniature brown onions): same flavour as brown onions but eaten whole

USES BY CUT

Minced: fast-cooking preparations where the texture of the onion must disappear and leave only its flavour (tomato sauce)
Thinly sliced: slow-cooked preparations where the texture of the onion must remain (French onion soup)
Rings: decoration, raw (hamburgers) or cooked (nage)
Whole: side dish (baby onions)
Mirepoix: aromatic flavouring

HOW DO RAW AND COOKED ONIONS DIFFER?

Raw onion: fresh, spicy flavour.
Cooked onion: lightly sweet flavour.

WHY DOES SLICED ONION MAKE US CRY?

Because of the sulphur it contains, which is released during cutting. Using a very sharp knife crushes the plant cells less and so reduces the release of sulphur.

WHY DOES ONION CARAMELISE?

In response to the heat, the proteins in the onion release amino acids that react with the sugars to yield a sweet, savoury but also nutty flavour.

HOW DO ONIONS DIFFER FROM FRENCH SHALLOTS?

Shallots have all the characteristics of onions without their spicy, even acrid taste.

Cutting and cooking onions

1 THINLY SLICED

What is it? Cutting into thin slices.

Cut the onion in half lengthways. Place the flat edge on a chopping board, then slice off the root (bottom) end. Slice thinly, in the same direction as the natural lines of the onion (lengthways).

2 MINCED

What is it? Cutting into small pieces.

Cut the onion in half lengthways. Place the flat edge on the board and slice thinly, in the same direction as the natural lines of the onion (lengthways), without cutting through the root (bottom) end. Hold the onion on top with bent fingers. Slice across the thickness two or three times (parallel to the board), without cutting through the root end, then thinly slice perpendicular to the natural lines.

3 RINGS

What is it? Cutting into thin circles.

Hold the onion with the root (bottom) end facing the centre of your hand. Cut into slices 2–3 mm thick. Separate the rings from each other.

4 'MELTED' OR SWEATED ONIONS

What is it? Pieces cooked until completely soft (they are melted in the sense that they have lost their water content). The finer the cut, the faster they 'melt'. A pinch of salt accelerates the process.

Melt 10 g butter per onion. Add the chopped onion and sweat over medium heat, stirring occasionally, until completely soft but not coloured.

5 CARAMELISED ONIONS

What is it? Melted onions, cooked until they colour.

Melt 10 g butter per onion. Add the onion and sweat until completely soft. Let it cook until the onion turns golden. Add sugar (½ teaspoon per onion) if you want to accentuate the caramelisation.

POTATOES

Understand

WHAT ARE THEY?

Herbaceous plants, from the same family as tomatoes, of which we eat the tubers.

CATEGORIES

New potatoes: harvested in spring, before they mature, eaten from October to December in the southern hemisphere (April to mid-August in the north). Thin skin, melting flesh, slightly sweet taste. To be eaten soon after purchase.
Storage potatoes: harvested at full maturity in January–February in the south (September–October in the north), they keep for several months in a dark room at 6°C.

ROLES

Binding (soups, green vegetable purées), thanks to their starch content
Base ingredient (for duchess potatoes, dauphine potatoes)
Accompaniment (mashed, steamed, sautéed)

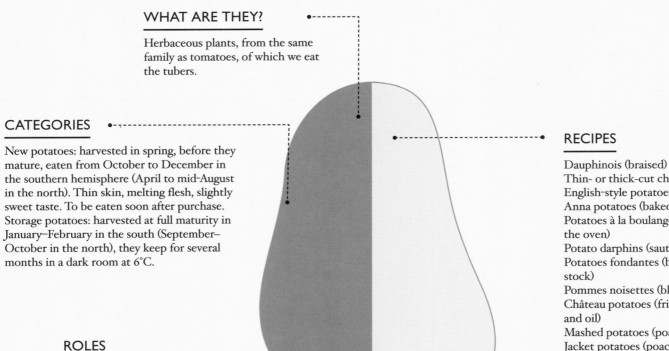

RECIPES

Dauphinois (braised)
Thin- or thick-cut chips (see opposite)
English-style potatoes (poached)
Anna potatoes (baked in a mould)
Potatoes à la boulangère (braised in the oven)
Potato darphins (sautéed in a frying pan)
Potatoes fondantes (braised in a white stock)
Pommes noisettes (blanched)
Château potatoes (fried in butter and oil)
Mashed potatoes (poached, page 60)
Jacket potatoes (poached or baked in their skin)

VARIETIES

BOILING (WAXY) POTATOES
Characteristic: hold together during cooking.
Uses: salads, steamed or sautéed potatoes.
Examples: cherie (red skin), roseval (pale pink skin, sweet yellow flesh), charlotte (popular), pompadour (de Picardie – Label Rouge), ratte (small, with a taste of chestnuts), kipfler (yellow skin, light yellow flesh).

ALL-PURPOSE POTATOES
Characteristic: multi-purpose.
Uses: stews (they absorb the flavour of sauces well), gratins.
Examples: monalisa, nicola (yellow skin and flesh), desiree (pink skin, pale yellow flesh).

ROASTING (FLOURY) POTATOES
Characteristic: fall apart during cooking (they are thus very crumbly, without structure).
Uses: chips, soups, roast potatoes.
Examples: bintje (large, widely grown), artemis (pale yellow flesh), agria (yellow skin and flesh).

PREPARATION

Peel the potatoes lengthways. Remove all spots and traces of bugs; complete several passes with the vegetable peeler, but avoid digging in. Keep the potatoes in cold water in the refrigerator until required.

WHAT ROLE DOES THE STARCH PLAY?

A complex sugar and the main energy storage product of potatoes, starch has a thickening property that can modify the consistency and structure of the liquids to which it is added.

Cutting potatoes

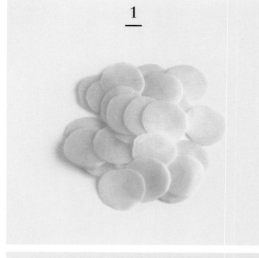

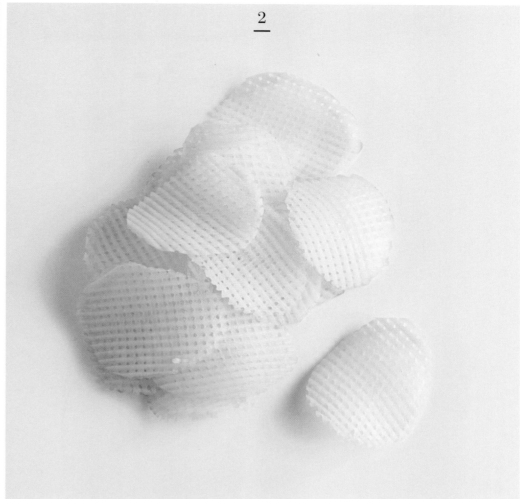

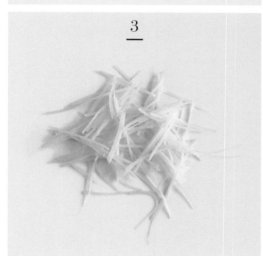

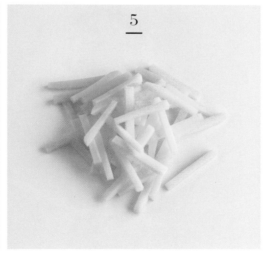

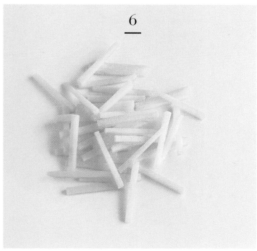

1 CRISPS

What are they? 1 mm thick rounds.

Lightly trim the ends of the potatoes to make them cylindrical. Cut them into 1 mm thick rounds using a mandoline.

2 GAUFRETTES (WAFER POTATOES)

What are they? Thin rounds with a lattice pattern.

Use medium potatoes of an even shape. Peel and round off the ends. Cut each with the wavy blade of a mandoline, rotating the potato a quarter turn between each pass to obtain an openwork lattice.

3 PAILLES (POTATO STRAWS)

What are they? Thin batons 1.5 mm thick.

Using a mandoline, cut the potatoes in 1.5 mm thick slices then in even batons 1.5–2 mm wide.

4 PONT-NEUF (THICK-CUT CHIPS)

What are they? Batons 1 cm thick and 6–7 cm long.

Trim the potatoes at their ends by 2 mm as well as along one side, to give them a stable base. Cut into even slices 1 cm thick and 6–7 cm long. Stack two or three slices on top of each other, then cut them into even batons 1 cm thick.

5 MIGNONETTES (CHIPS)

What are they? Batons 8 mm thick and 5 cm long.

Prepare as for pont-neuf potatoes but make the batons 8 mm wide and 5 cm long.

6 ALLUMETTES (MATCHSTICK CHIPS)

What are they? Batons 5 mm thick and 5 cm long.

Prepare as for pont-neuf potatoes but make the batons 5 mm thick and 5 cm long.

MASHED POTATO

Understand

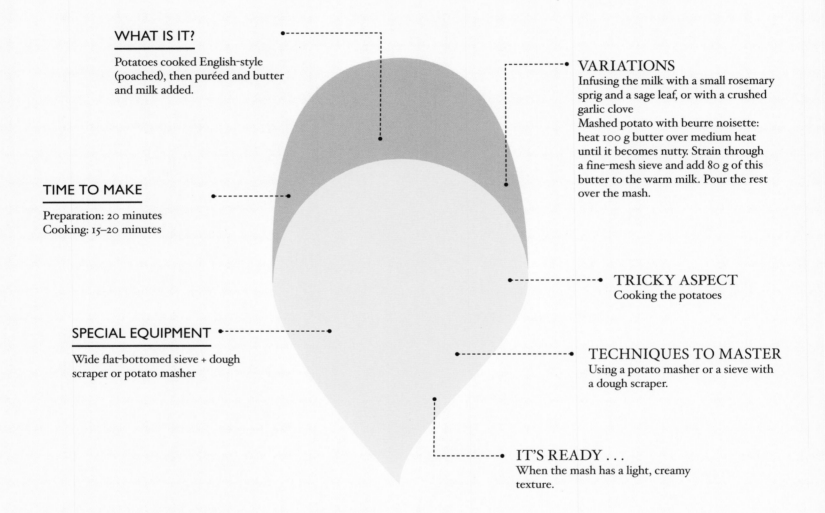

WHAT IS IT?
Potatoes cooked English-style (poached), then puréed and butter and milk added.

TIME TO MAKE
Preparation: 20 minutes
Cooking: 15–20 minutes

SPECIAL EQUIPMENT
Wide flat-bottomed sieve + dough scraper or potato masher

VARIATIONS
Infusing the milk with a small rosemary sprig and a sage leaf, or with a crushed garlic clove
Mashed potato with beurre noisette: heat 100 g butter over medium heat until it becomes nutty. Strain through a fine-mesh sieve and add 80 g of this butter to the warm milk. Pour the rest over the mash.

TRICKY ASPECT
Cooking the potatoes

TECHNIQUES TO MASTER
Using a potato masher or a sieve with a dough scraper.

IT'S READY . . .
When the mash has a light, creamy texture.

WHY SHOULDN'T YOU USE A FOOD PROCESSOR TO MAKE THE MASH?
The blade cuts the starch grains in the potato. When these starch grains burst, they release componenets that make the purée elastic.

WHY ADD THE FAT?
The fat content of the butter and the milk adds creaminess. The fat also absorbs the flavours; the melted butter therefore helps to enhance the flavours of the thyme and bay leaf.

TIP
Prepare the mash a few hours in advance and reheat it over medium heat while adding 100 ml of the potato cooking water.

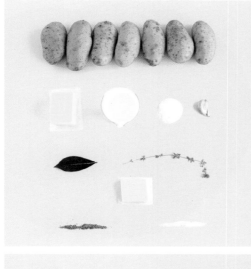
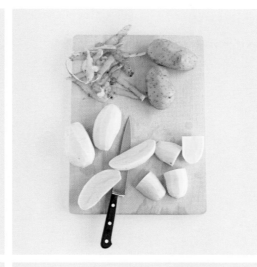

SERVES 4

900 g roasting (floury) potatoes
1 tablespoon coarse salt
1 garlic clove
180 ml milk
85 g butter
1 thyme sprig
1 bay leaf
½ teaspoon table salt
freshly ground black pepper (6 grinds)

TO FINISH

20 g butter

1 Peel the potatoes and cut into 5 cm pieces, then wash.

2 Transfer to a large saucepan and cover with 3 cm water. Bring to the boil, add the coarse salt and simmer (without boiling) for 15–20 minutes, until cooked through.

3 Peel the garlic clove and cut in half. Heat the garlic, milk, 85 g butter, thyme, bay leaf, salt and pepper in a small saucepan over medium heat until the butter has melted. Increase the heat to very high then remove from the heat as soon as the mixture starts to simmer.

4 Drain the potatoes. Dry them for 1 minute over low heat by stirring them and shaking the pan.

5 Crush the hot potatoes with a masher or push through a wide flat-bottomed sieve over the saucepan.

6 Remove the thyme, bay leaf and garlic from the milk with a skimmer or slotted spoon and gradually pour the infused milk over the mash while mixing with a wooden spoon. Adjust the seasoning.

7 Make a well in the top of the pile of mashed potato and add the 20 g butter. Stir until melted through.

DUCHESS POTATOES

Understand

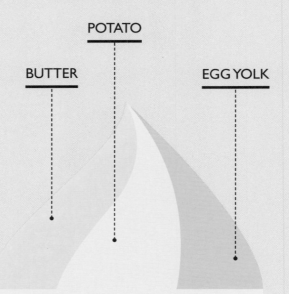

BUTTER

POTATO

EGG YOLK

WHAT ARE THEY?

Duchess potatoes mixture: cooked and mashed potatoes, with butter and egg yolk added.
Duchess potatoes: duchess potatoes mixture piped using a fluted piping nozzle, then baked until golden.
À la duchesse: dish served with duchess potatoes.

TIME TO MAKE

Preparation: 30 minutes
Cooking: 12–15 minutes

SPECIAL EQUIPMENT

Wide flat-bottomed sieve + dough scraper (or potato masher)
Piping bag + 1.5 cm fluted piping nozzle
Pastry brush

USES

Decoration of roast meat dishes
Small side dish

TECHNIQUE TO MASTER

Piping (page 281)

WHY COOK THE POTATOES ON COARSE SALT?

This method takes longer than boiling, but results in the flesh being less moist (the salt absorbs water on the surface of the potatoes). With drier flesh there is less chance of the mixture becoming elastic because the starch is less swollen with water.

VARIATIONS

Potato croquettes: duchess potatoes mixture shaped into cylinders, then coated with breadcrumbs and fried
Almond potato croquettes: duchess potatoes mixture shaped into almond shapes, then coated in flaked almonds
Dauphine potatoes (page 244): dauphine potatoes mixture + choux pastry

TIP

Use the duchess potatoes mixture hot – it will be easier to manipulate.

Learn

MAKES 35–40

500 g potatoes (bintje or similar)
100–150 g coarse salt
50 g butter
3 egg yolks
pinch of freshly grated nutmeg
½ teaspoon salt
freshly ground black pepper (6 grinds)

TO FINISH

20 g butter

1 Preheat the oven to 200°C. Wipe the potatoes with moist paper towel. Make a bed of coarse salt in an ovenproof dish or saucepan and sit the potatoes on top. Roast for 45 minutes to 1 hour, depending on their size. Check if the potatoes are cooked by cutting open the largest. Cook for a few more minutes if necessary.

2 Cut the 50 g of butter into pieces and refrigerate. Melt the 20 g of butter and use it to grease a baking tray with a pastry brush. Keep any remaining butter in the saucepan.

3 Remove the flesh from the potatoes using a spoon and push through a flat wide-bottomed sieve with a dough scraper, or mash with a potato masher.

4 Dry the mashed flesh in a saucepan over very low heat, stirring with a spatula to ensure that it doesn't stick. Add the cold pieces of butter and stir them in until melted.

5 Remove from the heat, then add the egg yolks one at a time, mixing well after each addition. Season with the nutmeg, salt and pepper.

6 Quickly stir the mixture over low heat for 1–2 minutes. Smooth the surface.

7 Fill a piping (icing) bag with the mixture and use a 1.5 cm fluted piping nozzle to pipe evenly spaced small heaps of mixture on the greased baking tray. Brush each duchess potato with a little of the leftover melted butter. Bake for 12–15 minutes, until lightly browned.

EGGS

Understand

WHAT ARE THEY?

Products laid by hens consisting of a shell containing two elements: the white and the yolk.

ROLES

EGG YOLK
Thickening, notably of sauces (sauce for veal frikassee)
Stabilisation: promotes the formation of and stabilises emulsions (mayonnaise, hollandaise sauce, etc.)

EGG WHITE (WHISKED)
Creates mousses and rises (cheese soufflé)

WHOLE EGGS
Binding set cream mixtures (quiche mixture)
Binding doughs (choux pastry, pasta dough)
Binding stuffings

PRODUCT

Weight (average egg) = 60 g (10 g for the shell, 35 g for the white and 15 g for the yolk).
Egg white: proteins.
Egg yolk: fats, including lecithin (which plays an important role in emulsions: binding oil and water).
'Extra-fresh' egg: laid less than 9 days before the purchase date.
'Fresh' egg: laid 9–28 days before the purchase date.

TASTE

Eggs have a characteristic flavour that remains after they are mixed with other ingredients and cooked. They capture the flavours of other ingredients formed during preparation.

HOW DO YOU STOP THE SHELL CRACKING DURING COOKING?

Place the egg very carefully in simmering but not boiling water.

HOW DO YOU ENSURE WELL-BEATEN EGG WHITES?

Use perfectly clean equipment and whites without any trace of yolk.

AT WHAT TEMPERATURES DOES AN EGG COAGULATE (COOK)?

The white begins to coagulate at 61°C, the yolk at 68°C.

WHY DOES EGG YOLK PROMOTE THE FORMATION OF EMULSIONS ?

During whisking, the fats and proteins it contains get 'activated'. The lecithin contained in the egg yolk acts as an emulsifier by binding oil and water, which creates and stabilises the emulsion.

TIPS

To make peeling easier: cool the egg by plunging it into very cold water for 5 minutes, then break the shell very delicately and peel the large end of the egg first, removing the shell membrane under the air chamber.
Extra-fresh eggs are harder to peel than fresh eggs (the air chamber is smaller).

COOKING VARIATIONS

Eggs at room temperature: allow 3 minutes for extra-soft-boiled eggs, 5 minutes for soft-boiled eggs and 10 minutes for hard-boiled eggs.

Cooking eggs

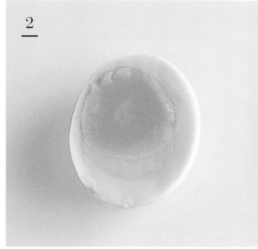

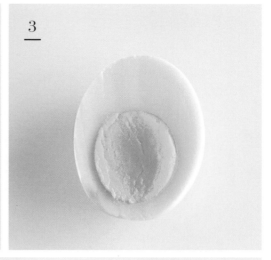

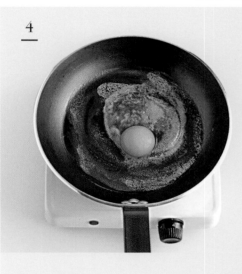

COOKING AN EGG IN ITS SHELL

Bring a large amount of cold water to the boil in
a small saucepan. Take an egg straight out of the
refrigerator and immerse it carefully in the water
using a skimmer or slotted spoon. Reduce the heat
to medium and let it cook.

1 EXTRA-SOFT-BOILED EGG

White semi-coagulated, yolk liquid. Cook for
4 minutes from when it starts simmering again.

2 SOFT-BOILED EGG

White coagulated, yolk creamy. Cook for 6 minutes
from when it starts simmering again.

3 HARD-BOILED EGG

White and yolk coagulated. Cook for 12 minutes
from when it starts simmering again.

COOKING A SHELLED EGG

4 FRIED EGG (FRYING PAN OR TRAY)

Unbeaten egg: white coagulated, yolk creamy.

Traditional eggs *sur le plat* are cooked on a small serving
tray in the oven.

Break the egg into a ramekin or cup. Melt 10 g butter
in a small non-stick frying pan over high heat. When

it starts to turn noisette (page 53), pour in the egg.
Reduce the heat to medium. Cook for 1–2 minutes,
until the white is lightly browned. Season the white
with a pinch of salt and a grind of pepper.

5 SCRAMBLED EGGS

Beaten eggs: soft and creamy.

Using a fork, beat four eggs with ¼ teaspoon salt and
a grind of pepper. Melt 10 g butter in a small frying
pan over medium heat until foaming. Add the eggs
when the butter stops foaming and stir quickly with
a silicone spatula until it leaves a trace in the pan.
Reduce the heat to low and stir for 1 minute. When
the eggs are still runny, remove from the heat and add
another 10 g butter. Stir.

ROLLED OMELETTE

Understand

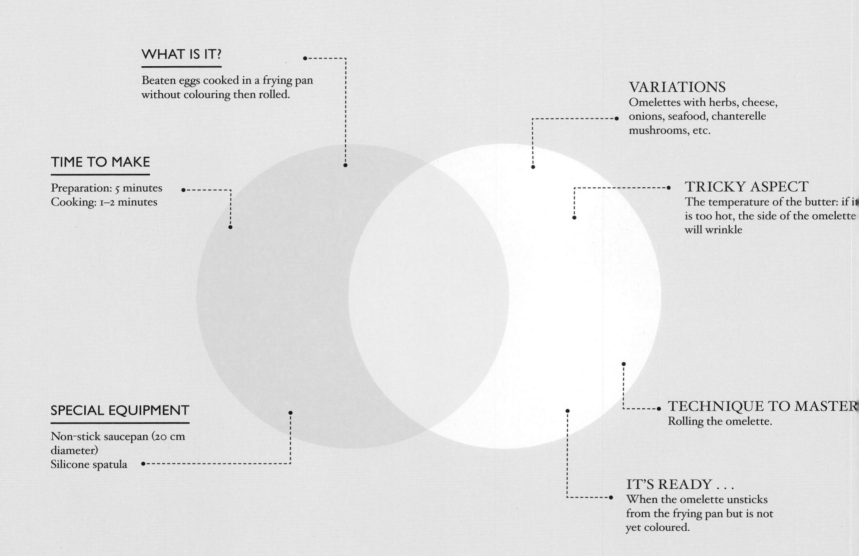

WHAT IS IT?

Beaten eggs cooked in a frying pan without colouring then rolled.

TIME TO MAKE

Preparation: 5 minutes
Cooking: 1–2 minutes

SPECIAL EQUIPMENT

Non-stick saucepan (20 cm diameter)
Silicone spatula

VARIATIONS
Omelettes with herbs, cheese, onions, seafood, chanterelle mushrooms, etc.

TRICKY ASPECT
The temperature of the butter: if it is too hot, the side of the omelette will wrinkle

TECHNIQUE TO MASTER
Rolling the omelette.

IT'S READY . . .
When the omelette unsticks from the frying pan but is not yet coloured.

WHY SHOULD THE EGG NOT BE OVER-BEATEN?

There is a risk that the base will be frothy, because the proteins capture air and create a foam that can give the omelette too airy a texture.

WHY MUST THE OMELETTE NOT COLOUR?

The browner it becomes, the more the egg proteins coagulate (they become overcooked), creating sulphur bonds between the proteins that emit an unpleasant aroma.

DEGREES OF COOKING
Runny (a thin 'sauce' seems to coat the coagulated egg): allow 1–2 minutes.
Soft (there is no more 'sauce' but the egg is still very soft): allow 1–2 minutes, remove from the heat, cover and wait 1 minute.
Well cooked (the coagulated egg is firmer): allow 1–2 minutes, remove from the heat, cover and wait 2 minutes.

TIPS
Retain a medium heat and move the eggs around constantly to ensure that they don't colour.
When cooking with gas, preheat the empty frying pan over low heat for 5 minutes before melting the butter over medium heat, as gas has a tendency to brown the omelette where the flame hits the pan.

MAKES I SMALL ROLLED OMELETTE

3 eggs
¼ teaspoon salt
freshly ground black pepper (3 grinds)
15 g butter

1   Using a fork, beat the eggs in a round-bottomed bowl with the salt and pepper until slightly foamy. Add 5 g of the butter, cut into small cubes.

2   Melt the remaining butter in a frying pan over medium heat. Pour in the egg, wait a few seconds, then mix using a silicone spatula with a rapid circular movement, for 1–2 minutes. Form the mixture into a round omelette without holes.

3   When the edges of the omelette can be lifted with the spatula, turn off the heat. Tip up the pan by lifting the handle, and fold over the third of the omelette nearest the handle. Slide the omelette slightly to the other side of the pan, fold the opposite third of the omelette over the first while turning it out onto a warm plate with the smooth side facing up.

4   Neaten the omelette with your hands if necessary so that it's slightly domed.

POACHED EGGS

Understand

WHAT ARE THEY?

Eggs cooked out of their shell in very hot water; the white is coagulated, the yolk creamy.

SPECIAL EQUIPMENT

Small saucepan
Skimmer or finely slotted spoon

TIME TO MAKE

Preparation: 5 minutes

WHY DRAIN THE EGG BEFORE COOKING?

To remove the liquid part of the white, which forms unattractive filaments during cooking, while retaining the viscous part of the white, which will coagulate better around the yolk. This technique means you can omit adding vinegar to the cooking water.

WHY IS VINEGAR SOMETIMES ADDED TO THE WATER?

The acidity provided by the vinegar accelerates the coagulation of the proteins and thus formation of a neat white around the yolk. In this recipe, the liquid part of the white is removed before cooking, so there is no risk of the white spreading out. In addition, the taste of the egg benefits from the absence of vinegar in the cooking water.

HOW DOES IT DIFFER FROM A SOFT-BOILED EGG?

For a soft-boiled egg, the egg is cooked in its shell (and so retains its shape during cooking).

WHY POACH AN EGG IN A WATER VORTEX?

The vortex gathers the white around the yolk and helps the egg retain its shape. During cooking, the proteins coagulate and the texture of the egg stiffens.

FOR 1 POACHED EGG

1 cold extra-fresh egg
pinch of salt
freshly ground black pepper (1 grind)

1 Heat a small saucepan filled with water. Break the egg into a small bowl.

2 Pour the egg onto a skimmer or finely slotted spoon set over a bowl. Let the fluid part of the white run through, then scrape the bottom of the spoon (the thick part of the white will cling to the yolk).

3 Pour the drained yolk back into the small bowl. When the water is simmering, reduce the heat to low and stir the water with a wooden spoon to create a small vortex. Pour the egg into the centre of the vortex and let it cook for 90 seconds to 2 minutes, over low heat, gently pushing the white over the yolk until the white is cooked.

4 Remove the egg using the slotted spoon, then place the spoon on paper towel to drain. Carefully transfer the egg to a serving plate. Season with the salt and pepper.

DEEP-FRIED EGGS

Understand

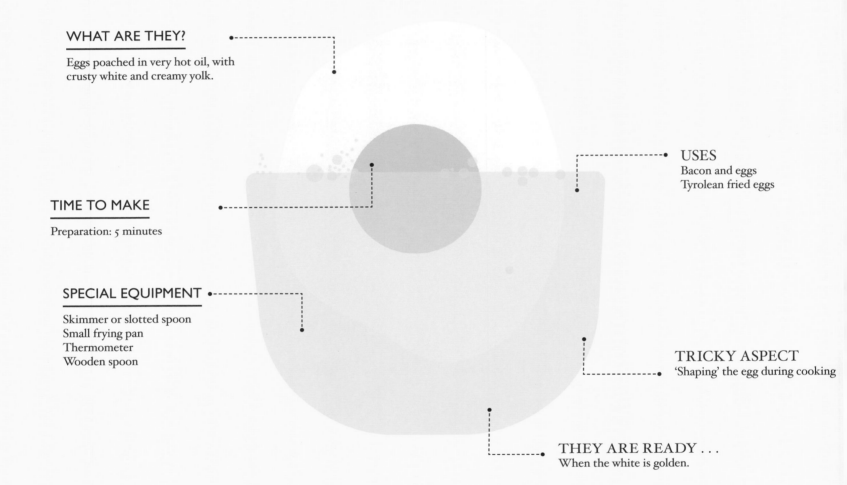

WHAT ARE THEY?

Eggs poached in very hot oil, with crusty white and creamy yolk.

TIME TO MAKE

Preparation: 5 minutes

SPECIAL EQUIPMENT

Skimmer or slotted spoon
Small frying pan
Thermometer
Wooden spoon

USES

Bacon and eggs
Tyrolean fried eggs

TRICKY ASPECT

'Shaping' the egg during cooking

THEY ARE READY . . .
When the white is golden.

WHY USE EXTRA-FRESH EGGS?

They have a crucial globular mass of white, which won't expand into the oil but will retain its form around the yolk.

WHY IS THE COOKING TIME SO SHORT?

Oil can be heated to a much higher temperature than water, which doesn't go above 100°C. At 190°C, the egg cooks much more rapidly.

HOW DOES THE CRUST FORM AROUND THE EGG?

The high temperature dries out the protein network on the surface of the egg and makes it crisp.

FOR 1 DEEP-FRIED EGG

1 cold extra-fresh egg
200 ml peanut oil
pinch of salt

1 Break the egg into a bowl.

2 Heat the oil in a deep frying pan or deep-fryer to 190°C. Gently pour in the egg.

3 The white will coagulate into large bubbles; push them quickly over the yolk using a wooden spoon while rolling the egg on itself to give it an even shape. Let it fry for a maximum of 1 minute: the yolk should be soft and the white golden.

4 Drain the egg using a skimmer or slotted spoon and place it on a plate lined with paper towel. Season with salt.

SAUTÉING

Understand

WHAT IS IT?

Pan-frying: cooking small pieces at very high temperatures in a frying pan, in a small quantity of fat, uncovered (dry heat).

SPECIAL EQUIPMENT

Frying pan, sautoir (straight-sided sauté pan) or sauteuse (slightly flared sauté pan) to suit the size of the food to be cooked

TIME TO MAKE

Quick (10–20 minutes)

TYPE OF COOKING
Heterogeneous: fast and well done on the outside, less cooked in the middle.

INGREDIENTS TO SAUTÉ
Small cut of tender meat (tournedos, veal cutlets, filet mignon, etc.)
Poultry pieces (escalopes, thighs, etc.)
Fish fillets
Offal
Eggs
Vegetables (potatoes, zucchini/courgettes, mushrooms, onions, etc.)

USES
Sautéed potatoes
Sautéed chicken chasseur
English-style calf's liver
Skirt steak with shallot sauce
Pepper steak
Sautéed veal chops in cream sauce
Sole meunière (page 150)
English-style whiting
Fried eggs

WHY IS THIS TECHNIQUE USEFUL?

It forms a very fragrant crust around the food during cooking (Maillard reactions, page 282), which provides crispness without overcooking the centre.

WHY BASTE THE FOOD DURING COOKING?

To improve the colouration on the surface and to moisten the food in its own juices and fat.

HOW DOES IT DIFFER FROM POT-ROASTING?

Pot-roasting cooks large ingredients, covered, in the oven in moist heat (thanks to the water content of the vegetables in the roast). Pot-roasting prevents food drying out by not exposing it to direct heat.

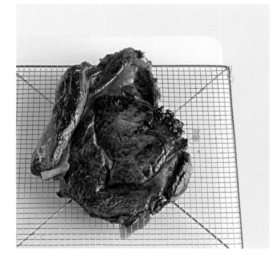

RIB-EYE STEAK WITH ROQUEFORT SAUCE

SERVES 2

1 French shallot
70 g rocket (arugula)
1½ tablespoons olive oil
1 × 600 g rib-eye steak
1 teaspoon table salt
30 g butter
100 g crème fraîche
50 g Roquefort
freshly ground black pepper (3 grinds)
¼ teaspoon fleur de sel

1   Peel and mince (page 280) the shallot. Wash and spin the rocket. Heat a frying pan over very high heat and add the oil. Pat the meat dry with paper towel then sprinkle with the table salt. When the oil is just smoking, add the meat and seal for 2 minutes.

2   Turn the meat over, reduce the heat to high and add the butter.

3   Cook for a further 2 minutes, basting the meat with the foaming butter.

4   Transfer to a wire rack and cover with foil.

5   Reduce the heat to medium and partially degrease (page 283) the pan. Add the shallot and let it sweat. Deglaze with 50 ml cold water. Scrape any stuck-on bits off the bottom of the pan, bring to the boil, then reduce until almost dry.

6   Stir in the crème fraîche and Roquefort, then add half the rocket. Stir until wilted, then add the rest.

7   Sprinkle the steak with the pepper and fleur de sel, then serve with the sauce.

ROASTING

Understand

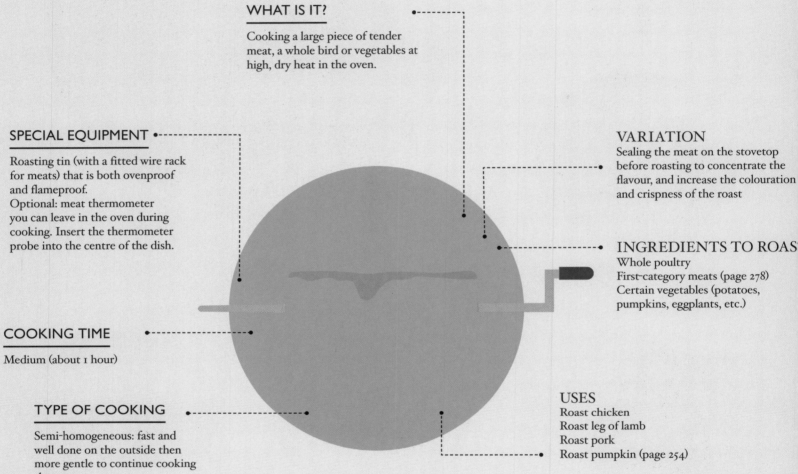

WHAT IS IT?

Cooking a large piece of tender meat, a whole bird or vegetables at high, dry heat in the oven.

SPECIAL EQUIPMENT

Roasting tin (with a fitted wire rack for meats) that is both ovenproof and flameproof.
Optional: meat thermometer you can leave in the oven during cooking. Insert the thermometer probe into the centre of the dish.

COOKING TIME

Medium (about 1 hour)

TYPE OF COOKING

Semi-homogeneous: fast and well done on the outside then more gentle to continue cooking the centre.

VARIATION

Sealing the meat on the stovetop before roasting to concentrate the flavour, and increase the colouration and crispness of the roast

INGREDIENTS TO ROAST

Whole poultry
First-category meats (page 278)
Certain vegetables (potatoes, pumpkins, eggplants, etc.)

USES

Roast chicken
Roast leg of lamb
Roast pork
Roast pumpkin (page 254)

WHY USE THIS TECHNIQUE?

To cook large ingredients without them drying out. First at high temperature to seal the outside, then more gently to cook the centre.

WHY BASTE THE MEAT?

To improve the colouration on its surface and to moisten the food with its own juices and fat.

WHY LET THE MEAT REST AFTER COOKING?

Let the meat rest on a wire rack to prevent it stewing in its own juices (which will soften the surface), to relax the muscle fibres and make the colour of the flesh even (by evenly redistributing the blood in the piece of meat). Let it rest for 10–20 minutes, depending on size.

OVEN TEMPERATURE

Large pieces: cook at high temperature (220°C), then at low temperature (160°C).
Small pieces: cook at high temperature (220°C).
Avoid temperatures that are too high (240°C and over); put the meat under the grill at the end of cooking to finish browning.

CORE TEMPERATURE

Take the meat out when the thermometer reaches 5°C below the desired final temperature.
Beef:
- very rare: 50°C
- rare: 55°C
- medium-rare: 60°C
- well done: 70°C
Pork:
- rare: 70°C
- medium-rare: 75°C
Lamb:
- rare: 60°C
- medium-rare: 70°C
Veal: 70°C
Poultry: 75–80°C
Fish: 50°C

ROAST PORK

SERVES 4

4 large French shallots
4 garlic cloves
5 sage leaves
5 thyme sprigs
1 kg boneless rolled and tied
pork loin, skin and fat on
2 teaspoons salt
freshly ground black pepper (12 grinds)
3 tablespoons olive oil

1   Preheat the oven to 220°C. Remove the outer layer of skin from the shallots. Peel the garlic cloves, then cut each into two or three slices. Wash the sage and thyme.

2   Pat the pork completely dry with paper towel. Score the fat with straight lines 1 cm apart, cutting through the entire thickness of the fat without touching the flesh.

3   Turn it over, season with salt and pepper, and rub well into the meat. Insert the garlic, thyme and sage under the strings of the loin.

4   Turn the loin over again, then season the fat with salt and pepper, particularly between the cuts. Pour 1 tablespoon of the oil over the whole loin and massage it in.

5   Heat the remaining oil in a roasting tin over very high heat on the stovetop, and brown the fat side of the loin. Transfer the loin to the wire rack of the tin, fat side up. Place the shallots in the bottom of the tin, place the rack in the tin and roast in the oven for 20 minutes. Reduce the oven temperature to 160°C and roast for a further 35 minutes. Finish by browning the fat for 1–2 minutes under the grill, until it puffs up slightly and becomes crisp. Rest the meat for 15 minutes on the rack, covered with foil.

6   Untie the loin. Remove the shallots from the tin. Partially degrease the cooking juices in the tin, then bring to the boil over very high heat on the stovetop. Pour in 150 ml very cold water and scrape any stuck-on bits off the bottom. Bring to the boil and simmer for a few minutes, until reduced to your liking. Season to taste. Strain through a fine-mesh sieve.

GRILLING

Understand

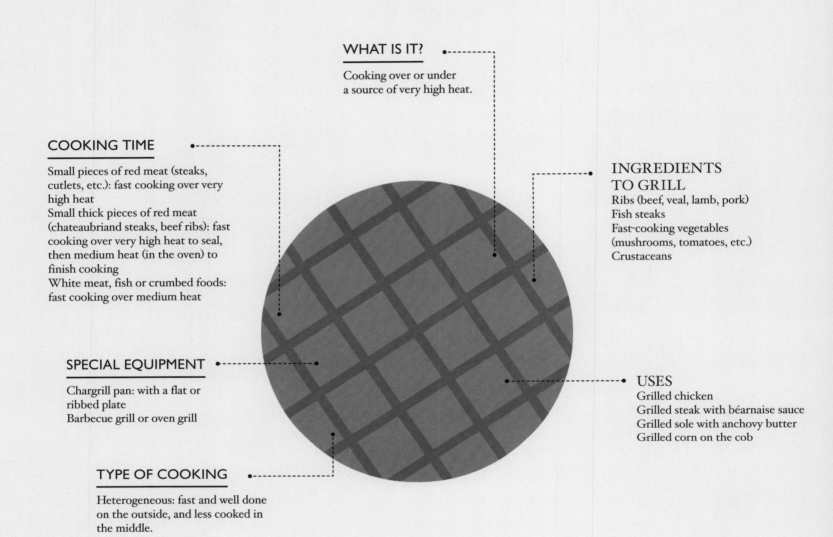

WHAT IS IT?
Cooking over or under
a source of very high heat.

COOKING TIME
Small pieces of red meat (steaks,
cutlets, etc.): fast cooking over very
high heat
Small thick pieces of red meat
(chateaubriand steaks, beef ribs): fast
cooking over very high heat to seal,
then medium heat (in the oven) to
finish cooking
White meat, fish or crumbed foods:
fast cooking over medium heat

**INGREDIENTS
TO GRILL**
Ribs (beef, veal, lamb, pork)
Fish steaks
Fast-cooking vegetables
(mushrooms, tomatoes, etc.)
Crustaceans

SPECIAL EQUIPMENT
Chargrill pan: with a flat or
ribbed plate
Barbecue grill or oven grill

USES
Grilled chicken
Grilled steak with béarnaise sauce
Grilled sole with anchovy butter
Grilled corn on the cob

TYPE OF COOKING
Heterogeneous: fast and well done
on the outside, and less cooked in
the middle.

WHY USE THIS TECHNIQUE?
*To form a very flavoursome crust around the food during cooking (Maillard reactions,
page 282), which adds crispness without overcooking the inside.*

WHY SHOULD YOU NOT GRILL FOOD AT TOO HIGH A HEAT?
*If over-seared, grilled meats take on a metallic taste and toxic compounds form. The meat
is what the French call* ferrée *(tasting of iron).*

RESTING
Let small thick pieces of red meat rest
under foil for 5–10 minutes to give the
flesh an even colour and promote relaxation
of the muscle fibres.

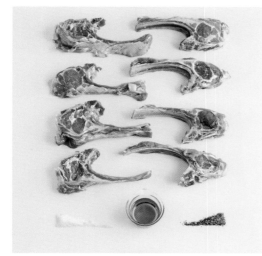

GRILLED LAMB CUTLETS

SERVES 4

8 lamb cutlets
1½ tablespoons olive oil
1 teaspoon salt
freshly ground black pepper (8 grinds)

1   Coat the lamb cutlets in a little of the oil. Season with salt.

2   Lightly oil the bars of a barbecue or chargrill pan using paper towel soaked with the remaining oil. Heat to very high heat.

3   Place the lamb cutlets diagonally across the bars and cook for 1 minute, give them a quarter turn, then cook for another 1 minute, then turn them over and cook in the same way to given them a criss-cross pattern. Transfer the cutlets to a wire rack to rest, and season with pepper.

BRAISING

Understand

WHAT IS IT?
Cooking a large piece of food slowly, covered, in a moistening liquid. In the case of meat, it is first browned (brown braising – colouring) or cooked until firm (white braising – no colouring).

SPECIAL EQUIPMENT
Flameproof casserole dish, sautoir (straight-sided sauté pan): preferably both heavy-based (which retains the heat), and with a tight-fitting lid.

COOKING TIME
Second- or third-category meat (page 278): 4–5 hours in a 150°C oven
Fish and vegetables (high water content): 30 minutes maximum

TYPE OF COOKING
Double cooking: fast and strong to colour the outside and then in a liquid to cook through

INGREDIENTS TO BRAISE
Large pieces of second- and third-category meat (page 278), firm, rich in collagen, which need time to tenderise (chuck roast, veal shoulder, ham, etc.)
Whole fish or fish fillets
Leaf vegetables

BRAISING RECIPES
Beef olives (paupiettes of beef) with carrots
White- or brown-braised calf sweetbreads
French-style jugged hare
Braised witlof (chicory), lettuce, fennel, cabbage
Stuffed trout
Fillet of sole or turbot bonne femme

WHY USE THIS TECHNIQUE?
To form a very flavoursome crust during the initial cooking in oil (Maillard reactions, page 282). The cooking then continues in a braising liquid.
- Meat: to form a very flavoursome crust that then dissolves in the cooking liquid, flavouring and colouring the braising stock.
- Fish: to transfer flavour to the cooking liquid.
- Vegetables: to gain flavour from an aromatic cooking liquid (wine, stock).

DOES THE SIZE OF THE MEAT HAVE AN IMPACT ON TASTE?
When meat is cut into pieces, it gives more of its flavour to the cooking liquid than when cooked whole. In the latter case, the meat retains more of its own flavour.

HEIGHT OF THE COOKING LIQUID
The greater the volume of the cooking liquid, the lighter the braising stock will be. The less liquid there is, the more full-bodied the braising stock will be. Traditionally, the braising stock is rather light, so the cooking liquid is high.

BRAISED CHUCK ROAST

SERVES 8

3 large onions
3 garlic cloves
500 ml (2 cups) red wine (Côtes du Rhône)
1 litre (4 cups) white poultry stock (page 10)
1 thyme sprig
1 bay leaf
10 black peppercorns
1 × 1.5 kg chuck roast
1 teaspoon table salt
2 tablespoons olive oil
40 g butter
½ teaspoon fleur de sel
freshly ground black pepper (8 grinds)

1   Preheat the oven to 150°C with a shelf placed on the lowest rung. Cut the onions in mirepoix (page 34). Peel and crush the garlic (page 280). Pour the wine and poultry stock into a saucepan. Add the thyme, bay leaf and peppercorns, then bring to a simmer.

2   Pat the meat dry with paper towel, then season with the table salt. Heat the olive oil in a flameproof casserole dish over very high heat. Brown the meat on all sides. Degrease the bottom of the dish, then decant the meat (page 282).

3   Melt the butter in the casserole dish over medium heat. Add the onion and garlic, and sweat.

4   Deglaze with half the red wine and poultry stock mixture. Scrape any stuck-on bits off the bottom. Bring to a simmer, then reduce by about one-third, skimming as the liquid reduces.

5   Return the meat to the casserole dish, then pour in the remaining wine and stock mixture. Bring to a simmer. Cover and transfer to the oven for 5–6 hours, or until the meat is very tender. Turn the meat halfway through the cooking time.

6   Decant the meat and transfer to a heatproof container. Strain the sauce through a fine-mesh sieve and pour it over the meat. Let it cool for at least 3 hours, or overnight.

7   Degrease the sauce. Decant the cold meat from its gravy. Bring the gravy to a simmer in a saucepan and reduce by one-third. Strain through a fine-mesh sieve. Adjust the seasoning. Put the meat and gravy in the pan, then bring to a simmer and reheat for 5 minutes over medium heat, basting the meat with the gravy.

8   Decant the meat, then sprinkle with the fleur de sel and pepper. Serve the sauce in a gravy boat.

STEWING

Understand

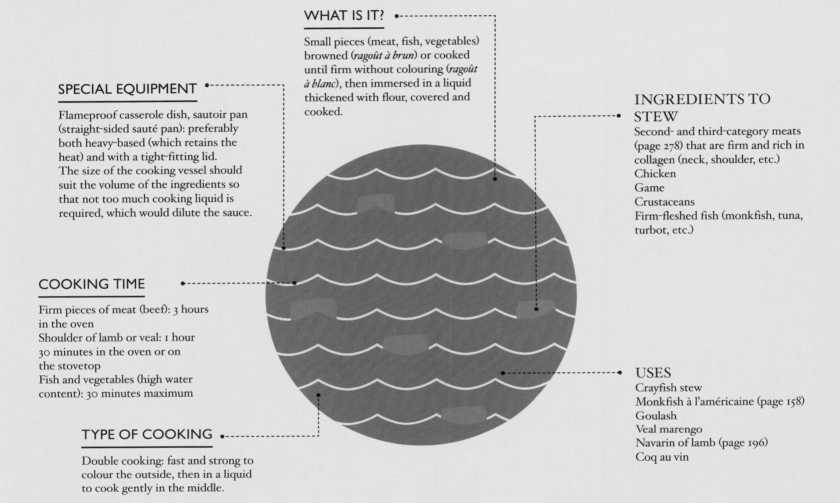

WHAT IS IT?

Small pieces (meat, fish, vegetables) browned (*ragoût à brun*) or cooked until firm without colouring (*ragoût à blanc*), then immersed in a liquid thickened with flour, covered and cooked.

SPECIAL EQUIPMENT

Flameproof casserole dish, sautoir pan (straight-sided sauté pan): preferably both heavy-based (which retains the heat) and with a tight-fitting lid. The size of the cooking vessel should suit the volume of the ingredients so that not too much cooking liquid is required, which would dilute the sauce.

INGREDIENTS TO STEW

Second- and third-category meats (page 278) that are firm and rich in collagen (neck, shoulder, etc.)
Chicken
Game
Crustaceans
Firm-fleshed fish (monkfish, tuna, turbot, etc.)

COOKING TIME

Firm pieces of meat (beef): 3 hours in the oven
Shoulder of lamb or veal: 1 hour 30 minutes in the oven or on the stovetop
Fish and vegetables (high water content): 30 minutes maximum

USES

Crayfish stew
Monkfish à l'américaine (page 158)
Goulash
Veal marengo
Navarin of lamb (page 196)
Coq au vin

TYPE OF COOKING

Double cooking: fast and strong to colour the outside, then in a liquid to cook gently in the middle.

WHY USE THIS TECHNIQUE?

To form a very flavoursome crust (more or less brown depending on whether it is a white or brown stew) by cooking in oil (the Maillard reactions, page 282). The cooking then continues gently, by simmering in a liquid. The crust dissolves in the cooking liquid, flavouring and colouring the sauce.

DOES THE SIZE OF THE MEAT HAVE AN IMPACT ON THE TASTE?

Meat cut into smaller pieces flavours the sauce more.

WHY DUST THE MEAT WITH FLOUR?

The flour helps to thicken the sauce.

HEIGHT OF THE COOKING LIQUID

The greater the volume of the cooking liquid, the more the flavour of the sauce will be diluted. The less liquid there is, the more full-bodied it will be. The sauce of a stew should be quite full-bodied, so the cooking liquid should half-fill the pan.

STEWED VEAL

SERVES 4

500 ml (2 cups) dry white wine
500 ml (2 cups) white poultry stock (page 10)
1 onion
½ teaspoon salt
30 g plain (all-purpose) flour
1 kg veal shoulder, cut into 15–20 pieces
60 g butter
10 g flat-leaf (Italian) parsley
1 garlic clove
1 unwaxed lemon

1 Mix the white wine with the poultry stock. Peel and mince the onion. In a large bowl, mix half the salt into the flour. Add the veal pieces, mix to coat in the flour and tap off any excess.

2 Melt the butter in a flameproof casserole dish over high heat, then reduce the heat to medium and brown the veal on all sides.

3 Remove the veal from the dish, degrease partially, then add the onion with the remaining salt. Sweat the onion, stirring.

4 Return the veal to the dish, stir, then pour in the wine and stock mixture to halfway, while scraping the bottom of the dish with a flat spatula. Bring to the boil and skim. Cover and simmer for 2 hours.

5 Wash, dry and finely chop the parsley. Peel and finely chop the garlic and zest the lemon. Mix these ingredients together in a small bowl.

6 Remove the meat from the dish and strain the sauce through a fine-mesh sieve without pushing. Adjust the seasoning.

7 Return the sauce to the casserole dish, add the meat and stir, then simmer for a few minutes. Add the garlic, parsley and lemon zest mixture and serve.

COOKING AT
LOW TEMPERATURE

Understand

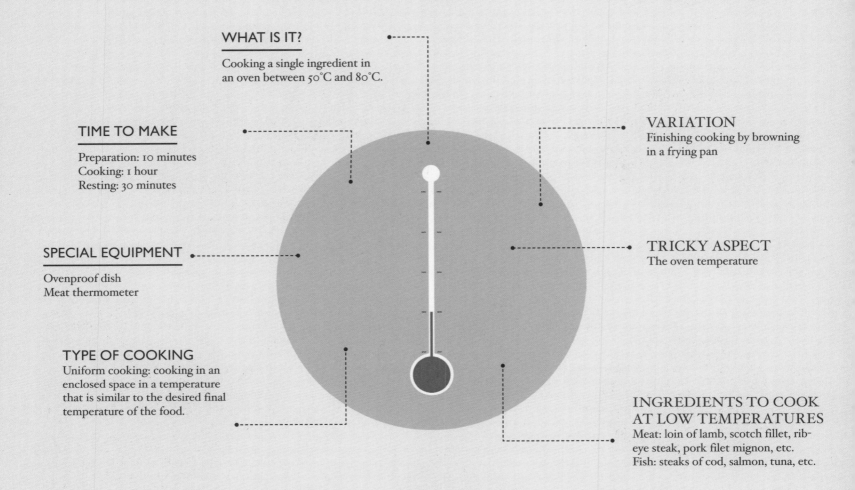

WHAT IS IT?

Cooking a single ingredient in
an oven between 50°C and 80°C.

TIME TO MAKE

Preparation: 10 minutes
Cooking: 1 hour
Resting: 30 minutes

VARIATION
Finishing cooking by browning
in a frying pan

SPECIAL EQUIPMENT

Ovenproof dish
Meat thermometer

TRICKY ASPECT
The oven temperature

TYPE OF COOKING
Uniform cooking: cooking in an
enclosed space in a temperature
that is similar to the desired final
temperature of the food.

**INGREDIENTS TO COOK
AT LOW TEMPERATURES**
Meat: loin of lamb, scotch fillet, rib-
eye steak, pork filet mignon, etc.
Fish: steaks of cod, salmon, tuna, etc.

WHY USE THIS TECHNIQUE?
The flesh is evenly cooked from the outside to the inside, without drying out.

TECHNIQUE TO MASTER
Cooking with a meat thermometer
(page 282)

TIP
To insert the thermometer, go through the
middle of the ribs, and position it so it does
not touch a bone.

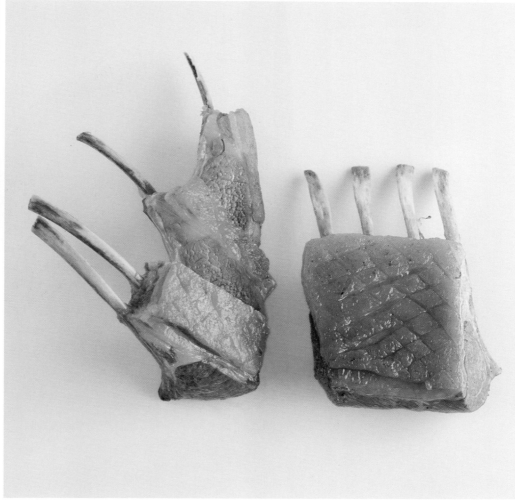

RACK OF LAMB

SERVES 4

2 × 400 g Frenched racks of lamb, refrigerated
1 teaspoon salt
3 tablespoons olive oil

1 Cross-score the fat on the lamb racks as soon as you remove them from the refrigerator, then leave to come to room temperature for 30 minutes. Place your baking dish, meat thermometer and four serving plates in the oven and preheat the oven to 70°C.

2 Season the lamb with the salt and brush each rack with a little of the olive oil. Put them in the baking dish, insert the thermometer in one, and cook in the oven for 1 hour, or until the core temperature reaches 55°C.

3 Heat the remaining oil in a large frying pan over high heat. Brown the lamb racks on all sides, particularly on the fat side, so that it partially melts. Cut into cutlets by passing a knife between the ribs.

POACHING IN
HOT WATER

Understand

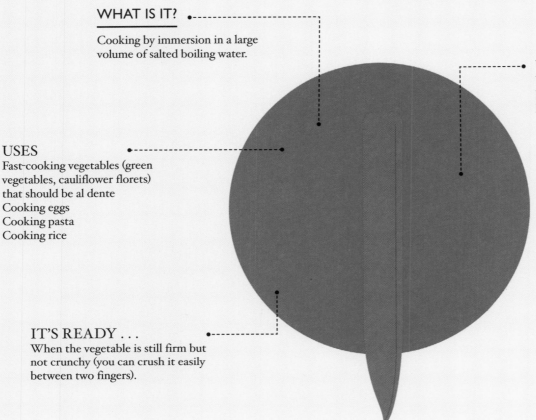

WHAT IS IT?
Cooking by immersion in a large volume of salted boiling water.

VARIATION
Vegetables served cold: cooked English-style (in boiling water) then refreshed in iced water (a large bowl of water and ice cubes)

USES
Fast-cooking vegetables (green vegetables, cauliflower florets) that should be al dente
Cooking eggs
Cooking pasta
Cooking rice

IT'S READY . . .
When the vegetable is still firm but not crunchy (you can crush it easily between two fingers).

WHY START WITH HOT WATER?

For fast tenderisation of the ingredient's structure.
For vegetables that don't need much softening and don't contain much starch, poaching in hot water is recommended because it is faster.
For meats, the temperature must be above 65°C to break down the collagen (and thus tenderise the meat). Poaching in hot water is thus recommended, because the meat benefits straight away from a temperature that allows it to tenderise.

ENGLISH-STYLE GREEN BEANS

SERVES 4

600 g green beans
40 g butter
coarse salt: 20 g per 1 litre (4 cups) water

1　Trim the beans, then wash and drain them.

2　Bring a large saucepan of salted water to a vigorous boil. Plunge in the beans in one go and cook for 5–10 minutes. Skim the surface if necessary. Drain. Serve with butter.

POACHING IN
COLD WATER

Understand

WHAT IS IT?

Cooking by immersion in a large volume of cold water that is then brought to the boil.

USES

Cooking foods with delicate flesh (fish fillets)

Cooking foods containing starch (potatoes)

Making sauce (blanquette): starting with cold water allows an exchange of flavours between the main ingredient and the aromatic flavourings while enriching the cooking liquid

Cooking in court bouillon or court mouillement (limited liquid; skate, turbot)

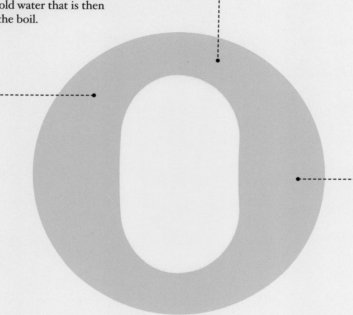

IT'S READY . . .

When the point of a knife plunged into the ingredient meets almost no resistance.

WHY START WITH COLD WATER?

For foodstuffs containing starch: it allows gelatinisation of the starch as the temperature rises, before the cell walls break down. If potatoes were plunged into boiling water, the starch would form a 'barrier' that would stop them cooking uniformly.

- Fish: with the slow rise in temperature, the proteins coagulate less, and the flesh doesn't stiffen straight away. It is close to the principle of cooking at low temperature. The flesh is moist.

ENGLISH-STYLE POTATOES

SERVES 4

1 kg firm-fleshed potatoes (charlotte or similar)
coarse salt: 20 g per 1 litre (4 cups) water

1   Peel and wash the potatoes, then put them in a large saucepan. Cover with cold water (fill to at least 5 cm above the height of the potatoes).

2   Bring to the boil, then add the salt. Simmer for 20 minutes. Skim. Stop the cooking process by pouring in a little cold water to keep them at about 90°C until ready to use.

DOUBLE
FRYING

Understand

WHAT IS IT?

Double cooking of a foodstuff that
is completely immersed in hot oil,
to ensure thorough cooking and the
formation of a crust.

SPECIAL EQUIPMENT

Heavy-based saucepan
Thermometer
Frying basket

WITH AN ELECTRIC DEEP-FRYER

Same procedure.
First fry: 130°C
Second fry: 175°C.

DEEP-FRYER TIP

If using an electric deep-fryer,
check the temperature of the oil
using a thermometer: the actual
temperature is often below the
temperature indicated by the
deep-fryer.

USES
Vegetable chips (potato, sweet
potato, parsnip, pumpkin)

WHY COOK TWICE?

*The first fry at 130°C cooks the potato and
the starch they contain swells in the heat.
The second fry at 175°C gives the potatoes
their colour. The surface of the batons is
dried out by the high temperature of the oil
bath, which makes the crisp crust.*

WHY A DIFFERENT OIL
TEMPERATURE EACH TIME?

*The first bath, which is more gentle, allows
the potatoes to cook without burning; the
second, which is hotter, forms the crust.*

WHY ISN'T IT NECESSARY TO
WASH THE CUT POTATO PIECES?

*Unlike single frying, frying at two
temperatures benefits from the starch
of the potatoes. It makes the chips crunchier.*

Learn

THICK-CUT CHIPS (PONT-NEUF)

SERVES 4

1 kg roasting (floury) potatoes (bintje or similar)
1.5 litres (6 cups) peanut oil
1 teaspoon salt

1   Cut the potatoes into pont-neuf-style batons (page 59). Don't wash them.

2   Heat the oil to 180°C. Immerse the potatoes, let the temperature fall, then cook until 'blond' at 120–130°C. Remove the chips after 5–6 minutes: the pulp of a baton pressed between two fingers (protected from the heat with paper towel) should crush easily. Drain well in a colander or frying basket and set aside to return to room temperature.

3   Increase the temperature of the oil to 190°C. Immerse the potatoes, let the temperature fall then keep it at 175°C and cook for 2–3 minutes. The chips should be crisp, with a dark golden colour.

4   Drain well, add the salt, mix and turn out onto paper towel.

MATCHSTICK CHIPS (ALLUMETTE)

Prepare and cut the potatoes as described on page 59.

Cook for 3 minutes in the first oil bath (130°C), until the pulp of a baton crushes easily when pressed between your fingers, then 1 minute in the second oil bath (175°C).

CHIPS (MIGNONETTE)

Prepare and cut the potatoes as described on page 59.

Cook for about 4 minutes in the first oil bath (130°C), until the pulp of a baton crushes easily when pressed between your fingers, then 2 minutes in the second oil bath (175°C).

SINGLE
FRYING

Understand

page 178

WHAT IS IT?

Cooking a food by completely immersing it in hot oil.

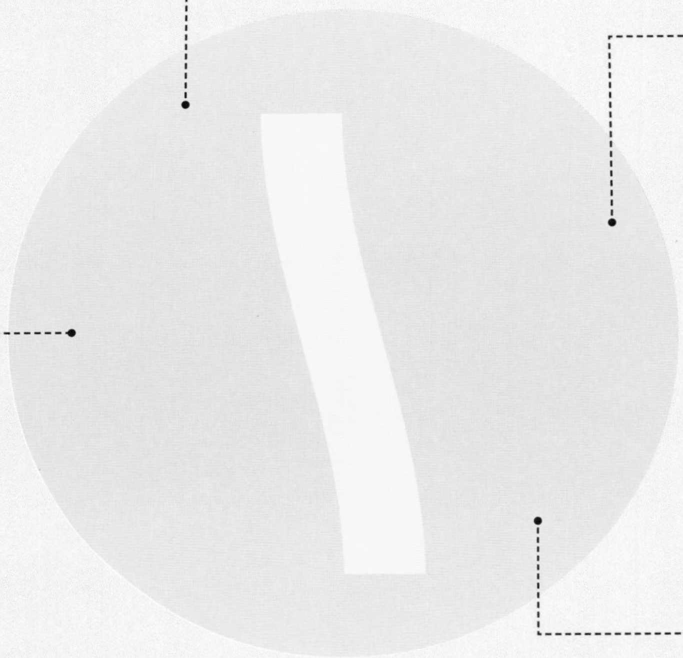

USES
Vegetable crisps (beetroot, carrot, etc.)
English-style breadcrumb coating (flour, egg wash and breadcrumbs)
Tempura
Battered food (fish and chips, page 178)

SPECIAL EQUIPMENT

Heavy-based saucepan
Thermometer
Frying basket

WITH AN ELECTRIC DEEP-FRYER
Same procedure but heat the oil to 130°C straight away.

WHY COOK ONLY ONCE?

The food being fried doesn't require a long cooking time (small pieces, soft vegetables), a single oil bath can suffice. It allows you to cook and brown at the same time.

WHY RUB THE POTATOES IN WATER?

To remove the starch released during cutting. Sliced potatoes can also be wiped with paper towel. This prevents the starch from getting into the oil.

CRISPS

SERVES 4

500 g potatoes (bintje or similar)
1.5 litres (6 cups) peanut oil
1 teaspoon salt

1   Cut the potatoes into 1 mm thick rounds. Soak
them in cold water for 10 minutes. Rub them with
your hands in the water. Drain and dry carefully with
a clean tea towel (dish towel).

2   Heat the oil to 160°C. Immerse the potato rounds,
ten at a time, and let the temperature drop to 120–
130°C. Stir the crisps in the oil with a spatula and cook
for 3–4 minutes until golden and crisp.

3   Drain on paper towel, then repeat with the
remaining rounds. Season well with the salt.

GAUFRETTES (WAFER POTATOES)

Prepare the potatoes as indicated on page 59.
Cooking time: 5 minutes.

PAILLE (POTATO STRAWS)

Prepare the potatoes as indicated on page 59.
Cooking time: 2–3 minutes.

CHAPTER 2
RECIPES

FRENCH ONION SOUP

Understand

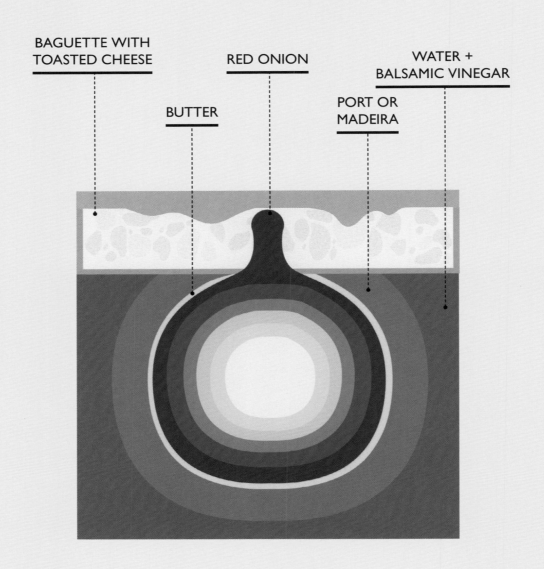

BAGUETTE WITH
TOASTED CHEESE

BUTTER

RED ONION

PORT OR
MADEIRA

WATER +
BALSAMIC VINEGAR

WHAT IS IT?

Onions stewed in butter, then cooked in water with port or Madeira and topped with toasted bread (croutons) and gruyère.

TIME TO MAKE

Preparation: 25 minutes
Cooking: 50–55 minutes

SPECIAL EQUIPMENT

Heatproof serving bowls

VARIATION

Normandy-style onion soup: stewed onions with flour added (page 282), then mixed with milk and thickened; croutons without cheese

TRICKY ASPECTS

Stewing the onions
The toasted cheese topping

TECHNIQUES TO MASTER

Scraping off stuck-on bits (page 283)
Slicing thinly (page 280)

TIP

If the onions stick to the bottom of the saucepan, add 1–2 tablespoons cold water.

IT'S READY . . .

When the soup is a sufficiently dark golden brown.

STORAGE

3 days in the refrigerator (without the bread or cheese). Reheat by bringing to a simmer, and wait until the last minute to prepare the croutons.

SERVES 4

SOUP

3 large red onions
60 g butter
½ teaspoon salt
60 ml (¼ cup) port or Madeira
1 tablespoon balsamic vinegar
freshly ground black pepper, to taste

CROUTONS

½ baguette
80 g gruyère, grated

1 Peel the onions and cut into 5 mm slices. Melt 20 g of the butter in a large heavy-based saucepan over medium heat. Add the onion and the salt. Cook for 25–30 minutes, stirring frequently, until the onion is dark golden brown.

2 Pour in 1.2 litres water and the port or Madeira, bring to the boil, then scrape any stuck-on bits off the bottom of the pan. Reduce the heat and simmer for 20 minutes, uncovered, skimming as necessary.

3 Cut the baguette half into slices about 1.5 cm thick. Melt the remaining butter in a large frying pan until it foams. Fry the slices of bread until golden on both sides. Drain on paper towel.

4 Preheat the grill to high. Add the balsamic vinegar to the soup, then taste and adjust the seasoning. Pour the soup into ovenproof serving bowls sitting on a baking tray, place one or two pieces of bread in each bowl and sprinkle with the gruyère. Place under the grill for 5 minutes, or until the cheese is melted and golden.

PRAWN BISQUE

Understand

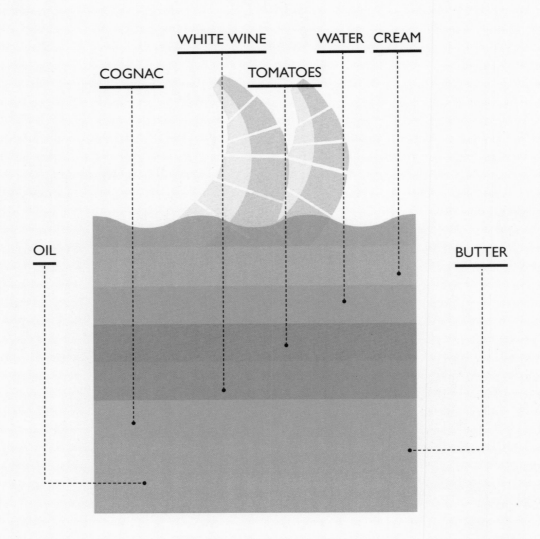

COGNAC

WHITE WINE

TOMATOES

WATER CREAM

OIL

BUTTER

WHAT IS IT?

Raw prawns browned with aromatic
vegetables then blended and strained.
The bisque is thickened with cream.

TIME TO MAKE

Preparation: 45 minutes
Cooking: 45 minutes

SPECIAL EQUIPMENT

Fine-mesh sieve
Blender or food processor

TRICKY ASPECT
The reduction

TECHINQUES TO MASTER
Reducing a sauce (page 283)
Pushing through a sieve (page 281)
Slicing thinly (page 280)
Decanting (page 282)
Skimming (page 283)
Deglazing (page 283)
Sweating (page 282)

TIP
To seal the prawns well, cook them in
several batches.

IT'S READY . . .
When the bisque is creamy.

STORAGE
2 days in the refrigerator in an airtight
container. Reheat over medium heat, stirring
constantly, until it boils.

WHAT DO THE PRAWN
SHELLS ADD?

*They contain chitin (a type of sugar
molecule) that breaks down into powerful
aromatic components at high temperatures.*

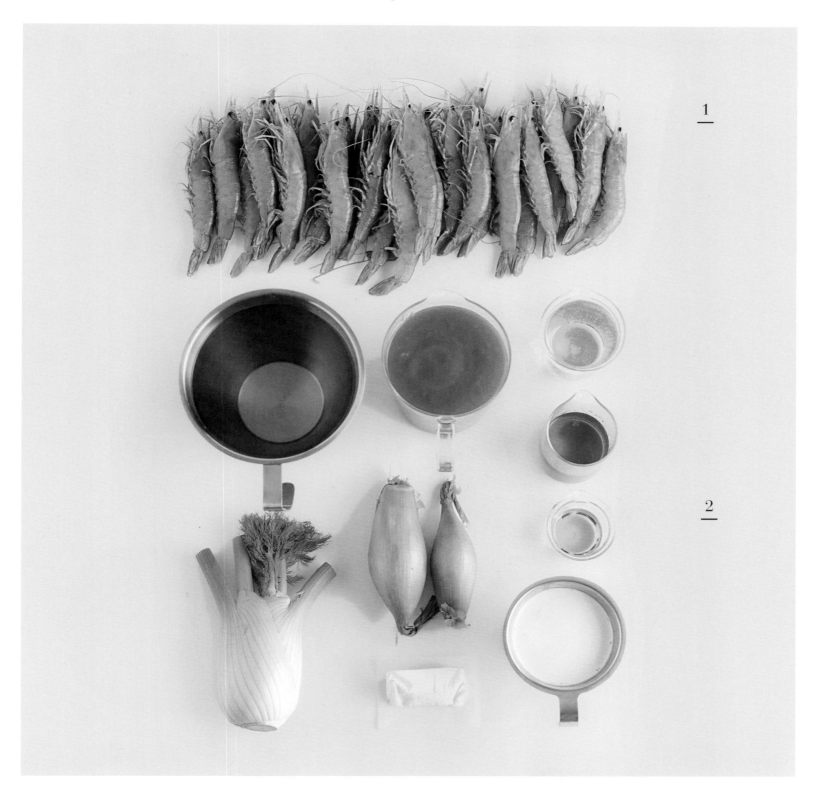

SERVES 4

1 PRAWNS

800 g raw prawns (shrimp), thawed
(30–50 prawns, depending on their size)

2 BISQUE

2 large French shallots
1 fennel bulb
1 tablespoon olive oil
30 g butter
80 ml (⅓ cup) cognac
200 ml white wine
600 g tinned chopped tomatoes
200 ml pouring (single) cream

continued on page 96

Making prawn bisque

1   Wash the prawns and dry them with paper towel. Peel and thinly slice the shallots. Wash and thinly slice the fennel.

2   Sear the prawns in the olive oil in a large saucepan over very high heat. Add the butter and let the prawns caramelise over medium heat for 2–3 minutes. Remove eight prawns, peel them, then return their shells to the pan. Set aside the flesh in an airtight container.

3   Remove the prawns from the pan, then sweat the shallot and fennel in the same pan for a few minutes. Return the prawns to the pan, then deglaze with the cognac and white wine. Reduce until no liquid remains.

4   Add the tomatoes and cook for 1 minute. Pour in 1 litre (4 cups) water, bring to the boil and simmer for 30 minutes, skimming regularly.

5   Blend or process the bisque to obtain a smooth purée. Push through a fine-mesh sieve. You should have 1–1.2 litres of bisque.

6   Pour the sieved bisque into a saucepan and reduce by half (10–15 minutes). Add the cream and stir over high heat. Reduce for 3–5 minutes. Purée for a few seconds with a hand-held blender.

7   Cut the reserved prawns in half crossways and serve on top of the bisque.

CHICKEN
CONSOMMÉ

Understand

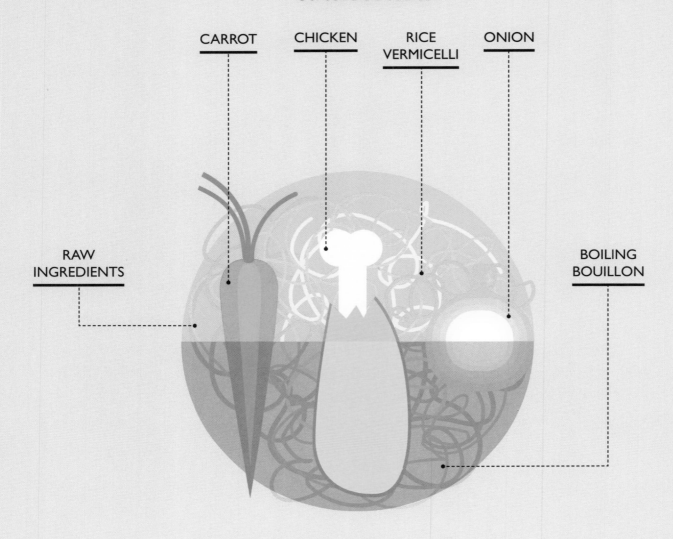

CARROT CHICKEN RICE VERMICELLI ONION

RAW INGREDIENTS

BOILING BOUILLON

WHAT IS IT?
Boiling white poultry stock poured over an assortment of raw chicken, carrot and rice vermicelli.

TIME TO MAKE
Preparation: 15 minutes
Resting: 5 minutes

SPECIAL EQUIPMENT
Meat tenderiser or heavy-based saucepan

VARIATION
Pot-au-feu bouillon

TRICKY ASPECT
The heat of the poultry stock must be very high to cook the vermicelli and the chicken, and to soften the carrot

TECHNIQUES TO MASTER
Flattening meat (page 278)
Cutting in brunoise (page 36)
Slicing thinly (page 280)
Mincing (page 280)

TIP
Let the stock boil for a few seconds so it is at the highest temperature possible.

IT'S READY . . .
When the rice vermicelli is soft and the chicken is cooked.

STORAGE
2 days in the refrigerator. Bring to the boil to reheat.

SERVES 4

70 g clear rice vermicelli
1 carrot
2 bulb spring onions (scallions)
1 x 150 g chicken breast fillet
10 g flat-leaf (Italian) parsley
1 litre (4 cups) white poultry stock (page 10)
3 tablespoons nuoc mam (Vietnamese fish sauce)
½ teaspoon salt
freshly ground black pepper (2 grinds)

1 Break the rice vermicelli in two. Peel the carrot and cut it in brunoise (page 36). Cut the green stems and the roots off the spring onion bulbs and remove the first layer of skin. Slice the bulbs thinly.

2 Flatten the thick parts of the chicken breast by hitting it with a meat tenderiser or the bottom of a heavy-based saucepan, then cut into thin strips 4–5 cm long.

3 Divide the ingredients among four bowls. Wash, dry, pick and finely chop the parsley leaves.

4 Add the nuoc mam, salt and pepper to the chicken stock and bring to a vigorous boil. Divide it between the four bowls, ensuring that all of the ingredients are immersed. Wait 5 minutes then scatter over the chopped parsley.

SOUP PIE

Understand

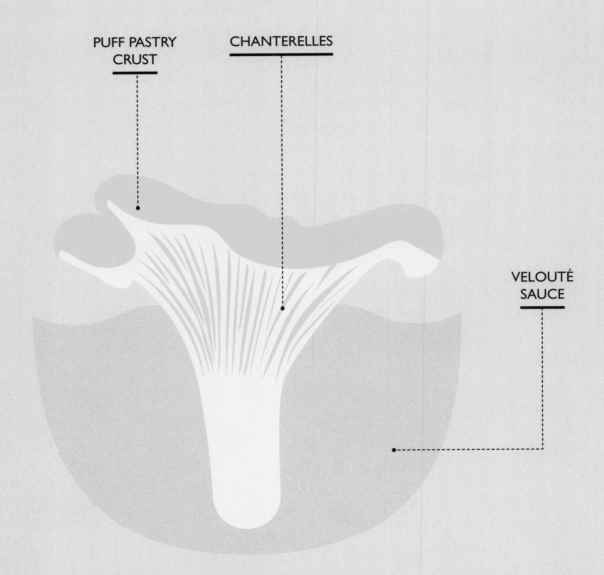

PUFF PASTRY
CRUST

CHANTERELLES

VELOUTÉ
SAUCE

WHAT IS IT?

Velouté sauce of button mushrooms and
chanterelles, thickened with cream, covered
with a disc of puff pastry then browned in
the oven.

TIME TO MAKE

Preparation: 35 minutes
Cooking: 40 minutes

SPECIAL EQUIPMENT

Ovenproof serving bowls
Pastry brush

TECHNIQUES TO MASTER

Slicing thinly (page 280)
Mincing (page 280)
Chopping finely (page 280)
Cutting in escalopes (page 280)
Sweating (page 282)

VARIATION

Traditional velouté sauce: béchamel sauce
base, thickened with cream and egg yolk

TIP

The puff pastry must be very cold to be
worked easily.

WHY DOES THE PUFF PASTRY
SWELL UP IN THE OVEN?

*Puff pastry contains water, which
evaporates into steam when heated.
This change triggers the swelling of
the pastry.*

Learn

SERVES 4

1 VELOUTÉ SAUCE WITH MUSHROOMS

300 g button mushrooms
200 g chanterelles
1 French shallot
1 garlic clove
40 g butter
600 ml white poultry stock (page 10)
150 ml pouring (single) cream

2 SEASONING

1 teaspoon salt
freshly ground black pepper (6 grinds)

3 PASTRY

250 g puff pastry (page 46), cold
plain (all-purpose) flour, for dusting

4 TO FINISH

1 egg yolk beaten with 1 teaspoon water

continued on page 102

101

Making soup pie

1   Cut the stems off the button mushrooms and slice the caps. Clean the chanterelles with a moistened pastry brush then slice them thinly. Peel and mince the shallot. Peel and finely chop the garlic.

2   Melt the butter in a large saucepan and sweat the shallot. Add the mushrooms, then stir constantly for 3–4 minutes, until the mushrooms have released their water. Add the garlic and cook for 30 seconds, or until fragrant. Season with salt and pepper.

3   In a separate saucepan, bring the white poultry stock to the boil then pour it over the mushrooms. Simmer for 20 minutes. Preheat the oven to 180°C.

4   Remove about half the mushrooms and set aside for the filling. Add the cream to the saucepan, then blend with a hand-held blender to obtain a smooth creamy sauce.

5   Roll out the puff pastry on a floured work surface. Cut out four discs with a diameter 3 cm larger than the top of your ovenproof serving bowls. Set aside in the refrigerator.

6   Divide the mushrooms among the serving bowls then pour in the cream sauce to 1.5 cm from the top.

7   Dampen the rim and the top of the bowls on the outside with a little water. Place a pastry disc over each bowl, pressing a little to seal. Brush with the mixed egg yolk and water.

8   Bake for 20 minutes, or until the pastry is golden. Cut the soup crust with the point of a knife.

SCALLOP
CARPACCIO

Understand

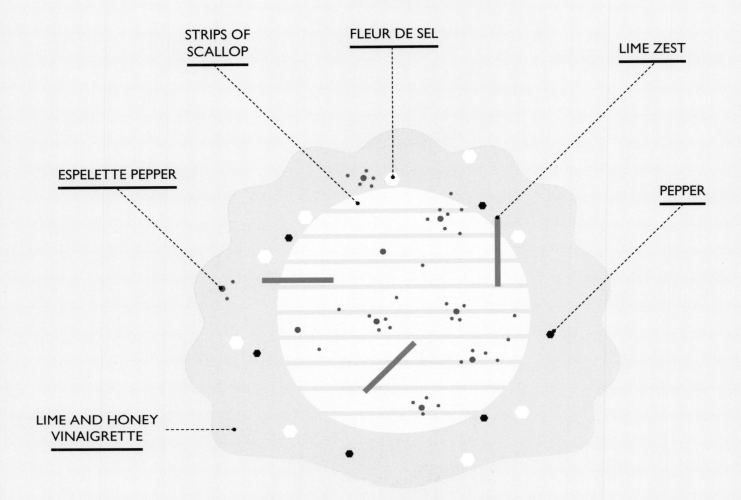

STRIPS OF SCALLOP

FLEUR DE SEL

LIME ZEST

ESPELETTE PEPPER

PEPPER

LIME AND HONEY VINAIGRETTE

WHAT IS IT?

Thin slices of raw scallop, seasoned at the last minute with a lime vinaigrette.

TIME TO MAKE

Preparation: 25 minutes
Resting: 30 minutes

SPECIAL EQUIPMENT

Very sharp, thin-bladed knife
Citrus zester

TRICKY ASPECT
Cutting the scallops

TECHNIQUES TO MASTER
Mincing (page 280)
Zesting (page 280)

TIP
With frozen scallops: slice them before they have completely thawed.

ORGANISATION
Prepare the plates up to 30 minutes in advance. Cover with plastic wrap and refrigerate. Season at the last minute.

WHY FREEZE THE SCALLOPS?

Freezing firms up the flesh and makes it easier to cut.

WHAT EFFECT DOES THE VINAIGRETTE HAVE ON THE SCALLOPS?

Unlike a tartare or marinated fish, here the vinaigrette is added at the last minute; it doesn't modify the texture of the scallop, simply dresses it.

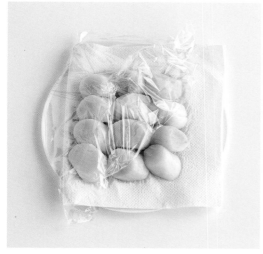

SERVES 4

12 scallops, without roe
1 lime (juice and zest)
½ teaspoon table salt
1 teaspoon honey
freshly ground black pepper (8 grinds)
2 ½ tablespoons olive oil
1 small French shallot (to serve)
pinch of espelette pepper (to serve)
¼ teaspoon fleur de sel (to serve)

1   Wash the scallops and dry with paper towel. Arrange on a plate, cover with plastic wrap and freeze for 30 minutes.

2   Wash and zest the lime using a citrus zester. Set aside the zest. Squeeze the juice into a small bowl with the table salt. Add the honey and pepper, then pour in the olive oil while mixing with a fork. Peel and mince the shallot.

3   Cut the scallops crossways into 2 mm thick slices.

4   Arrange the scallop slices on a plate. Mix the vinaigrette once more, then pour over the scallops. Sprinkle over the shallot, espelette pepper, fleur de sel and lime zest.

SALMON
TARTARE

Understand

SALMON RAW
IN THE MIDDLE

SALMON COOKED
BY THE MARINADE

MARINADE

AVOCADO

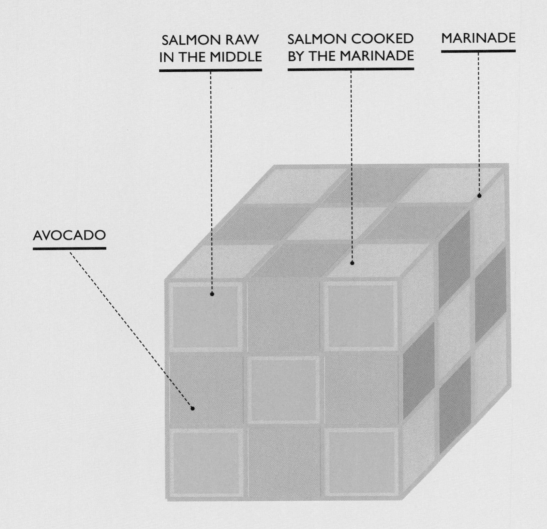

WHAT IS IT?

Diced raw salmon marinated in a mixture of lime juice, olive oil, shallot and dill, accompanied with diced avocado.

TIME TO MAKE

Preparation: 25 minutes; Resting: 5 minutes

SPECIAL EQUIPMENT

Chef's knife, fine-mesh sieve

VARIATIONS

Tartare minute (without resting time)
Gravlax (24 hours in the marinade) (page 108)

SERVING VARIATION

In a circle, alternating salmon and avocado

TRICKY ASPECT

Cutting the salmon

TECHNIQUES TO MASTER

Chopping finely and mincing (page 280)
Zesting (page 280)

TIP

Oil the knife to make cutting easier.

STORAGE

Prepare the salmon and the marinade separately, up to 1 hour before serving, and only bring them together 15 minutes before.

WHAT IS A MARINADE?

An aromatic liquid preparation intended to tenderise and flavour large ingredients before cooking or small pieces without cooking (instant marinades).

DOES THE ACIDITY OF THE LIME 'COOK' THE FISH?

The acidity modifies the proteins in the fish, which gives it a cooked appearance. In French, the word coction *is used for this process, to differentiate it from* cuisson *(cooking with heat).*

SERVES 4

400 g skinless salmon fillets
5 g dill
2 limes
1 French shallot
½ teaspoon salt
freshly ground black pepper (6 grinds)
2 tablespoons olive oil
1 avocado

1 Cut the salmon into very small dice. Set aside in the refrigerator. Wash, dry, pick and finely chop the dill. Wash, dry and zest one of the limes using a citrus zester, then squeeze both. Peel and very finely mince the shallot.

2 In a large round-bottomed bowl, dissolve the salt in the lime juice, then add the pepper, dill and half the shallot. Pour in the oil and stir. Add the salmon, stir, then refrigerate for 5 minutes.

3 Cut the avocado into small dice, then mix with the lime zest and the remaining shallot.

4 Drain the salmon over a bowl, reserving the marinade.

5 Dip the avocado into the marinade to coat, then drain.

6 Carefully mix the salmon and drained avocado and dress with a little of the marinade.

SALMON
GRAVLAX

Understand

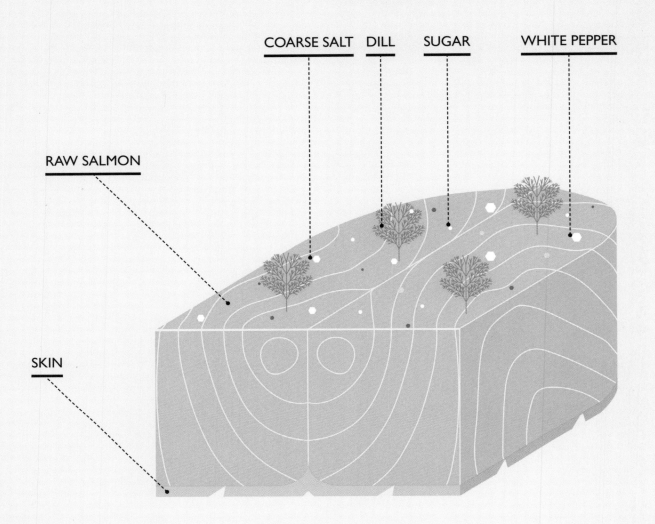

COARSE SALT   **DILL**   **SUGAR**   **WHITE PEPPER**

RAW SALMON

SKIN

WHAT IS IT?

Raw salmon marinated in salt and sugar, and seasoned with pepper and dill.

TIME TO MAKE

Preparation: 20 minutes (then overnight) + 30 minutes
Maceration: 24 hours

SPECIAL EQUIPMENT

Fishbone tweezers
Very sharp thin-bladed knife

TRICKY ASPECTS

Skinning the salmon
Removing bones without tearing the flesh

TECHNIQUES TO MASTER

Crushing spices (page 280)
Chopping finely (page 280)

TIP

Dip the tweezers in water before removing each bone.

IT'S READY . . .

When the salmon has released some of its water and has firmed up.

STORAGE

1 week in the refrigerator wrapped in baking paper then plastic wrap.

NOTE

For thicker, more uniform flesh, choose a piece from the centre of the salmon.

WHAT ROLE DOES THE
MARINADE PLAY?

The sugar and salt absorb water from the surface of the fish, which firms up the flesh. The dill, pepper and coriander seeds add aromatic notes that are captured by the fat in the fish and help to flavour it.

SERVES 4

GRAVLAX

20 g dill
20 g coarse salt
20 g sugar
½ teaspoon peppercorns
(preferably white), crushed
1 level teaspoon coriander seeds, crushed
1 × 400 g salmon fillet, scaled and pin-boned

GRAVLAX SAUCE

10 g dill
½ lemon
½ teaspoon salt
freshly ground black pepper (6 grinds)

30 g dijon mustard
20 g maple syrup
80 ml (⅓ cup) sunflower oil

1   To make the gravlax, wash, dry, pick and
finely chop the dill. Mix the coarse salt, sugar, dill,
peppercorns and coriander seeds in a small bowl. Wash
the salmon and dry with paper towel. Score the skin
with a sharp thin-bladed knife.

2   Spread one-third of the dill mixture in a baking
dish. Place the salmon fillet on top, skin side down,
and cover with the remaining dill mixture, pressing
with your hands to coat the fish well. Cover with
plastic wrap. Set aside in the refrigerator for 24 hours.
After 12 hours, pour off any liquid.

3   Rub the salmon with paper towel to dry it and
remove the seeds. Remove the skin by sliding a sharp
knife under it. Cut into thin slices, 1–1.5 cm thick.

4   To make the sauce, wash, dry, pick and finely
chop the dill. Squeeze the lemon half and mix with
the salt and pepper to dissolve the salt. Stir in the
mustard and maple syrup, then gradually pour in the
oil while whisking, to obtain a smooth sauce. Stir in
the chopped dill.

5   Place three slices of salmon on each plate, with a
little gravlax sauce to one side.

EGGS IN ASPIC

Understand

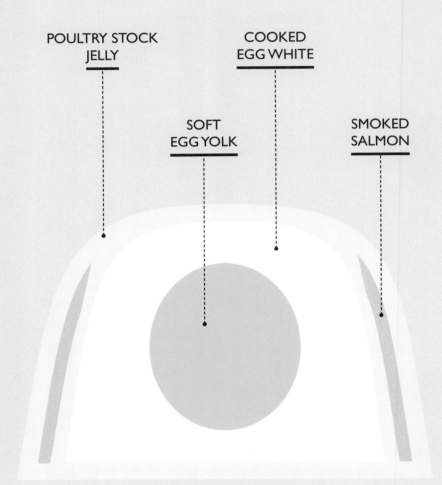

POULTRY STOCK JELLY

COOKED EGG WHITE

SOFT EGG YOLK

SMOKED SALMON

WHAT ARE THEY?

Soft-boiled eggs set in a moulded flavoured jelly and decorated with smoked salmon.

DEFINITION

Aspic: cooked preparation set in a moulded jelly. The egg is one of the traditional aspics, along with meat and fish aspics.

TIME TO MAKE

Preparation: 45 minutes
Resting: at least 1 hour

SPECIAL EQUIPMENT

Eggs in aspic moulds (or 6 cm water glasses)

ALTERNATIVE
With a poached egg (page 68)

VARIATIONS
Eggs in aspic with ham
Dressed eggs in aspic (cornichons + tarragon + capers)
Jelly flavoured with port, Madeira or cognac

TRICKY ASPECTS
The temperature of the jellied stock (if too hot it cooks the salmon, if too cold it starts to set)
Turning out the moulds

WHY REST FOR 1 HOUR IN THE REFRIGERATOR?

Once the gelatine is dissolved in a hot liquid, it must set into a jelly. This occurs at 10°C when the gelatine molecules bind together to form a network characteristic of gels.

SERVES 4

EGGS

4 soft-boiled eggs, shelled (page 65)

JELLY

500 ml (2 cups) white poultry stock (page 10)
½ teaspoon salt
8 gelatine leaves (15 g)

TO GARNISH

4 dill sprigs
50 g sliced smoked salmon

1   To make the jelly, heat the poultry stock. Add the salt (unless you're using purchased stock). Soften the gelatine by soaking in cold water for 5 minutes. Wring it out between your fingers, then add it to the hot stock. Whisk to dissolve it completely. Leave to cool.

2   Wash, dry and pick the dill. Cut the slices of salmon into strips as wide as the length of an egg (about 4 cm).

3   Place three or four dill fronds in the bottom of each mould. Pour over some still-warm stock to a depth of 2–3 mm. Refrigerate to set.

4   Dip the salmon slices in the stock and gelatine mixture. Stick them to the insides of the moulds without overlapping.

5   Cut a thin strip of egg white from each egg to stabilise it. Place an egg, cut side down, in the centre of each mould. Cover with the lukewarm poultry stock and refrigerate for at least 1 hour.

6   To unmould, slide a thin-bladed knife around the edge of each mould then invert onto a plate.

SEMI-COOKED
FOIE GRAS

Understand

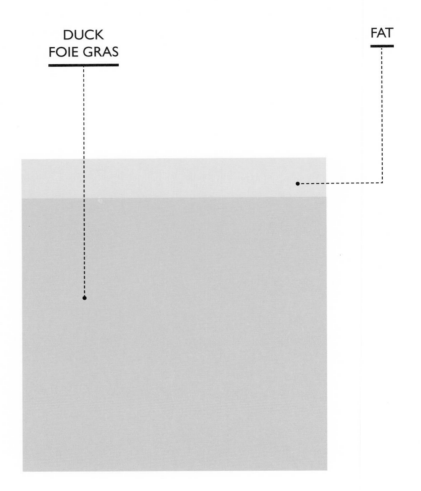

DUCK
FOIE GRAS

FAT

WHAT IS IT?

Raw duck liver seasoned with salt, pepper
and Noilly Prat, cooked in a terrine in
a bain-marie.

TIME TO MAKE

Preparation: 20 minutes
Cooking: 45 minutes
Resting: 3 hours + 48 hours (at least)

SPECIAL EQUIPMENT

Terrine (19 cm × 8 cm)
Small rigid tray (18 cm × 7 cm)
500 g weight

SEASONINGS

White port, cognac, calvados, armagnac
Espelette pepper, paprika, nutmeg

TRICKY ASPECT

Cooking

TECHNIQUE TO MASTER

Deveining foie gras (page 278)

IT'S READY . . .

When the tip of a knife comes out lukewarm
after being inserted into the middle for
5–10 seconds (45°C with an electronic meat
thermometer).

STORAGE

1 week in the refrigerator.

NOTE

Adjust the cooking and seasoning to the
weight: 8–10 minutes per 100 g foie gras;
10 g salt, 4 g pepper, and 2½ tablespoons
Noilly Prat per 1 kg foie gras.

WHY USE A BAIN-MARIE?

*It allows gentle cooking which prevents
the fat in the foie gras melting.*

WHY 'SEMI-COOKED'?

*Because it is cooked to 45°C at the
core (50°C once out of the oven), unlike
preserved foie gras (cooked to 100°C at
the core).*

SERVES 4

1 × 500 g lobe cold duck foie gras
1 teaspoon fine salt
freshly ground black pepper (15 grinds)
¾ tablespoon Noilly Prat
fleur de sel (to serve)
pepper mignonette (to serve)

1 Remove the foie gras from the refrigerator 1 hour before deveining so it is at 12–14°C. Preheat the oven to 120°C. Mix the salt and pepper. Separate the large and small pieces of the liver and carefully devein with your fingers or the rounded end of a spoon handle. Separate the edges of each piece and open them out. Remove the vein at the surface. Remove the second, deeper vein, cutting the liver gently to access it.

2 Season the two open faces of the liver with the salt and pepper mixture. Sprinkle over the Noilly Prat.

3 Place the pieces in the terrine, smooth side out, add any seasoning that fell out of the sides and tap down with the back of your hand to remove trapped air.

4 Place the terrine in a baking dish, add boiling water halfway up the sides and put the lid on the terrine. Bake for 45 minutes. Set aside to cool.

5 When the centre of the foie gras reaches 30–35°C, place the small tray on top and press to make the grease rise. Tip the terrine over a bowl to pour off the liquid and remove the blood that comes with it. Strain this liquid to remove the blood and set aside. Place the weight on the small tray. Refrigerate for at least 3 hours, or until the foie gras has solidified.

6 Remove the weight and the tray, smooth the surface with a spoon, then pour back the reserved grease. If it has solidified too much, liquefy in a bain-marie without overheating. Refrigerate for at least 48 hours.

7 Run the blade of a knife under hot water, dry it, then cut the terrine into slices 1 cm thick. Sprinkle with the fleur de sel and the pepper mignonette.

VOL-AU-VENTS

Understand

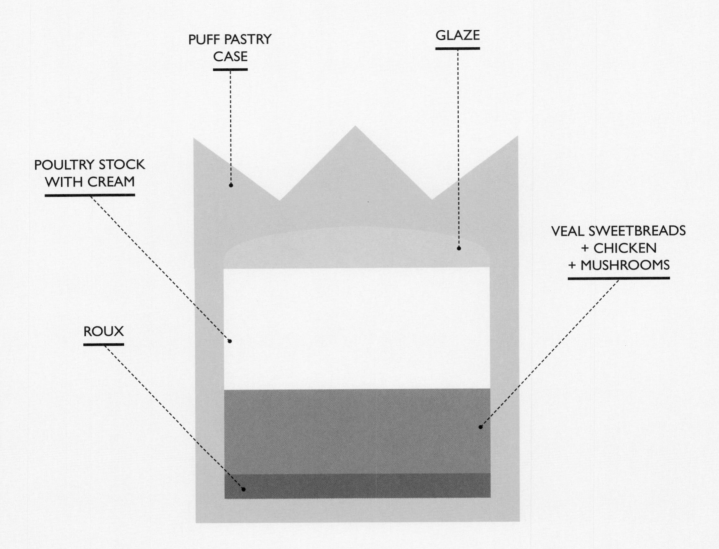

PUFF PASTRY
CASE

GLAZE

POULTRY STOCK
WITH CREAM

VEAL SWEETBREADS
+ CHICKEN
+ MUSHROOMS

ROUX

WHAT ARE THEY?

Case of puff pastry filled after cooking
with a salpicon (see below) of chicken, veal
sweetbreads and mushrooms, bound in
a creamy béchamel sauce.

DEFINITIONS

Vol-au-vent: traditionally, a puff pastry case of
15–20 cm, filled with a salpicon (see below).
Bouchée à la reine: mini puff pastry case filled
with creamy chicken purée or a salpicon of
chicken and mushrooms. These days, the two
are used interchangeably.
Salpicon: ingredients in small dice, bound in
a sauce.

TIME TO MAKE

Preparation: 45 minutes
Cooking: 1 hour
Resting: 20–30 minutes

SPECIAL EQUIPMENT

Rolling pin
Round biscuit cutter (5 cm diameter)
Round biscuit cutter (10 cm diameter)

TRICKY ASPECT

Cooking the pastry cases

TIP

The puff pastry must be very cold.
Refrigerate it for 20–30 minutes before
baking, to prevent it shrinking during
cooking.

STORAGE

2 days for the filling (in the refrigerator) and
the puff pastry cases (at room temperature).
Assemble and reheat for 8–10 minutes in a
150°C oven.

THEY'RE READY . . .

When the cases are golden and the sauce is
thick and creamy.

Learn

SERVES 4

1 PASTRY

600 g puff pastry (page 46)
plain (all-purpose) flour for dusting

2 FILLING

500 ml (2 cups) white poultry stock (page 10)
150 g veal sweetbreads, no skin
150 g chicken breast (fillet)
350 g button mushrooms
40 g butter
40 g plain (all-purpose) flour
100 ml pouring (single) cream

3 GLAZE

1 egg yolk beaten with 1 teaspoon water

4 SEASONING

1 teaspoon salt
freshly ground black pepper (6 grinds)

continued on page 116

Making vol-au-vents

1 Preheat the oven to 200°C. Roll the pastry out to 3 mm thick, regularly dusting the pastry, work surface and rolling pin with flour to prevent it sticking.

2 Cut out four 10 cm discs. Place them on a baking tray lined with baking paper. Cut out eight more 10 cm discs, then cut out the centres with a 5 cm biscuit cutter to create rings.

3 Glaze the pastry discs with the egg yolk mixed with the water, then place one ring on top of each disc, pressing gently to make it stick. Glaze the whole surface of the pastry. Place a second ring on top of the first, pressing gently. Glaze. Firm up the pastry by refrigerating for 20–30 minutes. Bake for 20 minutes, reducing the temperature to 160°C after 10 minutes.

4 Pour the poultry stock into a saucepan and add the veal sweetbreads and chicken breast. Bring to a simmer and cook for 25 minutes.

5 Remove the stalks from the mushrooms, then peel the caps and cut them into quarters. Add them to the stock and cook for a further 5 minutes. Remove the sweetbreads, chicken and mushroom using a skimmer or slotted spoon, and keep warm.

6 Make a roux (page 18) with the butter and flour in a large saucepan. Gradually incorporate the stock, whisking constantly. Add the cream and let it simmer for 10 minutes while whisking. Adjust the seasoning.

7 Cut the sweetbreads and chicken into small dice. Add them to the sauce with the mushrooms.

8 Using a utility knife, cut out the top layer of the pastry case bases (the first layer of pastry) on the inside of the cases, without piercing the bottom, and set aside. Fill the cases with the cream filling and reheat in the oven for 5 minutes.

9 Serve the vol-au-vents topped with their cut-out pastry 'lids'.

GOUGÈRES

Understand

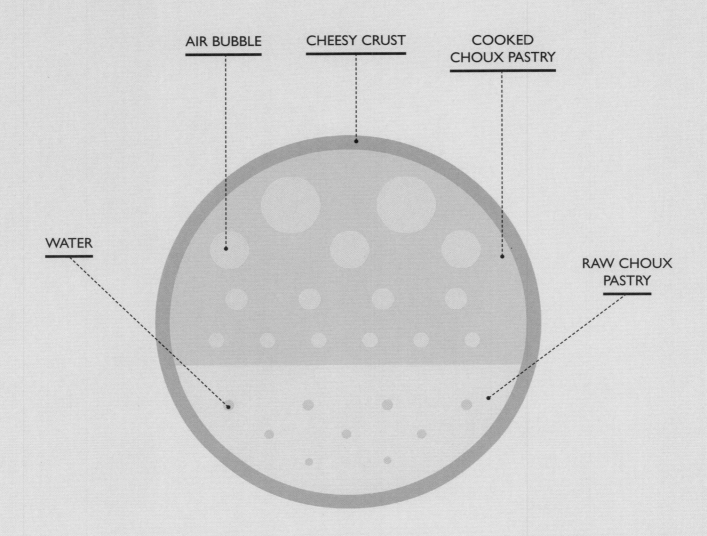

AIR BUBBLE

CHEESY CRUST

COOKED
CHOUX PASTRY

WATER

RAW CHOUX
PASTRY

WHAT ARE THEY?
Savoury cheese choux pastry, piped in balls.

TIME TO MAKE
Preparation: 30 minutes
Cooking: 25–30 minutes

SPECIAL EQUIPMENT
Piping bag + plain 12 mm decorating nozzle
Baking tray

VARIATION
Piping in a ring to make a wreath

TRICKY ASPECT
Cooking

TECHNIQUES TO MASTER
Drying out choux pastry (page 119)
Making a panade (page 119)
Piping (page 281)

TIP
Don't open the oven door before the gougères
have browned: there's a risk they will sink.

STORAGE
The gougères can be reheated for 2 minutes in
a 150°C oven.

HOW DO THE GOUGÈRES
SWELL UP?
*During cooking, the water in the pastry
evaporates as steam. As the pastry is
viscous, it retains the steam, which triggers
the swelling.*

WHY DO THEY SINK IF THE OVEN
IS OPENED TOO SOON?
*Because the temperature of the oven drops,
the steam returns to water, which takes
up less volume than steam, and so the
gougères sink.*

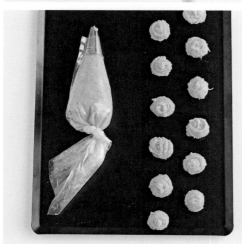

MAKES 30

CHEESE CHOUX PASTRY

70 g plain (all-purpose) flour
pinch of paprika
pinch of cayenne pepper
pinch of freshly grated nutmeg
freshly ground black pepper (6 grinds)
60 ml (¼ cup) milk
50 g butter, cut into dice
½ teaspoon salt
2 eggs, lightly beaten
100 g comté or beaufort cheese, finely grated

1   Preheat the oven to 180°C. Mix the flour with the spices. Combine 60 ml (¼ cup) water, the milk, butter and salt in a saucepan and place over medium heat. Stir with a wooden spoon until the butter melts, then bring to the boil, letting it boil for 2–3 seconds.

2   Remove from the heat, add the flour in one go and incorporate it gently. When the pastry pulls together, mix vigorously. Dry the pastry over medium heat while stirring for 30–60 seconds.

3   Transfer the panade (the dried pastry) to the bowl of an electric mixer and mix for a few seconds to cool it down (or stir it with a wooden spoon). Gradually add the egg, stopping after you have added two-thirds. If the choux pastry sticks to the spoon and falls off in one or several lumps, it is ready; if not, keep adding the egg.

4   Stir in the cheese.

5   Using a piping bag fitted with a plain 12 mm piping nozzle, pipe 30 gougères 3 cm in diameter, spacing them a minimum of 3 cm apart, on a baking tray lined with baking paper. Smooth them out (using a finger or a pastry brush) with the remaining beaten egg or even water.

6   Bake for 25–30 minutes, until the gougères are golden. Cool on a wire rack.

CHEESE
SOUFFLÉ

Understand

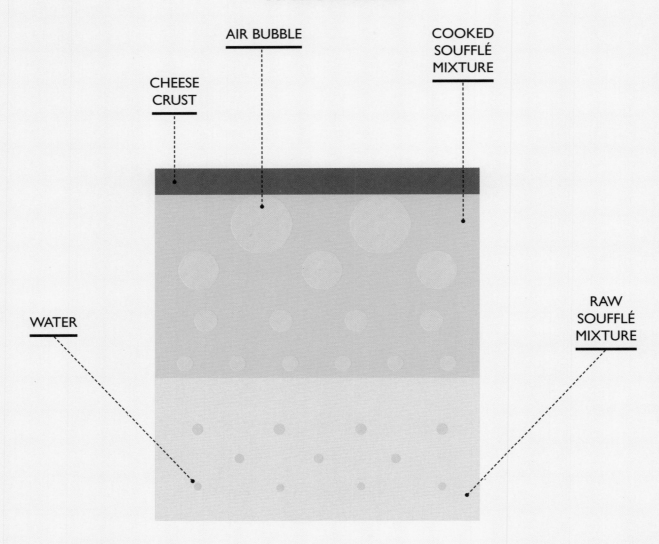

CHEESE
CRUST

AIR BUBBLE

COOKED
SOUFFLÉ
MIXTURE

WATER

RAW
SOUFFLÉ
MIXTURE

WHAT IS IT?

Mixture of mornay sauce (béchamel sauce
+ cheese + egg yolks) and beaten egg white,
which swells up during cooking.

TIME TO MAKE

Preparation: 30 minutes
Cooking: 45–50 minutes
Resting: 10 minutes

SPECIAL EQUIPMENT

Electric mixer (a stand mixer ensures a better
structure in the beaten egg white)
Soufflé dish (20 cm diameter)

VARIATIONS
Crab soufflé, sweet soufflés (with pastry
cream instead of béchamel sauce)

TRICKY ASPECT
Cooking

TECHNIQUES TO MASTER
Béchamel sauce (page 22), mincing (page 280)

TIP
If the soufflé sinks, rebake for 5 minutes. It will
swell up again and lose only 1 cm of its height.

IT'S READY . . .
When the soufflé is nicely browned and has
swelled up.

HOW DOES THE SOUFFLÉ SWELL?

*The water in the mixture evaporates. The
air bubbles make the mixture rise, while
at the same time being captured by the
coagulation of the egg proteins.*

WHY DO SOUFFLÉS SINK?

*Because the steam cools and condenses
back into water which takes up less
volume, plus the structural network formed
by the coagulation of the egg proteins isn't
always rigid enough.*

Learn

continued on page 122

SERVES 4

1 SOUFFLÉ MIXTURE (MORNAY SAUCE)

3–4 flat-leaf (Italian) parsley sprigs
40 g plain (all-purpose) flour
¼ teaspoon paprika
½ teaspoon salt
pinch of cayenne pepper
pinch of freshly ground black pepper
pinch of freshly ground nutmeg
40 g butter
330 ml (1 ⅓ cup) milk
170 g comté or beaufort cheese, grated
20 g parmesan, finely grated
6 egg yolks

2 EGG WHITES

6 egg whites

3 FOR THE SOUFFLÉ DISH

10 g butter, softened
20 g parmesan, finely grated

Making cheese soufflé

1 Preheat the oven to 180°C. Wash, dry, pick and mince the parsley. Generously butter a 20 cm diameter soufflé dish with the softened butter. Sprinkle the grated parmesan around the inside, tipping the dish to spread it around. Refrigerate.

2 Mix the flour, paprika, salt, cayenne pepper, black pepper and nutmeg in a round-bottomed bowl. Melt the butter in a small saucepan over medium heat. Add the flour mixture and cook for 1 minute, whisking, to make a roux (page 18). Pour in all the milk at once, continuing to whisk, and cook for 1 minute to make a béchamel sauce. Remove from the heat.

3 Add the comté or beaufort cheese and the parmesan (reserving 1 teaspoon), and stir through with a spatula until the cheeses have melted. Let the mixture cool for 10 minutes.

4 Add the egg yolks and the parsley to complete the mornay sauce.

5 Whip the egg whites to stiff peaks using an electric mixer. Add the mornay sauce and beat for a further 15 seconds.

6 Pour the mixture into the prepared soufflé dish, leaving 3 cm free at the top of the dish. Sprinkle with the reserved parmesan.

7 Bake for 45–50 minutes, reducing the oven temperature to 160°C after 20 minutes. Check if the soufflé is cooked by inserting a thin-bladed knife in the centre (going in from the side): the blade should come out clean.

SOUFFLÉ CREPES

Understand

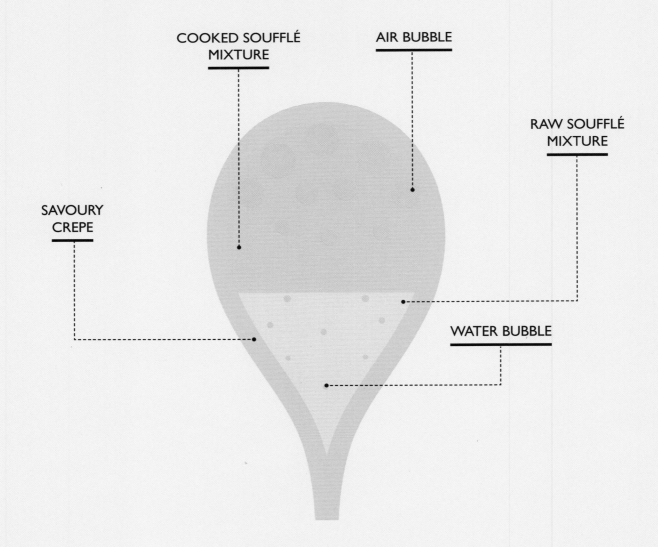

COOKED SOUFFLÉ MIXTURE

AIR BUBBLE

RAW SOUFFLÉ MIXTURE

SAVOURY CREPE

WATER BUBBLE

WHAT ARE THEY?

Crepes filled with a cheese soufflé mixture and mushrooms then cooked in the oven.

TIME TO MAKE

Preparation: 45 minutes
Cooking: 10–12 minutes
Resting: 10 minutes

SPECIAL EQUIPMENT

1 crepe pan (25 cm diameter)
2 baking trays
Electric mixer (a stand mixer ensures a better structure in the beaten egg white)

VARIATION

Soufflé crepes with roquefort and walnuts

TRICKY ASPECTS

Making thin crepes
Incorporating the béchamel sauce into the beaten egg white

TECHNIQUES TO MASTER

Chopping finely (page 280)
Cutting in escalopes (page 280)

STORAGE

1 day in the refrigerator, covered in plastic wrap. Reheat for 5 minutes in a 150°C oven.

THEY'RE READY . . .

When the crepes are slightly swollen and the soufflé mixture is cooked (a skewer inserted in the middle should come out clean).

SERVES 4

1 CREPE BATTER

80 g plain (all-purpose) flour
2 eggs (at room temperature)
½ teaspoon salt
170 ml milk (at room temperature)
25 g beurre noisette (page 53)
1 teaspoon peanut oil

2 SOUFFLÉ MIXTURE

40 g plain (all-purpose) flour
½ teaspoon salt
pinch of cayenne pepper
freshly ground black pepper (3 grinds)
pinch of freshly grated nutmeg
40 g butter, plus extra for greasing
250 ml (1 cup) milk
5 eggs, separated

3 FILLING

1 garlic clove
200 g button mushrooms
10 g butter
¼ teaspoon salt
freshly ground black pepper (3 grinds)
100 g emmental, grated

continued on page 126

Making soufflé crepes

1 Prepare the crepe batter. Make a well in the centre of the flour in a large round-bottomed bowl. Break the eggs into the well, add the salt and whisk. Gradually add half the milk, whisking until the batter is smooth. Add the beurre noisette, mix, then pour in the remaining milk.

2 Heat the crepe pan over very high heat. Grease the pan with paper towel soaked in the peanut oil. Pour a half-ladleful of batter into the centre and spread it out by tipping the pan. Turn the crepe over when the edges unstick and the bottom has coloured. Leave for a few seconds then invert onto a plate. Reduce the heat a little and repeat to make seven more crepes, oiling the pan between each if necessary.

3 Preheat the oven to 220°C. Butter two baking trays. To make the filling, peel, crush then finely chop the garlic. Remove the stems from the mushrooms, then peel the caps and cut them into 4–8 escalopes, depending on their size.

4 Sweat the mushrooms in 10 g butter over medium heat, until they lose some of their water. Stir in the garlic, then cook for 30–60 seconds. Season with salt and pepper.

5 Prepare the soufflé mixture. Mix the flour, salt, cayenne pepper, black pepper and nutmeg in a round-bottomed bowl. Make a béchamel sauce (page 22) with the 40 g butter, the flour mixture and the milk. Remove from the heat, add the emmental and the cooked mushrooms, stirring with a spatula. Let the mixture cool for 10 minutes. Beat the egg whites to stiff peaks. Incorporate the egg yolks into the

soufflé mixture, then pour the lot into the beaten egg whites and gently whisk together.

6 Slide four crepes onto each baking tray (allow them to hang over the edge of the tray a little, with the intention of folding them in half later). Fill half of each crepe with the soufflé mixture. Fold the crepe over without pressing. Transfer to the oven, reduce the temperature to 200°C and cook for 10–12 minutes. Reduce the temperature to 150°C halfway through the cooking time.

SEARED FOIE GRAS

Understand

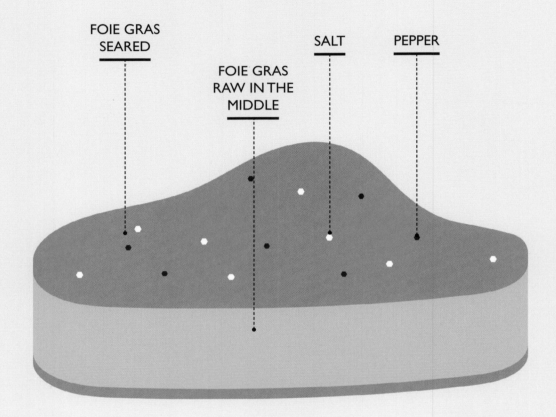

FOIE GRAS
SEARED

FOIE GRAS
RAW IN THE
MIDDLE

SALT

PEPPER

WHAT IS IT?

Escalopes of raw foie gras seared in a frying pan, served with a brunoise of apricots in port or Madeira.

TIME TO MAKE

Preparation: 25 minutes
Cooking: 10 minutes
Resting: 1 hour

SPECIAL EQUIPMENT

Ovenproof frying pan
Wire rack
Zester

VARIATIONS

Filling: fresh or dried figs
Serving: brunoise in a ring

TECHNIQUES TO MASTER

Degreasing a frying pan (page 283)
Whisking in butter (page 282)
Cutting in brunoise (page 36)
Reducing a sauce (page 283)

TIPS

Time the cooking of the foie gras
Use frozen escalopes of foie gras to avoid melting during cooking

IT'S READY . . .

When the foie gras is golden, the sauce shiny.

FOIE GRAS OPTIONS

Frozen escalopes of raw foie gras
(to use as is)
Fresh whole lobe of foie gras cut into escalopes
Vacuum-packed whole lobe of foie gras (separate the two parts and cut them in escalopes without deveining).

WHY DOES THE FOIE GRAS 'MELT' DURING COOKING?

The foie gras contains lots of fat. The fat melts very rapidly with the rise in temperature, which can cause a significant loss of substance.

SERVES 4

FOIE GRAS

8 escalopes raw duck foie gras
½ teaspoon salt
freshly ground black pepper (3 grinds)

SAUCE

80 g dried apricots
200 ml port or Madeira
1 unwaxed lemon
freshly ground black pepper (6 grinds)
1 tablespoon olive oil
40 g butter
½ teaspoon fleur de sel

1 Place the escalopes on a large plate lined with plastic wrap, then wrap tightly with another layer of plastic wrap. Freeze for 1 hour. Preheat the oven to 160°C. Start making the sauce. Cut the dried apricots in brunoise (page 36). Leave them to marinate for 5 minutes in the port or Madeira. Wash and dry the lemon, then remove the zest in long strips using a citrus zester; roughly chop the zest.

2 Drain the apricots, reserving the wine. Mix the apricots, lemon zest, pepper and olive oil.

3 Brown the foie gras escalopes in a hot non-stick frying pan for 30 seconds on each side. Season with the salt and pepper. Transfer the pan to the oven for 5 minutes. Switch off the oven. Transfer the foie gras to a wire rack over a baking tray and return to the switched-off oven.

4 Degrease the frying pan. Add the apricots and brown them over high heat, stirring constantly. Deglaze the pan with the reserved port or Madeira and reduce to three-quarters of its original quantity. Cut the butter into dice and gradually whisk into the sauce, then adjust the seasoning.

5 Serve the foie gras escalopes with a little of the apricot and port brunoise. Season with the fleur de sel.

ROASTED
BONE MARROW

Understand

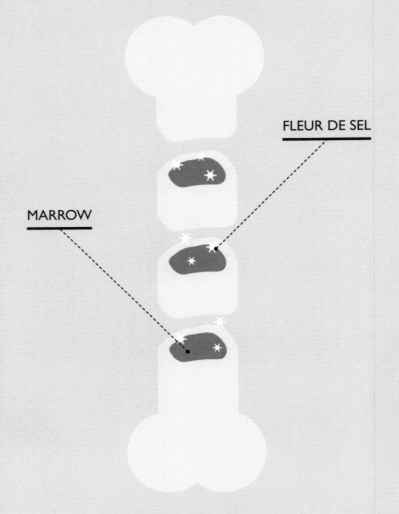

FLEUR DE SEL

MARROW

WHAT IS IT?
Hollow cylindrical bones (beef or veal shank) filled with soft marrow.

TIME TO MAKE
Preparation: 10 minutes
Cooking: 20 minutes

VARIATIONS
Bones cut in 'gutters' – i.e. in half lengthways (same cooking time)
Replace the fleur de sel with a salt flavoured with herbs or French shallot

TRICKY ASPECT
Cooking: overcooked marrow turns into oil

TIP
Rubbing the marrow with fleur de sel, at either end of the bone, prevents the marrow leaching out during cooking.

IT'S READY . . .
When the marrow has puffed up and browned.

STORAGE
Cooked: eat immediately.
Raw: 2–3 days in the refrigerator or several weeks in the freezer.

WHAT IS MARROW MADE OF?
Marrow is about 60 per cent fat. The remainder is made up of proteins and water.

WHY COVER THE MARROW WITH SALT?
The water contained in the marrow evaporates during cooking and makes it swell up. The salt absorbs water, and so reduces the swelling and prevents the marrow protruding from the bone.

SERVES 4

4 marrow bones (cut crossways by your butcher)
fleur de sel
1 teaspoon olive oil
freshly ground black pepper, to taste
100 g baguette (about ½ baguette)

1   Preheat the oven to 230°C. Rub the marrow with the fleur de sel, at either end of each bone, pressing hard to ensure it adheres well.

2   Coat a baking tray with the oil using paper towel. Bake the bones for 20 minutes, until the marrow is slightly swollen.

3   Cut the baguette into eight slices 1–1.5 cm thick. Toast them in the oven for 3–4 minutes, turning them once.

4   Check the marrow is cooked by inserting the blade of a knife in the middle: it should not meet any resistance and should come out warm. Remove the bones from the oven and serve with the toasted baguette, sprinkled with fleur de sel and pepper.

FOIE GRAS
RAVIOLI

Understand

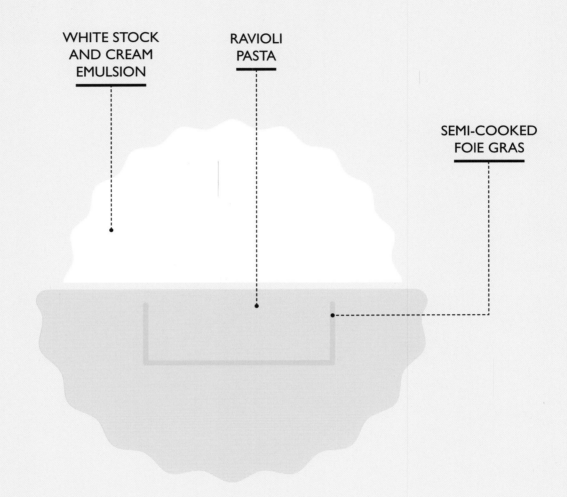

WHITE STOCK
AND CREAM
EMULSION

RAVIOLI
PASTA

SEMI-COOKED
FOIE GRAS

WHAT IS IT?

Squares of pasta, stuffed with foie gras and formed into half-moons, served in poultry stock with cream and flavoured with truffle oil.

TIME TO MAKE

Preparation: 20 minutes
Cooking: 10 minutes
Resting: 1–2 minutes

SPECIAL EQUIPMENT

Hand-held blender
Pastry brush
Round biscuit cutter (6 cm diameter)

TRICKY ASPECT
Making and cooking the ravioli

TECHNIQUES TO MASTER
Reducing a sauce (page 283)
Mincing (page 280)

IT'S READY . . .
When the ravioli are al dente and the cream foamy.

SERVES 4

16 won ton wrappers (10 cm × 10 cm)
160 g semi-cooked duck foie gras (page 112)
½ teaspoon fleur de sel
freshly ground black pepper (4 grinds)
2 tablespoons truffle oil
750 ml (3 cups) white poultry stock (page 10)
70 ml pouring (single) cream

TO FINISH

5 chives
truffle oil
½ teaspoon fleur de sel
freshly ground black pepper (4 grinds)

1 Cut the foie gras into sixteen even-sized cubes. Season with the fleur de sel and pepper. Drizzle truffle oil over each cube. Lay the won ton wrappers on a work surface with a corner facing you.

2 Moisten the top half of the wrappers with a little water using a pastry brush. Place a cube of foie gras on each wrapper, close to the bottom. Fold the wrapper into a triangle, leaving one side open. Press on the other edges to seal them and push out any trapped air, then seal the open side. Using a 6 cm biscuit cutter, trim the ravioli into half-moons.

3 Bring the poultry stock to the boil in a medium saucepan and add the ravioli. Reduce the heat to a simmer and cook for 1 minute, or until al dente. Remove the ravioli from the stock using a skimmer or slotted spoon, and divide among four soup bowls. Return the stock to the boil and reduce it by half.

4 Add the cream and reduce again, until you have a creamy but thick liquid. Foam up the sauce using a hand-held blender.

5 Wash and dry the chives, then mince. Pour the sauce over the ravioli and scatter over the chives. Drizzle with truffle oil, sprinkle over the fleur de sel and finish each plate with one grind of freshly ground black pepper.

EGGS
EN MEURETTE

Understand

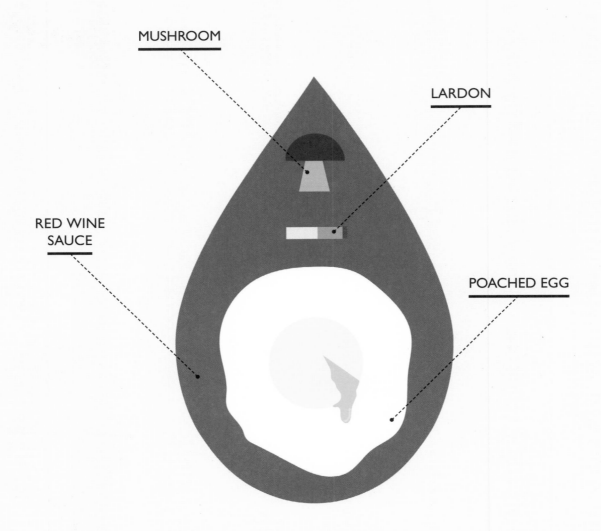

MUSHROOM

LARDON

RED WINE
SAUCE

POACHED EGG

WHAT ARE THEY?

Eggs poached in a red wine sauce, served
with the sauce and accompanied by lardons,
mushrooms and toasted bread.

TIME TO MAKE

Preparation: 40 minutes
Cooking: 20–25 minutes

SPECIAL EQUIPMENT

Fine-mesh sieve
Skimmer or finely slotted spoon

VARIATION

Eggs benedict: replace the red wine sauce
with hollandaise sauce (page 30) and the
mushrooms and lardons with smoked salmon

TRICKY ASPECTS

Poaching eggs in an opaque sauce
Incorporating the beurre manié (butter and
flour mixture) into the sauce

TECHNIQUES TO MASTER

Mincing (page 280)
Skimming (page 283)
Cutting in escalopes (page 280)
Draining egg whites (page 69)
Straining through a sieve (page 281)
Sweating (page 282)

NOTE

Use a full-bodied, tannin-rich wine (Côtes
du Rhône, Bordeaux Supérieur or
Languedoc, etc.).

THEY'RE READY . . .

When the reduced sauce is thick and the
garnish browned.

HOW DOES THE SAUCE THICKEN?

*Thanks to the beurre manié (butter +
flour). During cooking, the starch in the
flour swells up with the water in the sauce
(it gelatinises), then bursts and releases
two molecules (amylose and amylopectin)
that thicken the mixture.*

134

SERVES 4

1 EGGS

4 eggs

2 SAUCE

1 French shallot
50 g butter, softened
20 g tomato paste (concentrated purée)
500 ml (2 cups) red wine
500 ml (2 cups) brown veal stock (page 12)
2 teaspoons sugar
1 bay leaf
25 g plain (all-purpose) flour

3 TO GARNISH

150 g streaky bacon, cut into lardons
150 g button mushrooms
4 slices baguette

4 SEASONING

¼ teaspoon salt
freshly ground black pepper (6 grinds)

5 TO SERVE

2 flat-leaf (Italian) parsley sprigs

continued on page 136

Making eggs en meurette

1   Peel and mince the shallot. Melt 15 g of the butter in a medium-sized saucepan. Sweat the shallot with the salt, stirring constantly. Add the tomato paste and cook for 30 seconds, stirring constantly.

2   Add the wine, stock, sugar, bay leaf, and pepper (3 grinds), then reduce by half, for 10–15 minutes, skimming from time to time.

3   Place the lardons in a single layer in a frying pan over high heat. Cover with a little water, bring to the boil and reduce the heat to medium. Let the water evaporate then cook the lardons until they colour. Transfer to paper towel to drain. Remove the stems from the mushrooms, then peel the caps and cut them in two or four escalopes, depending on their size. Add 10 g of the butter to the pan and brown the mushrooms for 2–3 minutes. Add pepper (3 grinds) and remove from the heat.

4   In a small bowl, mix the remaining butter into the flour using a spoon, until the mixture is smooth (this is a beurre manié). Refrigerate. Toast the bread and place a slice on each plate.

5   One by one, break the eggs into a small bowl and drain off the liquid egg white using a skimmer or finely slotted spoon, keeping only the thick part of the white attached to the yolk. Transfer the stock and wine mixture to a small saucepan. Bring to the boil, then reduce the heat to low and make a small vortex by stirring the liquid with a spatula. Pour an egg into the centre and cook for 2 minutes over low heat, gently pushing the white over the yolk.

6   Remove from the heat and remove the egg using a skimmer or slotted spoon. Rest the skimmer on paper towel, then repeat with the remaining eggs. Place each drained egg on a slice of toast and transfer to four small bowls.

7   Strain the sauce through a fine-mesh sieve, then return it to the small saucepan and bring to the boil.

8   Add the beurre manié in small pieces while whisking the sauce to thicken it. Adjust the seasoning.

9   Wash and dry the parsley, then slice thinly. Pour the sauce over the poached eggs and around the slices of toast using a soup spoon. Add the mushrooms and lardons, and scatter over the parsley.

STUFFED MUSSELS

Understand

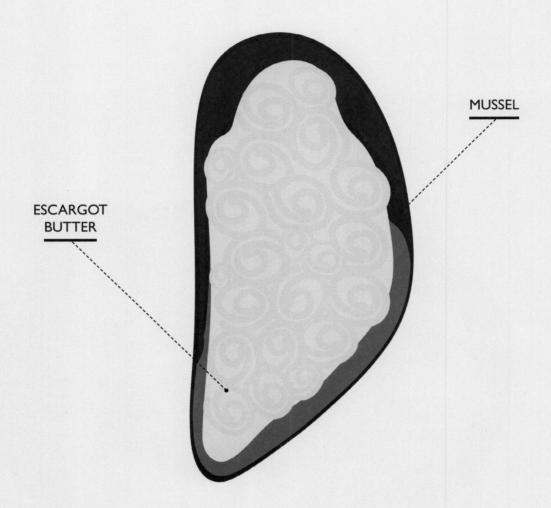

MUSSEL

ESCARGOT
BUTTER

WHAT ARE THEY?

Large mussels cooked in white wine,
then stuffed with an escargot butter
and browned in the oven.

TIME TO MAKE

Preparation: 45 minutes
Cooking: 10 minutes

SPECIAL EQUIPMENT

Chef's knife
Butter knife

VARIATION
Stuffed razor-shells

TRICKY ASPECT
Cooking the mussels: they toughen when
overcooked

TECHNIQUE TO MASTER
Mincing (page 280)

THEY'RE READY . . .
When the top is lightly browned and the
butter very soft.

ORGANISATION
Stuff the mussels 1–2 hours in advance, then
refrigerate. Brown them at the last minute.

WHY NOT CLEAN THE MUSSELS
IN A BOWL OF WATER?

*Because they could open and release their
sea water, which adds flavour during
cooking.*

SERVES 4

800 g large mussels
2 French shallots
180 g Escargot butter (page 41)
2 tablespoons white wine
freshly ground black pepper (6 grinds)

1 Wash the mussels under a trickle of cold water, removing the beards and discarding any mussels that are cracked or half-open, then drain.

2 Make the escargot butter.

3 Peel and mince the two shallots. Combine the mussels, shallot, white wine and pepper in a large saucepan. Cook over very high heat for 5–6 minutes, stirring frequently. Remove from the heat when the mussels have opened. Drain and set aside in the refrigerator.

4 Preheat the grill to high. Remove the top shell of each mussel. Cover each mussel with a little of the butter. Smooth the top with a butter knife. Brown under the grill for 2–3 minutes.

SCALLOPS WITH ORANGE
BUTTER

Understand

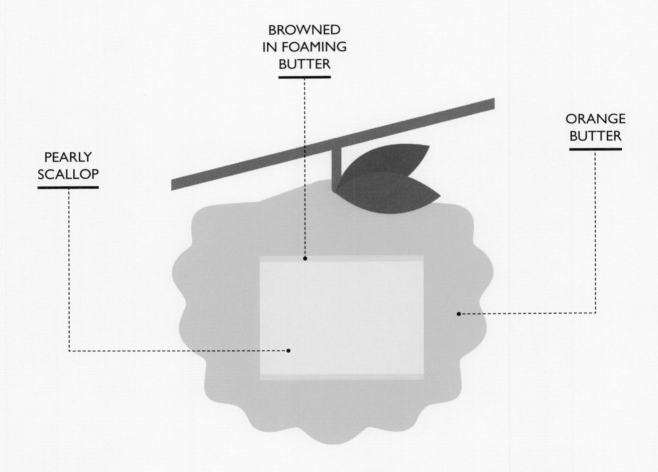

BROWNED
IN FOAMING
BUTTER

ORANGE
BUTTER

PEARLY
SCALLOP

WHAT ARE THEY?

Pan-fried scallops, served with a sauce of
reduced orange juice thickened with butter.

TIME TO MAKE

Preparation: 20 minutes
Cooking: 5–10 minutes

SPECIAL EQUIPMENT

Non-stick frying pan

VARIATION
Scallops in beurre blanc (page 28)

TRICKY ASPECT
Cooking the scallops: overcooking makes
them rubbery

TECHNIQUE TO MASTER
Whisking in butter (page 282)

TIP
The scallops must be very dry (well wiped)
to brown during cooking.

HOW DOES THE ORANGE JUICE
BECOME A SYRUP?

*During reduction, the water evaporates,
which results in the juice thickening to
a syrupy texture.*

WHY DOES THE BUTTER
FOAM UP?

*The water in the butter evaporates. The
proteins in the butter retain the water and
that forms the bubbles.*

SERVES 4

SCALLOPS

16 scallops without roe
1 teaspoon olive oil
30 g butter
½ teaspoon table salt
freshly ground black pepper (8 grinds)
½ teaspoon fleur de sel (to serve)

ORANGE BUTTER

3 oranges
50 g butter, cut into dice

1 Wash the scallops and dry them thoroughly with paper towel.

2 To make the orange butter, squeeze the oranges to obtain about 180 ml (¾ cup) juice. Bring to the boil in a small saucepan and continue boiling until it has a syrupy consistency (you should still have about 40 ml juice).

3 Over medium heat, add the diced butter, one piece at a time, to the reduced orange juice, swirling the pan to spread the butter around, or whisking, until almost melted. Cover and keep warm (over very low heat: 50°C maximum) until required.

4 Heat the oil in a frying pan over very high heat and quickly sear the scallops (1 minute on each side).

5 Reduce the heat to medium, add the butter and let it foam up. Baste the scallops with the butter for 1–2 minutes. Season with salt and pepper.

6 Place the scallops on serving plates, sprinkle with the fleur de sel and add a ribbon of orange butter.

FLAMBÉED PRAWNS

Understand

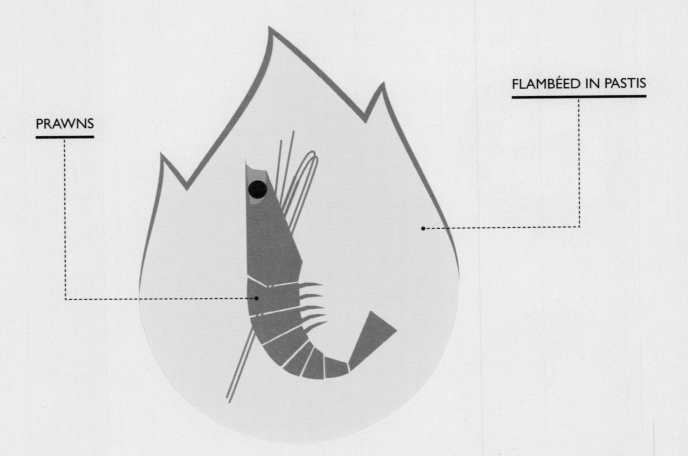

PRAWNS

FLAMBÉED IN PASTIS

WHAT IS IT?

Prawns marinated in herbs and garlic, pan-fried and flambéed in pastis.

TIME TO MAKE

Preparation: 25 minutes
Cooking: 5 minutes

SPECIAL EQUIPMENT

Large non-stick frying pan

VARIATIONS

Flambéed in whisky or cognac

TECHNIQUES TO MASTER

Shelling (page 279)
Slicing thinly (page 280)
Mincing (page 280)
Flambéing (page 282)
Zesting (page 280)

WHAT HAPPENS DURING FLAMBÉING?

Flambéing is setting the alcohol vapours alight. This accelerates its evaporation, and leaves aromatic notes of alcohol in the dish.

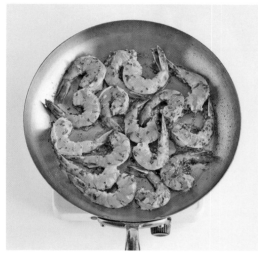

SERVES 4

FLAMBÉED PRAWNS

20 large raw prawns (shrimp), frozen
50 ml pastis

MARINADE

30 g flat-leaf (Italian) parsley
10 g coriander (cilantro)
1 large garlic clove
1 unwaxed lemon
¼ teaspoon espelette pepper
1 teaspoon salt
35 ml olive oil

1 Thaw the prawns in the refrigerator. Wash, shell and devein them (page 279), but leave the tail intact. Set them aside in an airtight container in the refrigerator while you prepare the marinade.

2 Wash and dry the parsley and coriander. Cut off the stems. Peel the garlic. Wash, dry and zest the lemon, then squeeze the juice into a small bowl. Purée the garlic, espelette pepper and salt in the bowl of a mini food processor. Add the herbs and blend to a rough paste. Add the lemon juice and the olive oil, stirring with a fork. Add half the lemon zest to the marinade.

3 Pour the marinade over the prawns.

4 Heat a large non-stick frying pan over high heat. Add the prawns one at a time, using tongs, and cook for 1 minute on each side. Reserve the marinade.

5 Sprinkle over 30 ml of the pastis then flambé (set it alight).

6 Transfer the prawns to a tray. Deglaze the pan with the remaining pastis. Stir in the reserved marinade. Return the prawns to the pan to finish cooking and sprinkle over the remaining lemon zest.

CRAYFISH
À LA NAGE

Understand

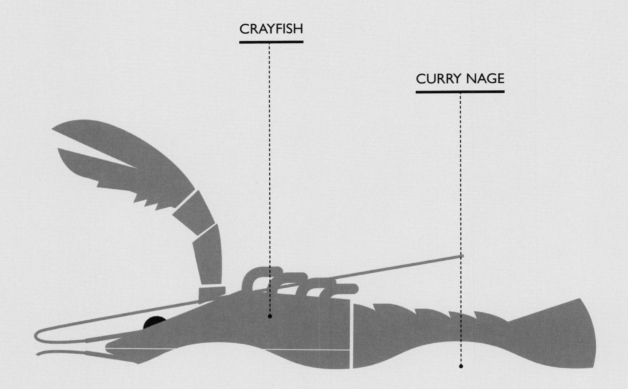

CRAYFISH

CURRY NAGE

WHAT IS IT?

Crayfish poached in a court bouillon flavoured with white wine, served with the cooking liquid flavoured with curry and foamed up with butter.

TIME TO MAKE

Preparation: 15 minutes (not including the court bouillon)
Cooking: 5–10 minutes

SPECIAL EQUIPMENT

Sieve
Hand-held blender

VARIATIONS

Traditional recipe: served with cooked carrots and onion rings
Scallops à la nage
Langoustines à la nage

TRICKY ASPECT

Cooking the crayfish

TECHNIQUES TO MASTER

Deveining crayfish (page 279)
Straining through a sieve (page 281)
Pushing through a sieve (page 281)

TIP

Devein just before cooking, otherwise the meat will pull away from the shell.

IT'S READY . . .

When the crayfish are cooked (taste one).

WHAT IS THE DIFFERENCE BETWEEN NAGE AND COURT BOUILLON?

Court bouillon is a base, nage is a dish. The recipe is the same.

SERVES 4

1 kg raw crayfish
1 litre (4 cups) court bouillon, made with 150 ml white wine instead of the vinegar (page 16)
50 g butter
½ teaspoon red curry paste

1 Wash and drain the crayfish. Devein them just before cooking.

2 Bring the court bouillon to the boil in a large saucepan and add the crayfish. Return to the boil then cook for 5–10 minutes, depending on the size of the crayfish, stirring frequently.

3 Remove the crayfish and keep warm. Strain the nage through a sieve without pushing. Peel the crayfish.

4 Melt 10 g of the butter in a medium saucepan, then add the curry paste. Mix by rubbing the paste against the bottom of the saucepan for 1 minute. Stir in the nage, then bring to the boil. Cut the remaining butter into pieces. Remove the pan from the heat, add the remaining butter, then foam up for a few seconds using a hand-held blender.

5 Pour the nage into serving bowls and sit the crayfish on top.

ROAST LOBSTER

Understand

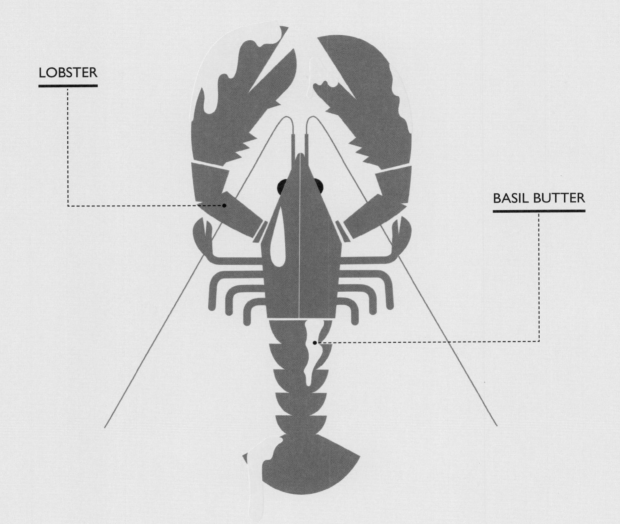

LOBSTER

BASIL BUTTER

WHAT IS IT?

Lobster cut in half, filled with a basil and mustard butter, pan-fried, then roasted.

TIME TO MAKE

Preparation: 20 minutes
Cooking: 7–8 minutes

SPECIAL EQUIPMENT

Thick-bladed knife
2 large ovenproof sauteuse pans (slightly flared sauté pans) or 2 large sauteuses and 1 roasting tin

TRICKY ASPECT
Cutting the lobster

TECHNIQUES TO MASTER
Mincing (page 280)
Chopping finely (page 280)

IT'S READY . . .
When the flesh of the pincers is cooked (which takes a bit longer than the flesh of the tail) and the shell is not completely red.

SERVES 4

4 × 500–600 g live lobsters
1 tablespoon olive oil
1 teaspoon fleur de sel (to serve)
pinch of esplette pepper (to serve)

BASIL BUTTER

1 basil branch sprig
4 semi-dried tomatoes
120 g butter, softened
80 g Meaux (wholegrain) mustard
1 teaspoon table salt
freshly ground black pepper (6 grinds)
pinch of espelette pepper

1 Start by making the basil butter. Pick, wash, dry and mince the basil leaves. Finely chop the semi-dried tomatoes. Mix with the butter and the mustard. Season with salt and pepper, and add the espelette pepper. Mix to make a uniform paste.

2 Place the lobsters in the freezer for 30 minutes to numb them. Kill the lobsters by inserting a knife in the middle of the head in one swift, sharp movement. Cut the lobsters in half lengthways, from head to the end of the tail. Remove the gut, roe, tomalley (green liver), any creamy parts and the gravel pouch in the head. Crack the pincers with the back of a knife to help them cook.

3 Preheat the oven to 200°C. Lift the tail meat of each lobster from the shell using a spoon, starting at the end of the tail. Put a layer of basil butter at the bottom of the shell then replace the meat. Reserve 2 tablespoons of the butter to serve and distribute the rest between the lobster heads.

4 Heat the olive oil in two sauteuse pans over high heat. Put the lobsters in, flesh side down, and cook for 1 minute, until lightly golden. Transfer the lobsters to a roasting tin. Roast for 6–7 minutes.

5 Sprinkle with the fleur de sel and espelette pepper. Serve with the reserved basil butter.

STUFFED SQUID

Understand

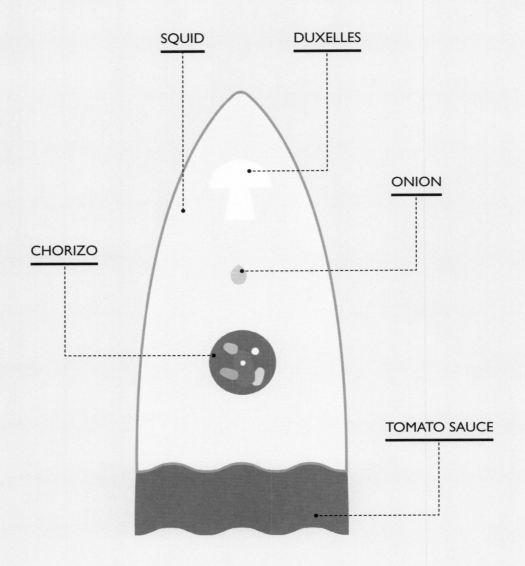

SQUID   DUXELLES

ONION

CHORIZO

TOMATO SAUCE

WHAT IS IT?

Whole squid stuffed with chorizo duxelles, pan-fried then roasted and served with a tomato sauce.

TIME TO MAKE

Preparation: 30 minutes
Cooking: 17–18 minutes

SPECIAL EQUIPMENT

Piping bag
4 toothpicks
Ovenproof frying pan

TRICKY ASPECTS
Cooking the squid
Stuffing the squid

TECHNIQUE TO MASTER
Chopping finely (page 280)

VARIATION
To intensify the squid taste, pan-fry the tentacles in olive oil with a little garlic, then chop and add to the duxelles

IT'S READY . . .
When the stuffed squid are golden and the flesh has softened.

SERVES 4

4 squid (about 20 cm long when whole), cleaned
¼ teaspoon salt
2 tablespoons olive oil

CHORIZO DUXELLES

3 French shallots
45 g butter
300 g button mushrooms
1 garlic clove
200 ml pouring (single) cream
30 g chorizo
½ lemon
¼ teaspoon salt
freshly ground black pepper (3 grinds)

ACCOMPANIMENT

350 ml tomato sauce (page 24)

1   Preheat the oven to 180°C. Make mushroom duxelles (page 43; minus the parsley) in a saucepan. Peel and chop the garlic, then add to the pan and stir for 30 seconds, until fragrant. Add the cream, bring to the boil, then simmer for about 10 minutes over low heat, stirring from time to time, until the mixture is smooth and thick.

2   Peel the chorizo and cut into thin slices then small dice. Season the duxelles with salt and pepper, squeeze over the lemon, then add the chorizo. Transfer to a heatproof bowl.

3   Wash the squid and stuff with three-quarters of the duxelles, using a well-filled piping bag. Close each squid by 'sewing' it shut with a toothpick.

4   Sprinkle a little salt over the squid and heat the olive oil in an ovenproof frying pan over very high heat. When the oil starts to smoke, brown the squid for 1 minute, then turn over one by one, with the help of the toothpicks.

5   Remove the squid from the pan, degrease and deglaze with 50 ml water then add the tomato sauce and bring to the boil. Add the squid and transfer the frying pan to the oven for 7–8 minutes. Season with pepper. Serve one squid per person with tomato sauce to one side of the plate.

SOLE MEUNIÈRE

Understand

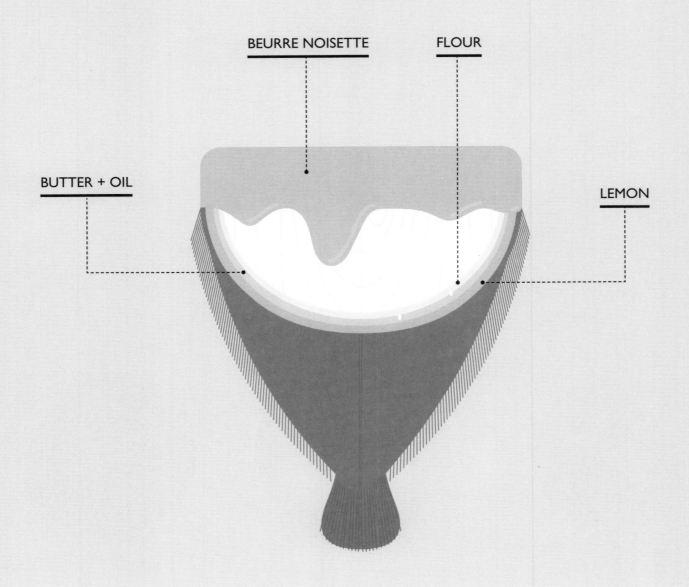

BEURRE NOISETTE

FLOUR

BUTTER + OIL

LEMON

WHAT IS IT?

Sole dusted with flour and pan-fried, sprinkled with beurre noisette, lemon juice and parsley.

TIME TO MAKE

Preparation: 15 minutes
Cooking: 5 minutes

SPECIAL EQUIPMENT

Two large frying pans

VARIATION

Trout meunière with almonds

TRICKY ASPECTS

Cooking
Plating up (sole is fragile after cooking)

TECHNIQUES TO MASTER

Making a beurre noisette (page 53)
Mincing (page 280)

TIP

To ensure the sole is well seared, dust it with flour just before cooking (otherwise the flour will absorb too much moisture and form a paste).

IT'S READY . . .

When pressing a finger into the base of the head (at the level of the gills) separates the fillets.

NOTE

In French cooking, a dressed sole has had the fins removed, and is skinned (white skin scaled and grey skin removed) and gutted.

WHAT DOES THE FLOUR DO?

The starch in the flour absorbs the water on the surface of the fish then gelatinises and dries with the application of heat. The dried flour adds to the crispness of the dish.

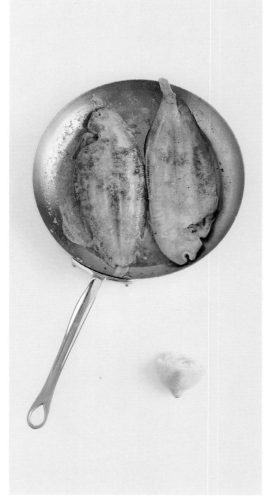

SERVES 4

10 g flat-leaf (Italian) parsley (to serve)
4 × 250 g dressed Dover sole portions
½ teaspoon salt
freshly ground black pepper (8 grinds)
80 g plain (all-purpose) flour
40 g butter
2 tablespoons sunflower or peanut oil
½ lemon
beurre noisette made from 80 g butter (page 53)

1   Wash, dry, pick and mince the parsley leaves. Wash the sole carefully and dry with paper towel. Season with salt and pepper.

2   Dust both sides of the sole with flour and tap gently to remove any excess.

3   Heat equal amounts of butter and oil in two large frying pans over high heat. When the butter foams up and turns slightly blond, brown the sole on the white-skinned side for 1–2 minutes.

4   Carefully turn the sole over using a spatula. Finish cooking over low heat for 2 minutes.

5   Transfer the sole to serving plates, white-skinned side up. Squeeze over the lemon half. Make a beurre noisette and pour over the fish. Scatter over the parsley.

SKATE GRENOBLOISE

Understand

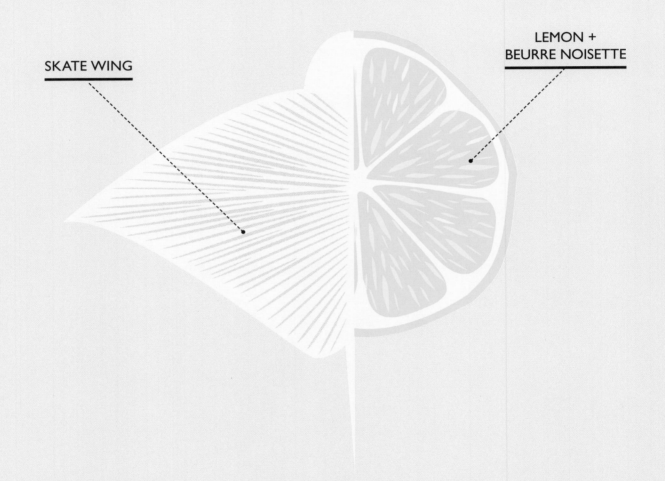

SKATE WING

LEMON +
BEURRE NOISETTE

WHAT IS IT?
Poached skate, served with beurre noisette, vinegar, capers, croutons and lemon segments.

TIME TO MAKE
Preparation (not including the court bouillon): 30 minutes
Cooking (not including the court bouillon): 10–15 minutes

TRICKY ASPECTS
Browning the croutons
Cooking the skate

TECHNIQUES TO MASTER
Peeling citrus for segments (page 280)
Cutting citrus segments (page 280)

VARIATION
Replace the court bouillon with salted water (15 g salt per 1 litre/4 cups water) brought to the boil then cooled and lemon juice added (the juice of 2 lemons per 1 litre/4 cups)

IT'S READY . . .
When the flesh of the fish comes away easily from the spine.

WHY MUST THE FISH BE COOKED AT A SIMMER RATHER THAN A VIGOROUS BOIL?
To prevent the flesh falling apart in the high heat.

Learn

SERVES 4

1 FISH

4 × 250 g skate wings or 4 fillets with spine
(thin skin left and thick skin removed)
2 tablespoons red wine vinegar

2 BEURRE NOISETTE (PAGE 53)

80 g butter

3 COURT BOUILLON (PAGE 17)

2 carrots
2 litres (8 cups) water
200 ml vinegar
30 g flat-leaf (Italian) parsley
6 thyme sprigs
2 bay leaves
2 onions
1 teaspoon peppercorns
30 g coarse salt

4 CROUTONS

80 g day-old white bread (no crusts)
20 g butter
2 tablespoons olive oil
¼ teaspoon salt

5 TO GARNISH

1 lemon
40 g capers

continued on page 154

Making skate grenobloise

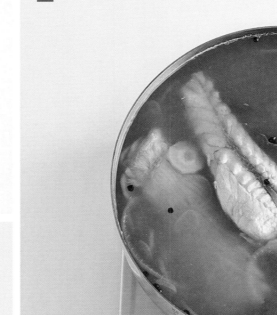

1 Make the court bouillon and let it cool.

2 To make the croutons, cut the bread into 1 cm dice. Heat the butter and olive oil together in a large frying pan over medium heat. When the butter stops foaming, add the bread cubes and stir for 5 minutes, until the croutons are golden. Drain on paper towel and season with the salt.

3 Peel the lemon for segments and cut into segments. Cut these into 1 cm dice. Wash and drain the capers.

4 Wash the skate wings to remove all trace of slime.

5 Immerse the wings in the cold court bouillon, then bring to the boil and simmer for 10–15 minutes.

6 Make the beurre noisette.

7 Drain the skate wings and transfer to serving plates. Remove the skin. Distribute the capers evenly over the fish. Coat in the beurre noisette. Deglaze the beurre noisette pan with the vinegar and pour immediately over the fish. Scatter over the croutons and the diced lemon.

TURBOT
BONNE FEMME

Understand

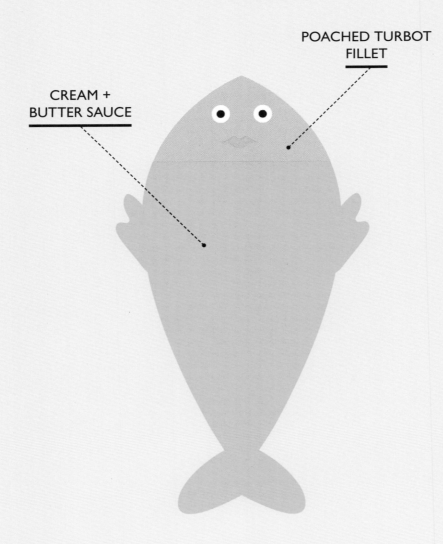

CREAM +
BUTTER SAUCE

POACHED TURBOT
FILLET

WHAT IS IT?

Turbot fillets poached in a court mouillement, then covered in the reduced cooking liquid, thickened with cream, foamed up with butter and browned under the grill.

TIME TO MAKE

Preparation: 20 minutes
Cooking: 7–9 minutes

SPECIAL EQUIPMENT

Roasting tin or ovenproof frying pan
Sieve

VARIATION
Sole bonne femme

TRICKY ASPECT
Cooking the fish

TECHNIQUES TO MASTER
Whisking in butter (page 282)
Mincing (page 280)
Slicing thinly (page 280)
Straining through a sieve (page 281)
Pushing through a sieve (page 281)
Reducing a sauce (page 283)

IT'S READY . . .
When the fish fillets are firm and the sauce is browned.

WHAT IS COOKING IN A COURT MOUILLEMENT?

Cooking in a limited volume of liquid – the fish is just covered (court mouillement is French for 'short wetting').

WHAT IS THE RIGHT COOKING TEMPERATURE?

The temperature at which the flesh of the fish is cooked is 50°C in the middle. At 160°C, this is reached very quickly, so the cooking phases must be short: 4–5 minutes in the oven then 3–4 minutes under the grill.

SERVES 4

FISH

2 × 1 kg or 1 × 2 kg turbots, filleted

COURT MOUILLEMENT

1 French shallot
20 g flat-leaf (Italian) parsley
100 g button mushrooms
5 g butter
1 teaspoon salt
freshly ground black pepper (4 grinds)
100 ml white wine

BONNE FEMME SAUCE

80 g butter
200 ml thick (double) cream

1 Preheat the oven to 160°C. Peel and mince the shallot. Wash, dry and roughly chop the parsley. Remove the stems from the mushrooms, then peel the caps and slice them thinly.

2 Butter a frying pan or flameproof roasting tin. Sprinkle in ¾ teaspoon of the salt, the pepper and the shallot. Add the parsley and mushrooms. Sprinkle the fillets with the remaining salt, fold in half and add to the pan. Pour in the wine and enough water to cover three-quarters of the height of the fish (100–200 ml). Cover with a sheet of baking paper cut to fit and bring to the boil on the stovetop.

3 Transfer to the oven for 4–5 minutes, until you meet resistance when you press the fish with a finger.

4 Remove the fillets with a skimmer. Strain the cooking liquid through a sieve, without pressing, into a small saucepan, then return the fillets to the empty frying pan. Cover with the baking paper and set aside.

5 Preheat the grill to high. Bring the cooking liquid to the boil. Reduce it to 3–4 tablespoons. Cut the butter for the sauce into dice.

6 Add the cream to the reduced liquid and reduce again until it coats the back of a spoon. Whisk in the butter over medium heat.

7 Pour the sauce over the fillets and brown under the grill for 3–4 minutes.

MONKFISH
À L'AMÉRICAINE

Understand

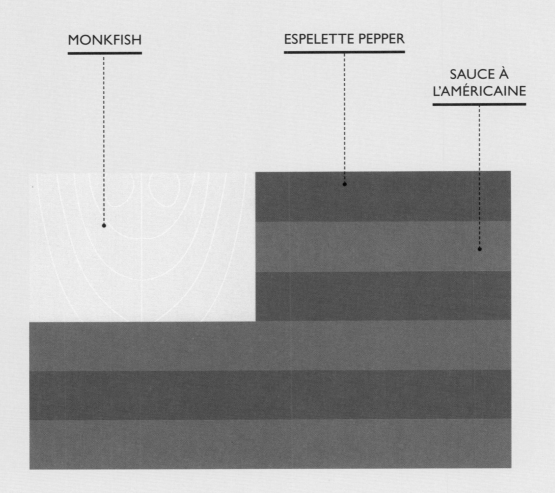

MONKFISH

ESPELETTE PEPPER

SAUCE À L'AMÉRICAINE

WHAT IS IT?

Monkfish and tomato stew: browned monkfish fillets, deglazed with cognac, then cooked in a tomato sauce.

TIME TO MAKE

Preparation: 35 minutes
Cooking: 30–35 minutes

SPECIAL EQUIPMENT

Chef's knife
Fine-mesh sieve
Flameproof casserole dish

VARIATION

Sauce à l'américaine made with crustaceans

TRICKY ASPECT

Cooking the monkfish in two phases

TECHNIQUES TO MASTER

Browning (page 282)
Reducing a sauce (page 283)
Whisking in butter (page 282)
Straining and pushing through a sieve (page 281)
Mincing (page 280)
Zesting (page 280)

IT'S READY . . .

When the monkfish is firm and the sauce is smooth and creamy.

SAUCE À L'ARMORICAINE . . .

Is the same as sauce à l'américaine.

WHY USE UHT CREAM?

The acidity provided by the wine, along with the reduction of the cream sauce, can curdle the cream. The heat treatment given to UHT cream (it is heated for 2 seconds at 150°C, then quickly cooled) and its high fat content (35 per cent) makes it very stable during cooking.

SERVES 4

1 FISH

1 × 1 kg whole headless, skinless monkfish
½ teaspoon salt
20 g butter
1½ tablespoons sunflower or peanut oil
2½ tablespoons cognac

2 SAUCE À L'AMÉRICAINE

140 g French shallots
1 garlic clove
¼ teaspoon salt
30 g tomato paste (concentrated purée)
200 ml dry white wine
350 g tinned chopped tomatoes
freshly ground black pepper (3 grinds)
pinch of cayenne pepper
100 ml UHT pouring (single) cream
20 g butter

3 TO SERVE

10 g flat-leaf (Italian) parsley
½ unwaxed lemon
pinch of espelette pepper

continued on page 160

Making monkfish à l'américaine

1   Break the monkfish spine into pieces. Peel and mince the shallots and garlic. Cut the monkfish into pieces. Dry the cut fillets with paper towel and sprinkle with the salt.

2   Heat the butter and the sunflower or peanut oil in a flameproof casserole dish over very high heat and brown the fish on all sides. Pour in the cognac and let it almost completely evaporate.

3   Remove the fish pieces. To make the sauce, fry the shallots with the salt in the casserole dish over medium heat. Add the monkfish spine and sweat for 1–2 minutes, then add the garlic. Stir for 30 seconds, mix in the tomato paste, then cook for about 1 minute. Pour in the wine and let it reduce by half.

4   Add the tomatoes, black pepper and cayenne pepper, then simmer, uncovered, for 15–20 minutes. Remove the spine pieces. Return the monkfish to the casserole dish, then cover and finish cooking by simmering for 2–3 minutes.

5   Remove the monkfish and keep warm. Strain the sauce through a fine-mesh sieve, pushing it through. Return the sauce to the pan and reduce it over high heat by about half. Reduce the heat to medium and stir in the cream, then reduce until thickened. Whisk in the butter. Adjust the seasoning.

6   Wash, dry, pick and mince the parsley leaves. Wash, dry and zest the lemon. Return the monkfish to the pan and sprinkle over the espelette pepper, lemon zest and parsley.

COD WITH A
HERB CRUST

Understand

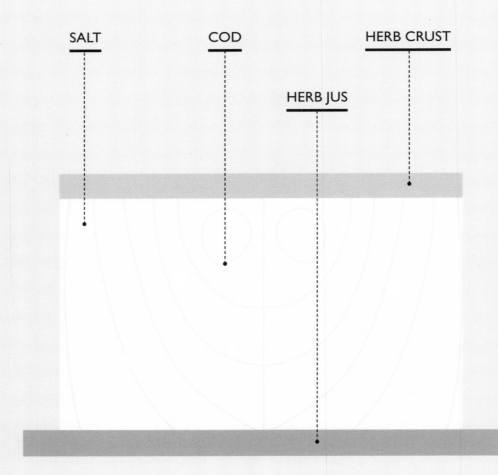

SALT   COD   HERB CRUST

HERB JUS

WHAT IS IT?

Semi-salted cod steak (pre-cooked in a marinade based on salt and sugar), pan-fried, then coated with a herb butter and browned.

TIME TO MAKE

Preparation: 35 minutes
Cooking: 5 minutes
Resting: 50 minutes

SPECIAL EQUIPMENT

Food processor
Rolling pin

VARIATION

Chorizo crust: replace the herbs with 100 g chorizo mixed with fresh breadcrumbs

TRICKY ASPECT

Coating with the herb crust

TECHNIQUES TO MASTER

Mincing and chopping finely (page 280)

IT'S READY . . .

When the herb butter is golden.

STORAGE

Freeze the herb butter for 3 weeks, covered with baking paper and plastic wrap.

WHY PRE-COOK IN SALT?

The salt absorbs water from the surface of the fish. The flesh of the fish firms up slightly and holds together better during cooking.

WHY 'SEMI-SALTED'?

The pre-cooking is called semi-salting because the fish is fresh and undried (unlike salt cod, for example).

SERVES 4

1 FISH

100 g coarse salt
10 g sugar
1 × 600 g skinless cod steak
1 tablespoon olive oil
50 g butter
½ teaspoon fleur de sel

2 HERB CRUST

100 g day-old white bread (no crusts)
2 French shallots
30 g flat-leaf (Italian) parsley
10 g tarragon
10 g basil
200 g butter, softened
¾ teaspoon salt
freshly ground black pepper (6 grinds)

3 GREEN JUS

40 g flat-leaf (Italian) parsley
1 teaspoon coarse salt
freshly ground black pepper (4 grinds)

continued on page 164

Making cod with a herb crust

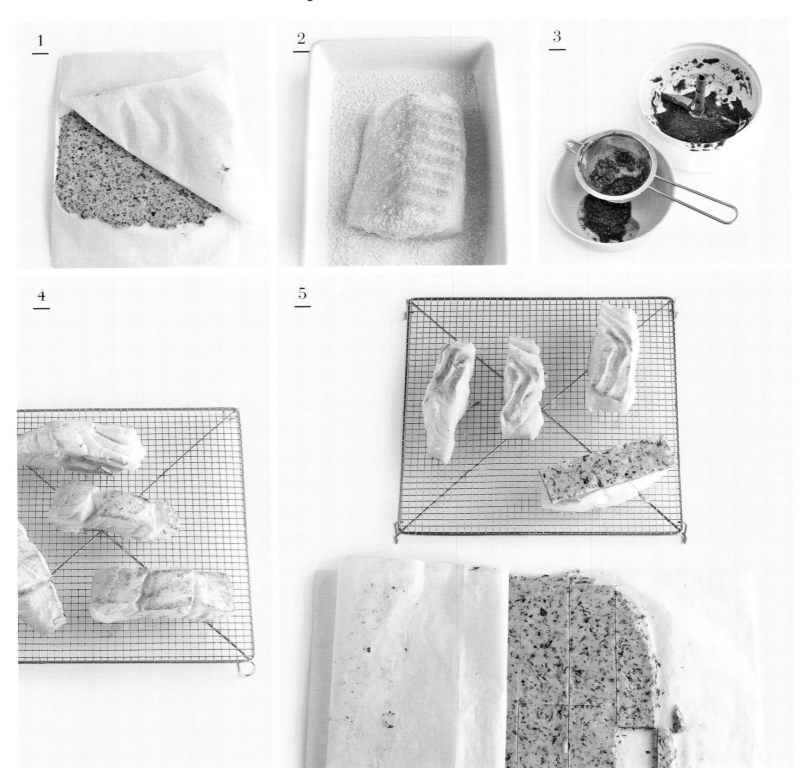

1 To make the herb crust, process the bread to fine crumbs. Peel and mince the shallots. Wash, dry, pick and chop the herbs. Mix all of the ingredients in a bowl. Using a rolling pin, roll the herb butter between two sheets of baking paper to 3–4 mm thickness. Freeze for at least 30 minutes to harden.

2 Mix the coarse salt with the sugar. Spread a thin layer of the mixture in a baking dish. Place the cod steak on top. Cover with the remaining salt mixture. Cover with plastic wrap and refrigerate for 20 minutes to firm up the flesh.

3 To make the green jus, wash and pick the parsley leaves. Plunge the leaves into boiling water with the salt. Cook for 2 minutes. Drain, retaining 1 teaspoon of the cooking water. Process the cooked leaves with the reserved cooking water and the pepper to form a sauce. Adjust the seasoning, then push the sauce through a fine-mesh sieve to obtain a smooth consistency.

4 Wash the cod under cold water. Dry with paper towel. Cut into four even slices. Preheat the grill to high. Heat the olive oil in an ovenproof frying pan over high heat and brown the cod pieces for 1 minute. Reduce the heat to low, turn the cod over, add the butter and cook for 5–6 minutes, basting the cod constantly with the foaming butter. Transfer to a wire rack.

5 Cut the herb butter into four pieces 1–2 mm larger than the cod slices. Place a slice on each piece of cod using a thin spatula.

6 Grill the cod until the crust is golden. Sprinkle over the fleur de sel. Serve with the green jus.

SLOW-COOKED
COD

Understand

50°C IN THE CENTRE   60°C AT THE SURFACE

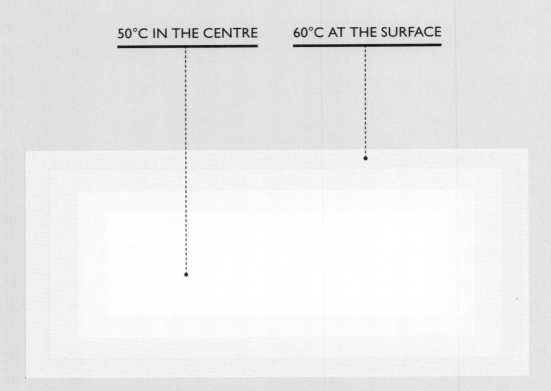

WHAT IS IT?

Cod steak roasted at low temperature (60°C), served with fried brown shrimp and a warm olive vinaigrette.

TIME TO MAKE

Preparation: 25 minutes
Cooking: 30 minutes
Resting: 20 minutes

SPECIAL EQUIPMENT

Large roasting tin
Deep-fryer or frying basket
Thermometer

TRICKY ASPECT
The oven temperature

TECHNIQUES TO MASTER
Cooking with a meat thermometer (page 282)
Chopping finely (page 280)
Mincing (page 280)

INGREDIENT TIP
Fry the shrimp if raw.

COOKING TIP
Use an electronic meat thermometer to check if the fish is cooked: the core temperature should reach 50°C.

WHY COOK AT A LOW TEMPERATURE?

The flesh doesn't dry out and cooks while staying soft and moist.

Learn

SERVES 4

1 ROAST COD

1 × 500 g skinless cod steak
¾ teaspoon salt
1 tablespoon olive oil

2 VINAIGRETTE

40 g (¼ cup) pitted kalamata olives
1 small French shallot
5 flat-leaf parsley sprigs
½ lemon
½ teaspoon salt
freshly ground black pepper (6 grinds)
2 ½ tablespoons olive oil

3 FRIED PRAWNS

500 ml (2 cups) peanut oil
200 g cooked brown shrimp
200 ml milk
1 teaspoon table salt
80 g plain flour
½ teaspoon fleur de sel
freshly ground black pepper (3 grinds)

continued on page 168

Making slow-cooked cod

1 Cut the fish into four even-sized pieces. Wash, and bring the fish to room temperature for 20 minutes on paper towel. Preheat the oven to 60°C (not fan-forced) and place the roasting tin and four serving plates on a lower shelf. Season the fish with the salt, brush with the olive oil, and place in the hot roasting tin in the oven. Cook for about 30 minutes, until the fish is opaque on the outside and translucent in the middle.

2 To make the vinaigrette, cut the olives into thin slices. Peel and mince the shallot. Wash, dry, pick and chop the parsley leaves. Squeeze the lemon. Dissolve the salt in the lemon juice. Mix all the vinaigrette ingredients except the olive oil.

3 To make the fried prawns, pour the peanut oil into a heavy-based saucepan and heat to 180°C or until a cube of bread dropped into the oil browns in 15 seconds. Wash and drain the prawns, then dry on a clean tea towel. Coat the prawns in the milk, then drain and season with the table salt. Dip them in the flour, then roll between your palms.

4 Plunge the prawns into the hot oil for 10 seconds. Drain the prawns and wait for the oil to reach 180°C again. Plunge the prawns into the oil again for 5 seconds, to make them really crisp, then drain on paper towel.

5 Season the prawns with the fleur de sel and the pepper.

6 Heat the olive oil in a small saucepan over medium heat. Add the vinaigrette ingredients and stir.

7 Place a piece of cod on each warm serving plate, then top with the hot vinaigrette and place the fried prawns on the side.

SEARED TUNA

Understand

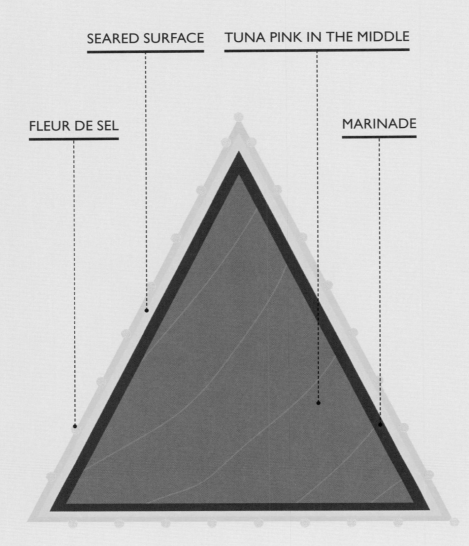

FLEUR DE SEL

SEARED SURFACE

TUNA PINK IN THE MIDDLE

MARINADE

WHAT IS IT?

Marinated tuna seared on all sides at high temperature and raw in the middle.

TIME TO MAKE

Preparation: 30 minutes
Cooking: 5 minutes, Resting: 30 minutes

SPECIAL EQUIPMENT

Flat-top grill or cast-iron frying pan

TRICKY ASPECTS

Cooking: searing the tuna to form a crust without cooking in the middle
Cutting: if the triangles are too large, the flesh won't be warm in the middle

TECHNIQUES TO MASTER

Zesting (page 280)
Slicing thinly (page 280)
Cutting a baking paper disc (page 285)

IT'S READY . . .

When the tuna is browned on the outside and warm in the middle.

HOW DOES THE MARINADE
AFFECT THE FISH?

It flavours the fish but doesn't pre-cook it because it contains no acidity.

SERVES 4

600 g bluefin tuna top loin, cut in
3 triangular pieces with 7–10 cm sides
100 ml soy sauce
2½ tablespoons peanut oil or grapeseed oil
2½ tablespoons toasted sesame oil
15 g sesame seeds
freshly ground black pepper (6 grinds)

SALAD

1 fennel bulb
iced water
50 g rocket (arugula)
1 lime

TO FINISH

½ teaspoon fleur de sel
freshly ground black pepper, to taste
1½ tablespoons olive oil

1   In a large baking dish, coat the tuna pieces in the soy sauce. Add the oils, sesame seeds and pepper. Mix well, then cover with plastic wrap and leave to marinate for 20 minutes at room temperature.

2   Cut the fennel in half then in half again. Remove the core, then cut the fennel into very thin slices using a knife or mandoline. Plunge the fennel slices into the iced water, then drain.

3   Wash and drain the rocket. Zest then squeeze the lime.

4   Drain the tuna, reserving the marinade. Heat a frying pan lined with a disc of baking paper cut to fit over very high heat for 1–2 minutes. Brown each side of the tuna then reduce the heat to low and cook for 2–3 minutes, turning the pieces regularly. You want the middle to stay pink, almost raw. Cut each piece into three or four slices 5 mm thick.

5   Mix the marinade with the lime zest and juice, then add the fennel and the rocket.

6   Arrange the tuna on one side of each plate and the salad on the other. Sprinkle with the fleur de sel and pepper, then drizzle with the olive oil.

CONFIT OF SALMON

Understand

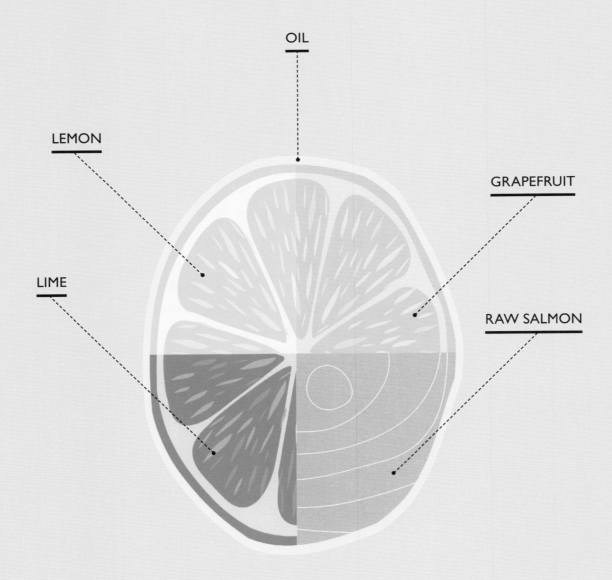

OIL

LEMON

GRAPEFRUIT

LIME

RAW SALMON

WHAT IS IT?

Salmon cooked in an oil bath at 60°C, served with thin strips of raw vegetables and citrus segments.

TIME TO MAKE

Preparation: 25 minutes
Cooking: 40 minutes

SPECIAL EQUIPMENT

Ovenproof saucepan or baking dish (large enough to fit the fish pieces side by side)
Zester
Mandoline

VARIATION

Confit of cod

TECHNIQUES TO MASTER

Peeling citrus for segments (page 280)
Cutting citrus segments (page 280)
Using a mandoline (page 284)
Zesting (page 280)

STORAGE

The salmon can sit in the oil for 30 minutes after cooking. Eat at room temperature.

IT'S READY . . .

When the flesh of the salmon is slightly pale and very soft.

WHY COOK IN OIL?

Oil and water don't mix, so the water in the flesh of the fish remains concentrated, which prevents it drying out.

WHY COOK AT LOW TEMPERATURE?

This minimises contraction of the muscles and so prevents the flesh hardening.

WHAT IS 'CONFITING'?

Cooking slowly in sugar or fat until the cooking liquid (syrup or oil) penetrates to the centre of the foodstuff.

SERVES 4

1 unwaxed lemon
1 unwaxed lime
1 unwaxed grapefruit
4 × 150 g skinless salmon fillets
300–500 ml olive oil
2 pinches of espelette pepper
about 15 red radishes
2 bulb spring onions (scallions)
½ teaspoon each of table salt and fleur de sel

1   Preheat the oven to 60°C. Wash and zest the citrus fruits. Place the salmon steaks side by side in an ovenproof saucepan or baking dish. Pour in enough olive oil to just cover the fish. Remove the salmon from the oil and drain over the saucepan or dish, then set aside on paper towel. Mix the citrus zests into the olive oil and season with one pinch of the espelette pepper. Put the pan or dish in the oven for 20 minutes.

2   Immerse the salmon fillets in the oil and return to the oven for a further 20 minutes. Remove from the oven and leave the salmon in the oil.

3   Squeeze half the lime into a small bowl, then stir in the table salt until dissolved. Add the remaining pinch of espelette pepper and pour in 2½ tablespoons of the oil used to cook the salmon. Stir.

4   Peel the lemon and grapefruit for segments, then cut out the segments of the whole lemon and half the grapefruit. Cut them in half lengthways if they are very thick.

5   Trim and wash the radishes. Cut off half the green stem on the spring onions. Using a mandoline, slice the vegetables into very thin slices, 1–2 mm thick, then mix with the citrus segments. Add the lime juice dressing.

6   Drain the salmon. Place the fillets whole or cut into cubes on one side of the serving plates with the salad on the other side. Season with the vinaigrette and the fleur de sel.

KOULIBIAC

Understand

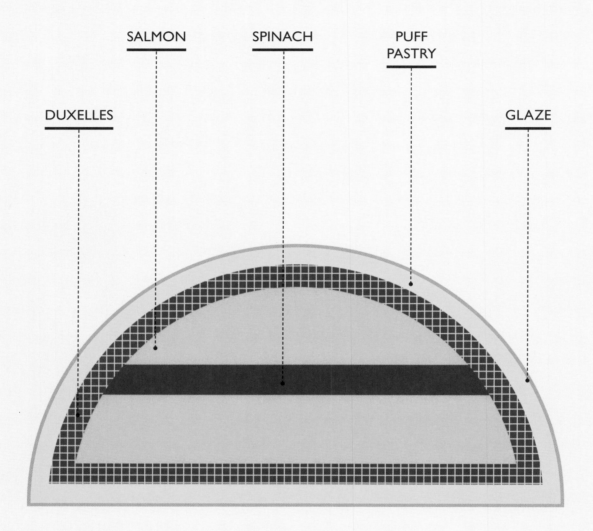

SALMON   SPINACH   PUFF PASTRY

DUXELLES   GLAZE

WHAT IS IT?

Salmon in a puff pastry crust stuffed with spinach and mushroom duxelles.

TIME TO MAKE

Preparation: 50 minutes
Cooking: 30 minutes
Resting: 1 hour 5 minutes

SPECIAL EQUIPMENT

Fishbone tweezers
Rolling pin
Pastry brush
Lattice pastry roller

VARIATIONS

Traditional stuffing: hard-boiled eggs and cooked rice
Assembly: laying a crepe between the stuffing and the puff pastry to avoid the pastry going soggy

TRICKY ASPECT

Assembling the pastry

TIPS

Roll out the pastry in a cold room to prevent it sticking.
If you don't have a lattice roller, create the decoration by hand (see boeuf en croûte, page 232).

STORAGE

2 days in the refrigerator; reheat for 10 minutes in a 150°C oven.

ACCOMPANIMENT

Beurre blanc (page 28)

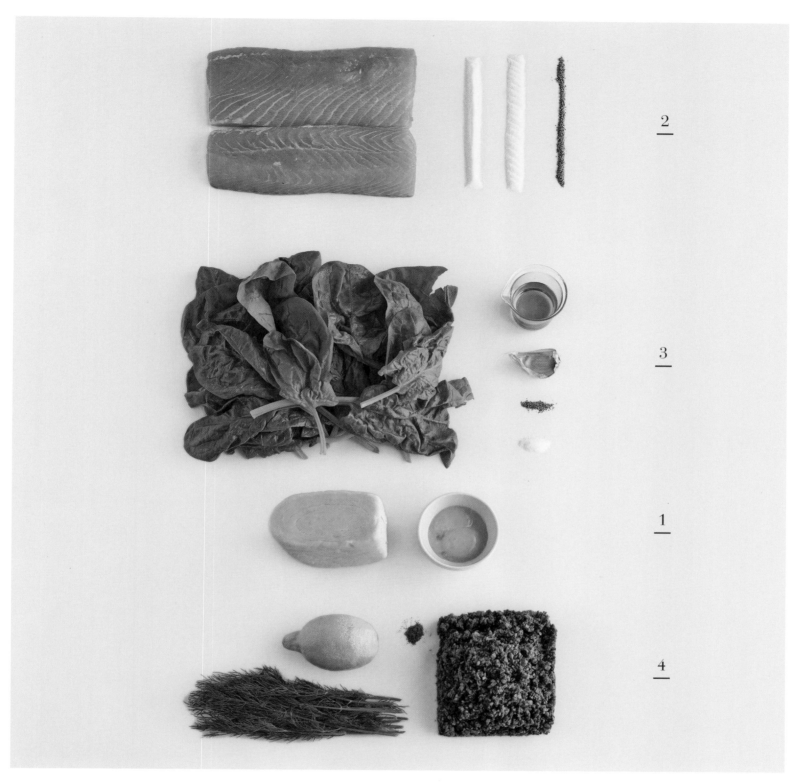

SERVES 4

1 CRUST

660 g puff pastry (page 46)
plain (all-purpose) flour, for dusting
2 egg yolks beaten with 2 teaspoons water

2 SALMON

1 × 800 g skinless salmon fillet, cut in half
lenthways into two 30 cm × 8 cm pieces

3 STUFFING

200 g spinach leaves
1 garlic clove
2 tablespoons olive oil
¼ teaspoon salt
freshly ground black pepper (3 grinds)

4 DUXELLES

300 g dry duxelles (page 42)
pinch of cayenne pepper
grated zest of 1 unwaxed lemon
30 g dill, finely chopped
2 teaspoons salt
freshly ground black pepper (8 grinds)
2 teaspoons sugar

continued on page 176

Making koulibiac

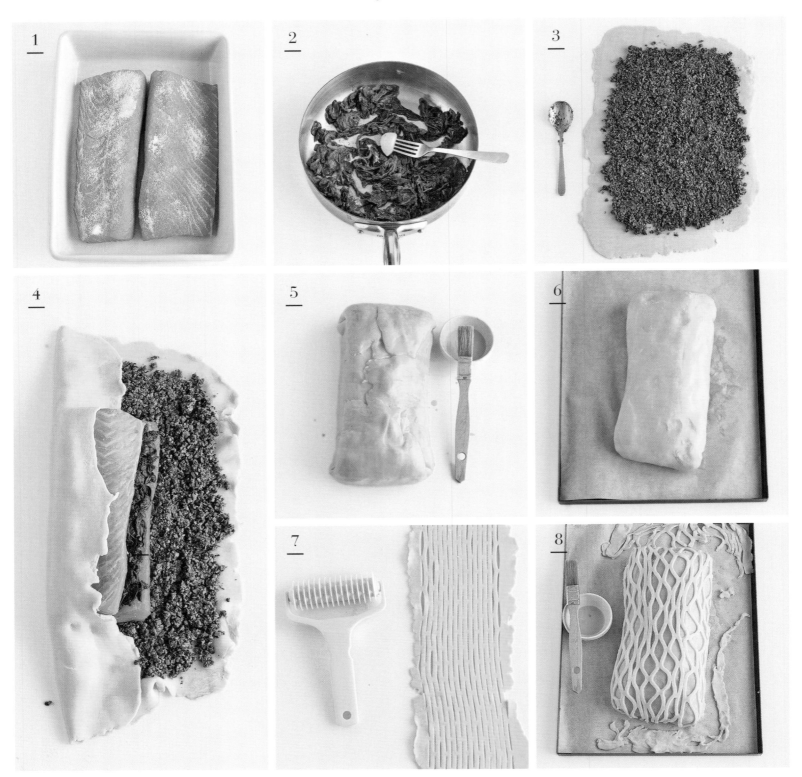

1 Cook the duxelles, then add the cayenne pepper, lemon zest and dill. Season with the salt, pepper and sugar. Refrigerate for 1 hour. Preheat the oven to 200°C.

2 Wash the spinach in plenty of water, then remove the stalks and any tough fibres. Peel the garlic, place it on the end of a fork and make an incision with the point of a knife. Heat the olive oil in a large frying pan over high heat and add the spinach. Stir and rub with the garlic. When the spinach has wilted, remove from the heat, then season with salt and pepper. Stir again with the garlic. When the spinach is lukewarm, squeeze it with your fingers to remove as much liquid as possible.

3 Line a baking tray with baking paper. Wash the salmon under a trickle of water, then drain on paper towel. Cut the puff pastry into two pieces, a larger one of 460 g and a smaller one of 200 g. Set the smaller piece aside in the refrigerator. Dust a work surface with flour and roll out the larger piece into a rectangle 3–4 mm thick and large enough to comfortably cover the two salmon pieces placed on top of each other. Spread the duxelles over the pastry, leaving a 3 cm gap around the edge.

4 Sit a piece of salmon in the middle of the pastry then cover with the spinach. Sit the second piece of fish on top. Enclose the salmon in the pastry, ensuring there are no air bubbles.

5 Using a pastry brush, glaze the pastry with the mixed egg yolk and water.

6 Transfer the koulibiac to the prepared baking tray, with the pastry join on the bottom. Set aside in the refrigerator.

7 Roll out the smaller piece of puff pastry into a rectangle as wide as a lattice pastry roller (about 12 cm). Run the roller over the whole length of the pastry, pressing hard.

8 Glaze the pastry of the koulibiac once more, then place the latticed rectangle over the top. Trim and glaze. Bake at 200°C for 30 minutes (the pastry must be golden). Let it rest for 5 minutes before cutting into thick slices.

FISH AND CHIPS

Understand

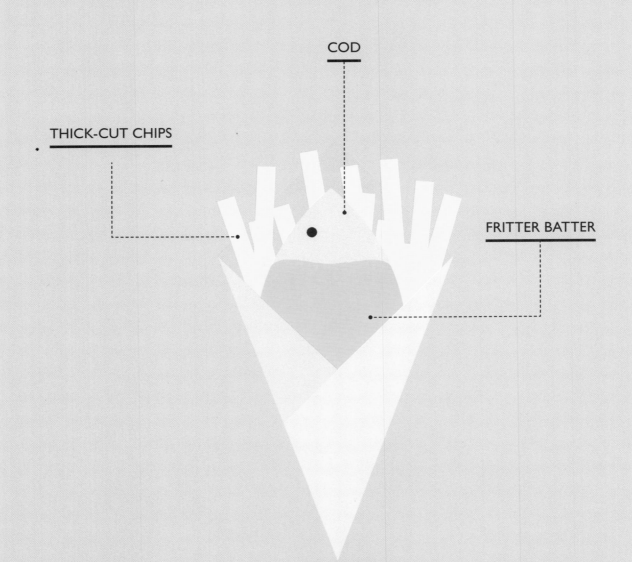

COD

THICK-CUT CHIPS

FRITTER BATTER

WHAT IS IT?

Battered cod served with chips and tartare sauce.

TIME TO MAKE

Preparation: 40 minutes
Cooking: 10 minutes
Resting: 30 minutes

SPECIAL EQUIPMENT

Pastry brush
Thermometer

VARIATIONS

Battered whiting or pollack
Crisps

TRICKY ASPECTS

Cooking the chips
Cooking the fish

TECHNIQUES TO MASTER

Chopping finely (page 280)
Mincing (page 280)

TIP

You can reheat the thick-cut chips by plunging them into oil at 180°C for a few seconds.

IT'S READY . . .

When the battered fish and the chips are golden and crisp.

WHAT DOES THE BEER DO?

It adds gas to the mixture, which aerates the batter and makes it light and crisp.

WHY MARINATE THE FISH IN COARSE SALT?

To season the flesh of the fish deeply and to firm it up. In addition, the salt dries the surface of the fish and makes the batter stick more easily.

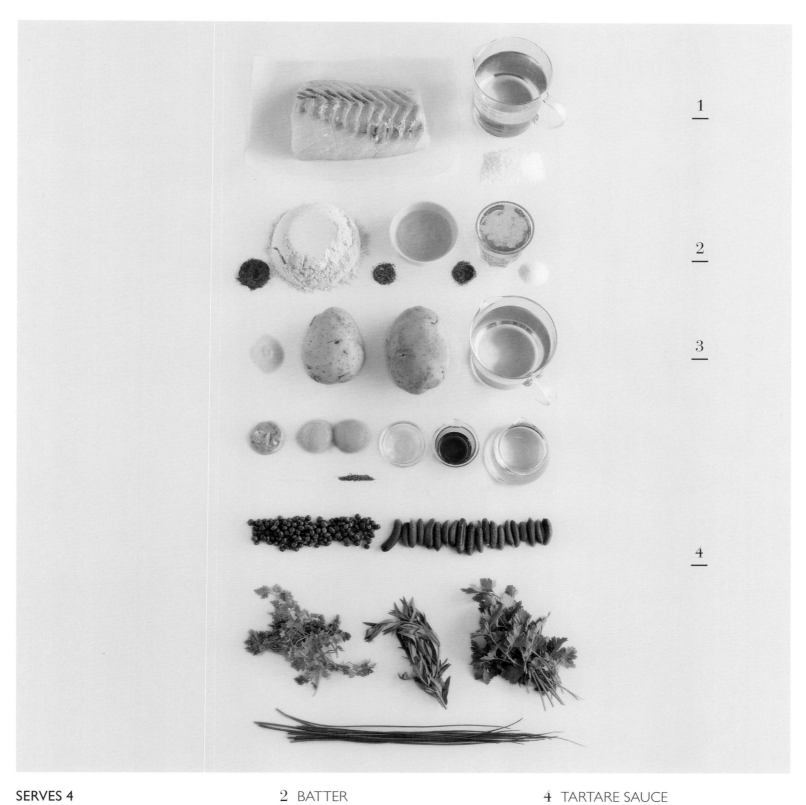

SERVES 4

1 FISH

30 g coarse salt
1 × 650 g skinless cod steak
500 ml (2 cups) peanut oil

2 BATTER

200 g plain (all-purpose) flour
1 teaspoon paprika
½ teaspoon cayenne pepper
¼ teaspoon ground black pepper
2 teaspoons salt
2 egg whites
250 ml (1 cup) beer

3 THICK-CUT CHIPS

1 kg roasting (floury) potatoes (bintje or similar)
1.5 litres (6 cups) peanut oil
1 teaspoon salt

4 TARTARE SAUCE

Mayonnaise
1 tablespoon mustard
1 tablespoon white vinegar
2 egg yolks
300 ml olive oil
½ teaspoon salt
¼ teaspoon ground black pepper

Tartare flavouring
20 g flat-leaf (Italian) parsley
5 g chervil
5 g tarragon
5 g chives
40 g capers
40 g cornichons

Making fish and chips

1   Sprinkle the bottom of a baking dish with half the coarse salt. Cut the piece of cod in half, sit the cod on top of the salt, then sprinkle with the remaining coarse salt. Cover with plastic wrap and refrigerate for 30 minutes.

2   To make the tartare sauce, wash, pick and finely chop the parsley, chervil and tarragon leaves. Wash and mince the chives. Cut the capers into small pieces and finely chop the cornichons. Make a mayonnaise with ¾ tablespoon water, the mustard, vinegar, egg yolks and oil (page 27), using the mustard and vinegar in place of the lemon juice. Stir in the herbs, capers and cornichons, then season with the salt and pepper, cover with plastic wrap and set aside in the refrigerator.

3   Cut the potatoes for thick-cut chips (pont-neuf potatoes, page 59) and deep-fry them in the peanut oil (page 87). Drain on paper towel and season with salt. Add the 500 ml (2 cups) peanut oil for the fish to a deep-fryer or heavy-based saucepan and heat to 180°C, or until a cube of bread dropped into the oil browns in 15 seconds.

4   To make the batter, mix the flour, paprika, cayenne pepper, black pepper and salt in a large round-bottomed bowl. Add the egg whites and the beer, then mix just enough for the batter to be smooth but still very foamy.

5   Wash the fish under cold water and carefully pat dry with paper towel. Cut into batons 8–10 cm long and 1.5–2 cm wide.

6   Using tongs, dip each piece of fish into the batter, then drop carefully into the oil in batches. Let the oil temperature fall when you add the fish and fry for 5 minutes. Drain on paper towel. Return the oil to 180°C before adding the next batch.

7   Serve the fish very hot, with the chips and tartare sauce.

BOEUF BOURGUIGNON

Understand

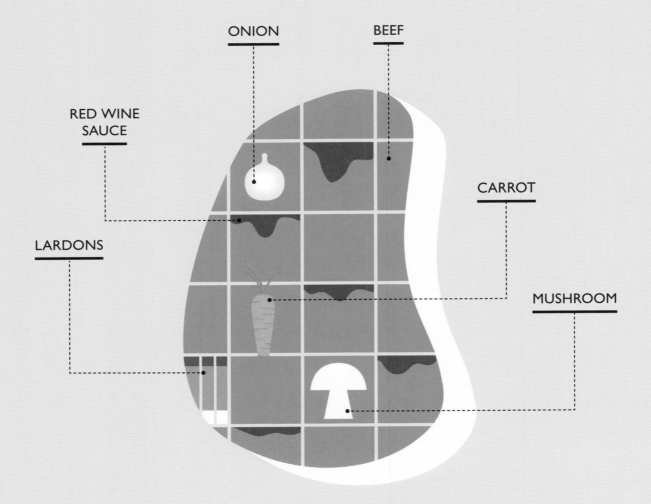

ONION

BEEF

RED WINE
SAUCE

CARROT

LARDONS

MUSHROOM

WHAT IS IT?

Brown beef stew: pieces of beef slowly cooked in a brown sauce with a red wine base.

TIME TO MAKE

Preparation: 40 minutes
Cooking: 2 hours 30 minutes to 3 hours

SPECIAL EQUIPMENT

Fine-mesh sieve
Cast-iron casserole dish

TRICKY ASPECTS

Not burning the bits stuck to the bottom
Retaining sufficient sauce

TECHNIQUES TO MASTER

Degreasing a frying pan (page 283)
Decanting (page 282)
Browning (page 282)
Scraping off stuck-on bits (page 283)
Reducing a sauce (page 283)
Straining through a sieve (page 281)
Adding flour to stews (page 282)
Toasting flour (page 281)
Cutting in escalopes (page 280)
Cutting in mirepoix (page 34)

IT'S READY . . .

When the sauce is smooth and thick.

STORAGE

Refrigerate the meat covered with the sauce.

NOTE

Use a full-bodied, tannin-rich wine (Côtes du Rhône, Bordeaux Supérieur, Languedoc, etc.).

ACCOMPANIMENT

Brown-glazed baby onions (page 252) (added with the mushrooms)

WHAT DOES CHOCOLATE ADD?

Rounded aromatic notes.

SERVES 4

1 MEAT

1 onion
2 carrots
1 celery stalk
1 orange
¾ teaspoon salt
2 tablespoons sunflower or peanut oil
1 kg chuck steak, cut into 40–50 g pieces
20 g plain (all-purpose) flour
350 ml full-bodied red wine
1 tablespoon tomato paste (concentrated purée)
10 g dark chocolate (70% cocoa)

2 AROMATIC FLAVOURING

½ teaspoon ground ginger
½ teaspoon paprika
pinch of freshly grated nutmeg
1 thyme sprig
1 bay leaf

3 GARNITURE BOURGUIGNONNE

150 g button mushrooms
150 g streaky bacon, cut into lardons
2 teaspoons olive oil
¼ teaspoon salt
freshly ground black pepper (3 grinds)

continued on page 184

1 Preheat the oven to 180°C and place a shelf on the lowest rung. Peel the onion and cut in mirepoix. Peel the carrots and cut in half lengthways, then in 5 mm slices. Cut the celery in 1.5 cm slices. Zest half the orange. Pat the meat dry with paper towel, then season with ½ teaspoon of the salt.

2 Heat 1½ teaspoons of the sunflower oil in a casserole dish over high heat. Brown the pieces of beef on all sides. Remove the meat, degrease the casserole dish, then pour in the remaining oil. Add the carrot and onion, then season with the remaining salt. When the onion is soft, sprinkle in the flour and toast in the oven for 5 minutes.

3 Heat the wine with 350 ml water in a saucepan until simmering. Remove the casserole dish from the oven, mix the vegetables well and reduce the oven temperature to 150°C. Add the tomato paste and the ginger, paprika and nutmeg to the casserole dish, then cook for 1 minute over high heat on the stovetop, stirring constantly. Stir in the meat.

4 Cover the meat to three-quarters of its height with the wine and water mixture. Add the celery, orange zest, thyme and bay leaf. Scrape the bottom of the casserole dish to remove any stuck-on bits. Bring to a simmer, then cover and transfer to the oven for 2 hours 30 minutes to 3 hours, until the meat is tender. After 1 hour 30 minutes, add more of the reheated wine and water mixture or hot water if necessary. Stir from time to time and check the concentration of the sauce every 45 minutes.

5 Cut the stalks off the mushrooms, then peel the caps and cut them into two or four escalopes, depending on their size. Put the lardons in a non-stick frying pan and cover with 200 ml water. Bring to the boil and let the water almost completely evaporate. Add half the olive oil and brown the lardons over medium heat, stirring frequently. Drain in a colander.

6 In the same frying pan, cook the mushrooms, adding the remaining oil if necessary. Season with the salt and pepper.

7 Decant the beef and carrots, then strain the sauce through a sieve into a bowl. Off the heat, return the meat and carrots to the casserole dish, along with the lardons and the mushrooms. Add the chocolate to the sauce and stir to melt. Adjust the seasoning, then pour into the casserole dish and serve.

POT-AU-FEU

Understand

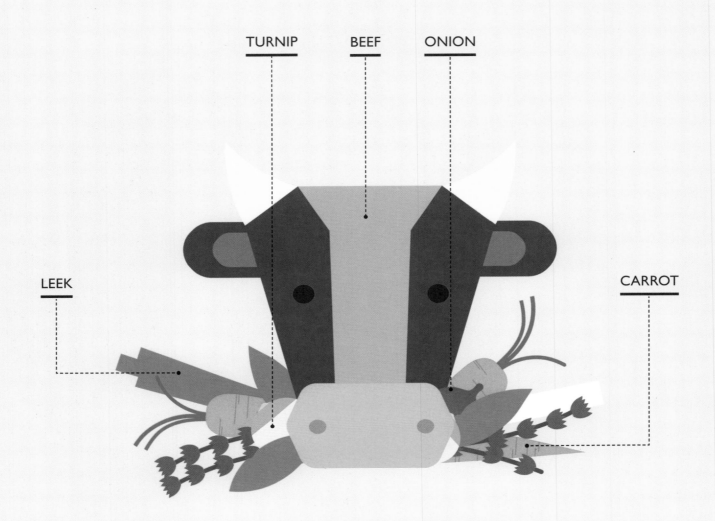

TURNIP   BEEF   ONION

LEEK

CARROT

WHAT IS IT?

Beef poached in an aromatic bouillon (cooking liquid) over very low heat, served with the vegetables it was cooked with and a condiment.

TIME TO MAKE

Preparation: 30 minutes
Cooking: 3–4 hours

VARIATION

Replace the herb cream with traditional condiments: mustards (strong and Meaux/ wholegrain), cornichons and fleur de sel (or coarse salt)

TECHNIQUES TO MASTER

Skimming (page 283)
Mincing (page 280)
Chopping finely (page 280)
Crushing garlic (page 280)
Making a bouquet garni (page 34)

TIP

To flavour and colour the bouillon, add a burnt onion (cut in half and blackened on foil in a frying pan over very high heat)

IT'S READY . . .

When the stock is clear and the meat and vegetables are tender.

SERVES 4

1 kg beef: chuck steak and
boned brisket (thick rib)
1 bay leaf
3–4 flat-leaf (Italian) parsley leaves
2 thyme sprigs
4 baby leeks
8 carrots
2 onions
6 cloves
4 garlic cloves
20 g coarse salt
4 peppercorns
8 small turnips

HERB CREAM

150 g fromage blanc
12 chives, minced
12 flat-leaf (Italian) parsley leaves, finely chopped
¼ teaspoon salt
freshly ground black pepper (6 grinds)

TO FINISH

½ teaspoon fleur de sel
freshly ground black pepper (6 grinds)

1   Prepare a bouquet garni (page 34) with the bay leaf, parsley leaves, thyme sprigs and one green leaf from a leek to wrap it up. Put the pieces of meat in a casserole dish and cover with 2.5 litres (10 cups) water. Bring to the boil, then reduce the heat and let it simmer. Skim all the foam off the surface.

2   Peel the carrots and onions and trim the leeks. Stud the onions with the cloves, pushing them in near the root end. Peel and crush the garlic cloves. Add the carrots, onions and garlic to the casserole dish with the salt, peppercorns and bouquet garni. Skim off any foam and leave it to simmer, uncovered, for 3–4 hours, until the meat is tender.

3   Peel the turnips and wash the leeks, then add them whole to the casserole dish 1 hour before the end of cooking.

4   To make the herb cream, mix the fromage blanc with the chives and parsley. Season with salt and pepper, then set aside in the refrigerator.

5   Cut the meat and serve with the vegetables. Sprinkle over the fleur de sel and pepper. Serve with the herb cream.

BLANQUETTE OF VEAL

Understand

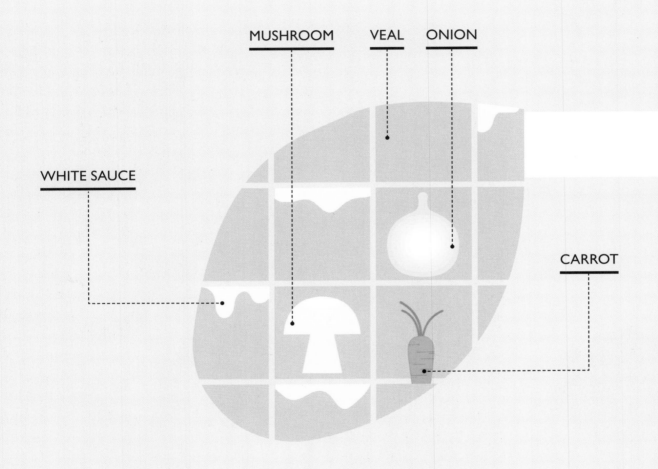

MUSHROOM · VEAL · ONION

WHITE SAUCE

CARROT

WHAT IS IT?

Veal stew: pieces of browned veal, poached in an aromatic stock, then served with a white sauce made with a roux of the cooking stock thickened with cream and egg yolk.

TIME TO MAKE

Preparation: 45 minutes
Cooking: 1 hour 55 minutes

SPECIAL EQUIPMENT

Fine-mesh sieve
Whisk

VARIATION

Traditional recipe: meat blanched then poached in cold water (no browning)

TRICKY ASPECTS

Browning the meat
Thickening the sauce

TECHNIQUES TO MASTER

Mincing (page 280)
Making a roux (page 18)
Scraping off stuck-on bits (page 283)
Skimming (page 283)
Cutting in escalopes (page 280)
Decanting (page 282)
Straining through a sieve (page 281)
Cutting a baking paper disc (page 285)

IT'S READY . . .

When the sauce is velvety.

STORAGE

2 days in the refrigerator.

HOW CAN THE CREAM BOIL WITHOUT THE EGG YOLKS COAGULATING?

When the yolk is mixed into the cream, it is diluted in the liquid. The proteins are more widely spaced, so the risk of coagulation is reduced. Adding the velouté sauce gradually heats the cream and egg yolk mixture gently and dilutes the preparation.

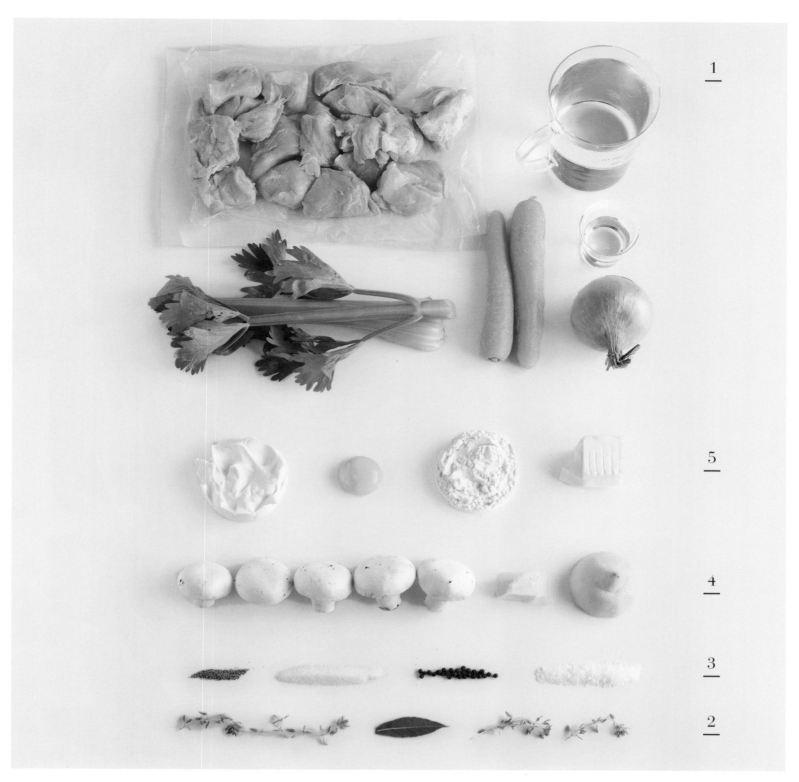

SERVES 4

1 MEAT

1 onion
2 carrots
1 celery stalk
800 g veal neck, cut into pieces of about 50 g
1 ½ tablespoons sunflower or peanut oil

2 AROMATIC FLAVOURING

2 thyme sprigs
1 bay leaf

3 SEASONING

1 teaspoon table salt
1 teaspoon coarse salt
½ teaspoon black peppercorns
freshly ground black pepper, to taste

4 MUSHROOMS

250 g button mushrooms
10 g butter, cut into dice
½ lemon

5 TO THICKEN

50 g butter
50 g plain (all-purpose) flour
1 egg yolk
100 g thick (double) cream

continued on page 190

Making blanquette of veal

1 Preheat the oven to 150°C and place a shelf on the lowest rung. Peel and mince the onion. Peel the carrots and cut into 1 cm thick rounds. Wash the celery and cut into 8–10 cm lengths. Pat the meat dry with paper towel, then season with half of the table salt.

2 Heat the sunflower oil in a flameproof casserole dish over very high heat and brown the meat on all sides. Decant the meat, add the onion, carrot and the remaining table salt, then reduce the heat to medium and sweat the vegetables.

3 Return the meat to the casserole dish, stir, then pour in 1.25 litres (5 cups) water. Return the heat to very high and bring to a simmer, scraping the bottom to remove any stuck-on bits. Skim the surface. Add the coarse salt, thyme, bay leaf, celery and peppercorns. Cover and transfer to the oven for 1 hour 30 minutes.

4 Cut the stalks off the mushrooms, then peel the caps and cut them into two or four escalopes, depending on their size. Place the mushrooms in a saucepan and just cover with some cooking liquid from the casserole dish. Add the butter and 1 teaspoon of juice from the lemon half. Bring to the boil, then simmer for 10 minutes, covered with a disc of baking paper cut to fit and with a vent. Drain the mushrooms, reserving the liquid.

5 Decant the meat and vegetables from the casserole dish. Discard the celery, thyme, bay leaf and peppercorns. Strain the cooking liquid through a sieve. Keep the meat and vegetables warm, with the mushrooms, in the covered casserole dish.

6 Make a roux with the butter and flour (page 18). Add about 500 ml (2 cups) of the strained cooking liquid along with 400 ml of the reserved mushroom-

cooking liquid. Bring to the boil while whisking. Let it thicken into a velouté sauce over low heat for 15 minutes.

7 Mix the egg yolk and cream in a small bowl, then add a little of the velouté sauce. Off the heat, gradually add this mixture to the hot velouté sauce. Return to the heat and bring to the boil, then let it boil for a few seconds while whisking. Check the thickness of the sauce (it should coat the back of a spoon) and adjust the seasoning. Add a few drops of lemon juice, if desired.

8 Pour the sauce into the casserole dish. Let it simmer for 5 minutes, then keep over very low heat until ready to serve.

ROLLED LAMB
WITH SPICES

Understand

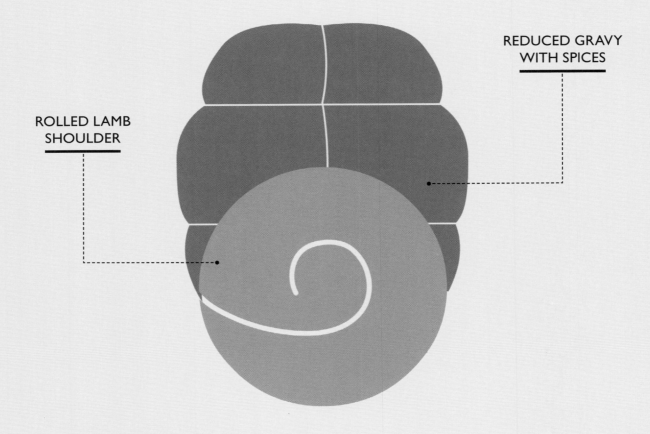

ROLLED LAMB
SHOULDER

REDUCED GRAVY
WITH SPICES

WHAT IS IT?

Lamb shoulder rolled with spices, cooked in gentle heat and basted regularly with the cooking liquid until almost completely reduced.

TIME TO MAKE

Preparation: 25 minutes
Cooking: 2 hours 35 minutes

SPECIAL EQUIPMENT

Kitchen string

VARIATION

Seven-hour leg of lamb: longer cooking time (7 hours), more gentle (120°C) and covered

TRICKY ASPECT

Not burning the bits stuck to the bottom

TECHNIQUES TO MASTER

Tying meat (page 278)
Mincing (page 280)
Sweating (page 282)

IT'S READY . . .

When the meat has a nice shiny crust and the gravy is well concentrated.

ACCOMPANIMENT

Couscous (page 236)

WHY COOK UNCOVERED?

To obtain a shiny sauce at the end of cooking.

SERVES 4

1 MEAT

800 g–1 kg boned lamb shoulder
(1.6 kg with bones)

2 MARINADE

½ teaspoon ras el hanout
½ teaspoon salt
60 ml (¼ cup) olive oil

3 TO COOK

50 g raisins
30 g fresh ginger
1 onion
1 garlic clove
1 tablespoon olive oil
30 g honey
2 pinches of saffron threads
300 ml white poultry stock (page 10)

4 TO FINISH

50 g (⅓ cup) blanched almonds
freshly ground black pepper (6 grinds)

continued on page 194

Making rolled lamb with spices

1 Roll the meat tightly and secure with kitchen string then transfer to a baking dish or roasting tin. Sprinkle with the ras el hanout and the salt, then coat with the 60 ml (¼ cup) olive oil. Preheat the oven to 150°C. Soak the raisins in warm water.

2 Peel and grate the ginger. Peel and mince the onion. Peel and crush the garlic. Drain the raisins.

3 Heat the 1 tablespoon of olive oil in a flameproof casserole dish over high heat and brown the lamb shoulder on all sides. Remove from the dish.

4 Reduce the heat to medium and sweat the onion for a few seconds. Stir in the ginger, the oil remaining from the marinade and the honey.

5 Return the shoulder to the casserole dish, then add the saffron, garlic and raisins. Pour in half the poultry stock. Transfer to the oven and cook, uncovered, for 2 hours to 2 hours 30 minutes, basting the meat from time to time with the cooking liquid. The gravy should reduce and become shiny by the end of cooking; add the remaining stock if it evaporates too quickly.

6 Toast the almonds in a dry frying pan over medium heat then roughly chop.

7 Remove the string from the lamb. Scatter over the almonds, season with the pepper and coat the lamb in its gravy.

NAVARIN OF LAMB

Understand

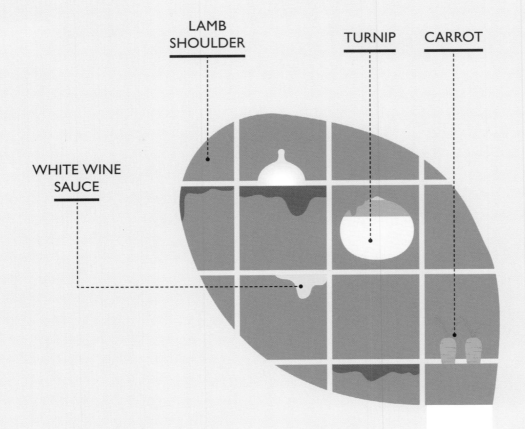

LAMB SHOULDER

TURNIP   CARROT

WHITE WINE SAUCE

WHAT IS IT?
Brown lamb stew: piece of lamb shoulder browned then cooked slowly in a white wine sauce. Served with seasonal vegetables.

TIME TO MAKE
Preparation: 25 minutes
Cooking: 1 hour 30 minutes to 1 hour 45 minutes

VARIATION
Original recipe: served with turnips

TRICKY ASPECT
The sauce: it must be thick without adding flour or reduction

TECHNIQUES TO MASTER
Mincing (page 280)
Scraping off stuck-on bits (page 283)
Decanting (page 282)
Browning (page 282)

TIP
If the vegetables are prepared in advance, keep them in the refrigerator under damp paper towel to prevent them drying out.

IT'S READY . . .
When the meat is tender, the vegetables soft and the sauce thick.

STORAGE
3 days in the refrigerator. Reheat, covered, over low heat with a little added water.

WHY REDUCE THE WINE?
To concentrate the sugars it contains, which makes it seems less acidic (in fact, its acidity is unchanged, but is camouflaged by the sugar).

SERVES 4

1 MEAT

1 garlic clove
1 onion
1 boned lamb shoulder (about
1.3 kg), cut into 16 pieces
3 tablespoons olive oil
3 teaspoons tomato paste (concentrated purée)
80 ml (⅓ cup) dry white wine

2 AROMATIC FLAVOURING

1 bay leaf
1 thyme sprig

3 VEGETABLES

6 thin carrots
5 turnips
300 g firm-fleshed potatoes

4 SEASONING

1½ teaspoons salt
freshly ground black pepper (6 grinds)

continued on page 198

Making navarin of lamb

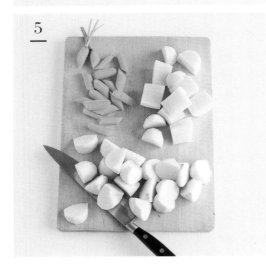

1 Preheat the oven to 150°C and place a shelf on the lowest rung. Peel the garlic and onion. Cut the garlic in half and mince the onion. Pat the meat dry with paper towel, then season with ½ teaspoon of the salt.

2 Heat the olive oil in a flameproof casserole dish over very high heat and brown the pieces of lamb. Decant the meat.

3 Reduce the heat to medium and add the onion, garlic and another ½ teaspoon of the salt, then sweat, stirring frequently. Add the tomato paste and stir for 1–2 minutes.

4 Add the lamb and stir. Pour in the wine and let it reduce to 2–3 tablespoons of liquid while scraping any stuck-on bits off the bottom of the dish. Pour in 200 ml water, add the bay leaf and thyme, then bring to the boil. Cover and transfer to the oven for 1 hour.

5 Peel and wash the carrots, turnips and potatoes. Cut the carrots on an angle into 3 cm lengths. Cut the turnips in half or quarters depending on their size. Cut the potatoes into 3 cm pieces. Season with the remaining ½ teaspoon of the salt.

6 Remove the garlic, bay leaf and thyme from the casserole dish, then stir in the vegetables. Return to the oven for another 30–45 minutes. Add the pepper and more salt if necessary.

LACQUERED DUCKLING

Understand

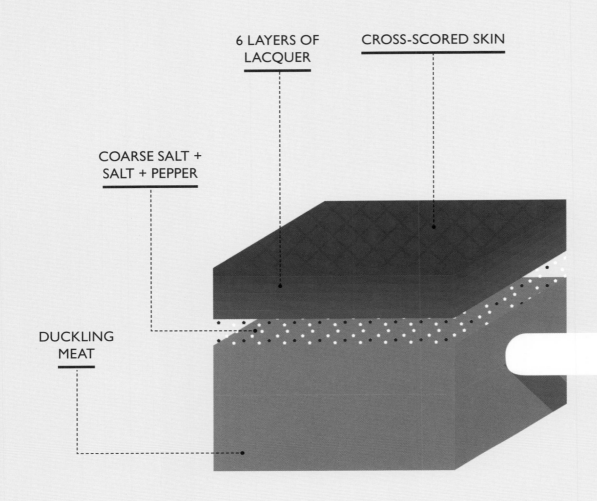

6 LAYERS OF LACQUER

CROSS-SCORED SKIN

COARSE SALT +
SALT + PEPPER

DUCKLING
MEAT

WHAT IS IT?

Roast duckling painted with lacquer
(sugar + vinegar) during cooking.

TIME TO MAKE

Preparation: 35 minutes
Cooking: 1 hour 10 minutes

SPECIAL EQUIPMENT

Pastry brush
Baking dish or roasting tin

VARIATION

Lacquered duck (adapted to serve 8)

TRICKY ASPECT

Preparing the lacquer

TECHNIQUE TO MASTER

Scraping off stuck-on bits (page 283)

TIPS

Use the natural pattern of the skin to help
you cross-score it evenly.
The baking dish or roasting tin shouldn't
be too large or the meat might burn.

IT'S READY . . .

When the skin is dark and shiny, without
being burnt.

WHAT MAKES THE LACQUER SHINE?

*At high temperatures, the sugar
is transformed into caramel
which adds a sheen.*

WHY IS IT NECESSARY TO CROSS-SCORE THE SKIN?

*To create small spaces where the
lacquer can become trapped before
caramelising in the oven.*

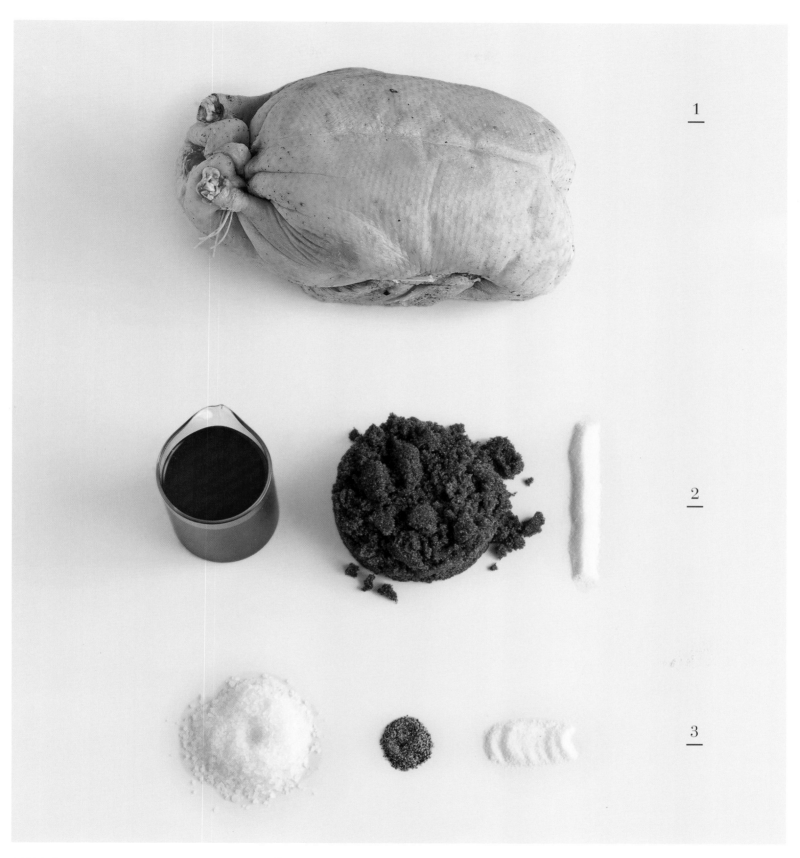

SERVES 4

1 MEAT

1 × 1.5–1.8 kg duckling (dressed weight)

2 LACQUER

135 g muscovado sugar
150 ml sherry vinegar
1 teaspoon table salt

3 SEASONING

½ teaspoon table salt
20 g coarse salt
½ teaspoon freshly ground black pepper

continued on page 202

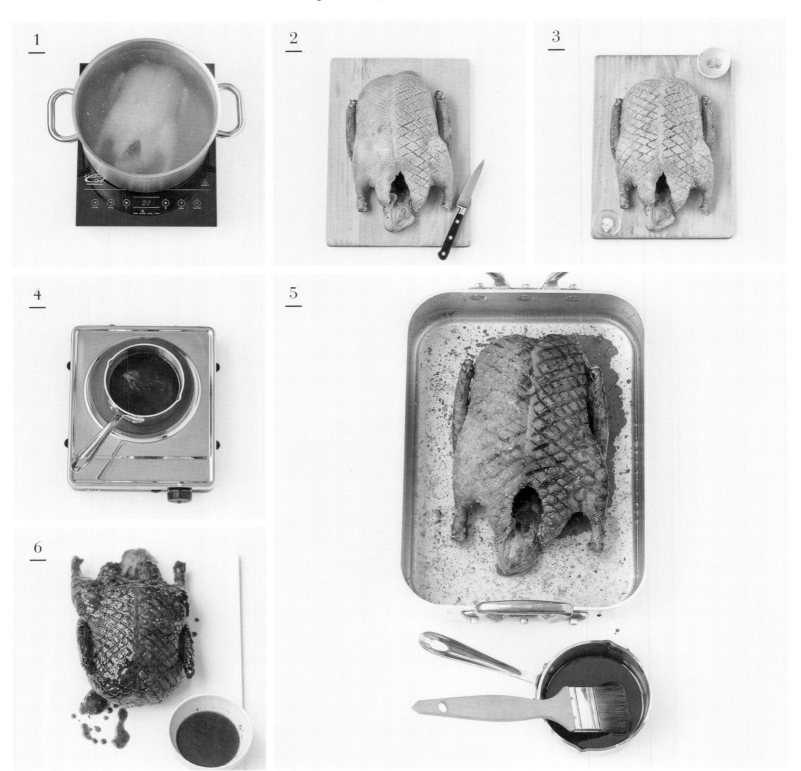

1 Preheat the oven to 180°C. Prepare a stockpot of simmering water, then turn off the heat and plunge the duckling into the water for 5 minutes.

2 Remove the duckling from the water by inserting a spatula into the rear end. Drain, shaking it a little. Cross-score the skin with a thin-bladed knife.

3 Season the cavity of the duckling with the ½ teaspoon of table salt. Mix the coarse salt with the pepper. Rub the skin with this mixture. Put the duck in a roasting tin and roast for 30 minutes.

4 Prepare the lacquer. Mix the sugar, vinegar and salt in a small saucepan and bring to the boil, then simmer for about 15 minutes, until the mixture becomes syrupy. You should have about 170 ml (⅔ cup) of liquid.

5 Increase the oven temperature to 220°C. Using a pastry brush, coat the duckling with two layers of lacquer then roast for 5 minutes. Repeat this process four times. Increase the oven temperature to 270°C, or its highest setting, and lacquer one last time (two coats). Roast for a maximum of 5 minutes, watching carefully as it colours.

6 Remove the duckling from the roasting tin. Discard the grease and any burnt residues. Pour in about 300 ml of hot water and scrape the stuck-on bits off the bottom with a spatula. Reduce this liquid in a small saucepan until the gravy has reduced to the desired concentration.

DUCK BREAST WITH
ORANGE SAUCE

Understand

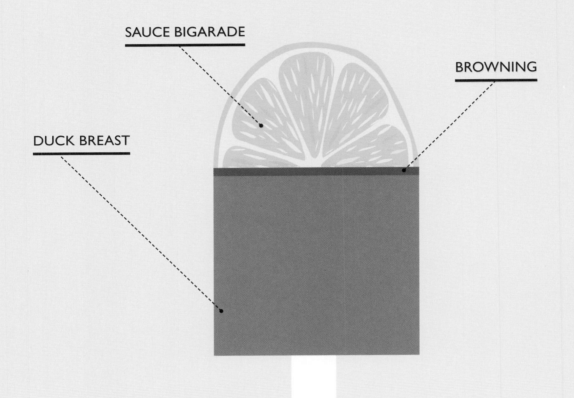

SAUCE BIGARADE

BROWNING

DUCK BREAST

WHAT IS IT?

Duck breast fillets pan-fried then cooked in the oven, served with a caramelised sauce and seasoned with citrus fruits.

TIME TO MAKE

Preparation: 20 minutes
Cooking: 20 minutes

SPECIAL EQUIPMENT

Ovenproof frying pan
Zester
Small fine-mesh sieve

TRICKY ASPECT

Cooking the caramel: if it is too dark it will be bitter

TECHNIQUES TO MASTER

Zesting citrus (page 280)
Crushing spices (page 280)
Reducing a sauce (page 283)
Deglazing (page 283)
Degreasing a frying pan (page 283)
Making a gastrique (page 55)

TIP

Use a frying pan with a pale base (stainless steel) for the caramel, to make it easier to control the colouration.

WHY COOK THE SKIN OF THE DUCK FILLETS FIRST?

To partially melt the fat, so it can be used to cook the flesh later on.

WHY TWO COOKING PHASES?

Cooking in the frying pan allows browning (and the development of aromatic notes); roasting in the oven cooks the duck through to the centre.

Learn

SERVES 4

MEAT

2 × 400 g duck breast fillets with fat (*magrets*)

ORANGE SAUCE

1 unwaxed orange
1 unwaxed lemon
40 g sugar
1½ tablespoons sherry vinegar

SEASONING

¾ teaspoon salt
freshly ground black pepper (8 grinds)
10 peppercorns
½ teaspoon fleur de sel

1   Wash, dry and zest the orange and lemon. Strain 80 ml (⅓ cup) of orange juice and two tablespoons of lemon juice into separate small bowls.

2   Make a gastrique with the sugar and vinegar in a small frying pan. Add the orange and lemon juice and let the liquid reduce by half over medium heat for 8–10 minutes. Add the zests and remove from the heat. Preheat the oven to 240°C.

3   To prepare the duck, remove the membrane, the fatty parts on the skin side of the breasts, and any superfluous fat. Cross-score the fat side of the breast, cutting on the diagonal. Season with ½ teaspoon of the salt and one grind of pepper per breast.

4   Heat an ovenproof frying pan over medium heat and cook the breasts, fat side down, for 2 minutes. Season the flesh side with the remaining salt and

pepper (one grind per breast). Turn the breasts over then transfer the pan to the oven for 6–8 minutes, until the duck is pink in the middle. Drain on paper towel.

5   Degrease the pan and deglaze with 2–3 tablespoons water. Over medium heat, reduce the liquid to almost nothing. Strain through a fine-mesh sieve and return to the pan. Stir in the orange sauce, then remove from the heat. Crush the peppercorns.

6   Cut the breasts into 5 mm slices. Arrange them on a plate, flesh side down. Remove the zests from the orange sauce and spread them over the meat. Coat with the sauce. Sprinkle over the fleur de sel and the crushed peppercorns.

PULLED PORK

Understand

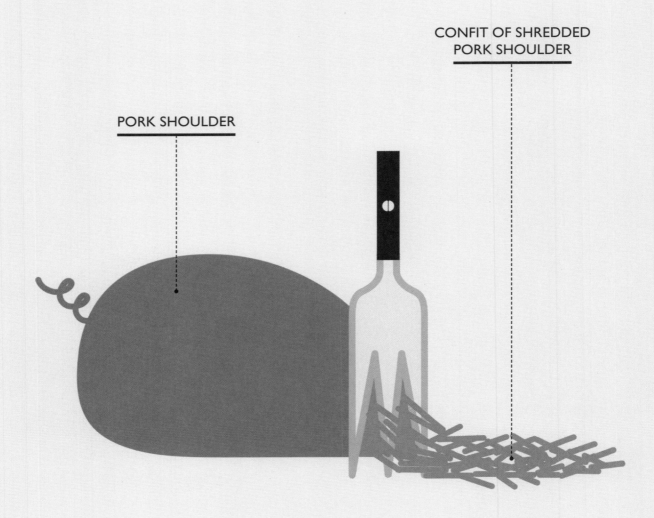

PORK SHOULDER

CONFIT OF SHREDDED
PORK SHOULDER

WHAT IS IT?
Piece of pork shoulder slow-roasted at low heat, then grilled, shredded and served with barbecue sauce.

TIME TO MAKE
Preparation: 30 minutes
Cooking: 2 hours 10 minutes

SPECIAL EQUIPMENT
Ovenproof saucepan

TECHNIQUES TO MASTER
Decanting (page 282)
Reducing a sauce (page 283)
Straining through a sieve (page 281)

VARIATION
Whole shoulder: rub it with mustard, sprinkle with paprika, salt, pepper, sugar and cayenne pepper. Cook for 3 hours in the saucepan, then 1 hour 30 minutes in the oven on a wire rack over a roasting tin.

IT'S READY . . .
When the top of the meat is well browned (but not burnt) and the corners are crisp

STORAGE
In the refrigerator for 2 days. Reheat for 10 minutes at 150°C.

ACCOMPANIMENT
Roast pumpkin (page 254)

WHY A FIRST COOKING PHASE STARTING FROM COLD?
Starting from cold means the meat takes longer to cook. This allows time for the extraction of aromatic components from the meat into the cooking liquid, without overcooking the meat, which results in a more flavoursome dish.

SERVES 4

1 MEAT

1 small onion
1 orange
1 kg pork shoulder (with a 2–4 mm
layer of fat), cut into 5 cm dice
1 teaspoon salt
½ teaspoon freshly ground black pepper
1 bay leaf
1½ tablespoons lime juice

2 BARBECUE SAUCE

120 ml (½ cup) bottled tomato sauce (ketchup)
20 g treacle
1½ teaspoons Worcestershire sauce
½–1 teaspoon hot sauce (Sriracha or Tabasco)
pinch of smoked paprika
⅓ teaspoon salt
freshly ground black pepper (10 grinds)

continued on page 208

Making pulled pork

1   Preheat the oven to 150°C. Peel the onion and cut it in half. Wash and squeeze the orange into a large ovenproof saucepan. Add the pork, salt, pepper, bay leaf, onion, lime juice and the whole peel of the orange (seeds removed), and enough water to just cover the meat. Place over high heat and stir from time to time until it simmers.

2   Cover and transfer to the oven for 2 hours, until the meat is tender. Turn the pieces over halfway through the cooking time.

3   Decant the meat. Discard the orange peel, onion and bay leaf. Reduce the liquid over high heat until it is syrupy. Strain two tablespoons of this syrup through a fine-mesh sieve and set aside. Reserve the remainder of the syrup. Preheat the grill to high.

4   In a roasting tin or baking dish, shred the meat using two forks. Mix the remaining syrup with the meat. Adjust the seasoning.

5   Spread the pieces of meat over a wire rack resting on a baking tray (or the wire rack and tray of your grill). Brown under the grill for 8–10 minutes, turning the meat over after 4 minutes.

6   Whisk the reserved syrup with all the barbecue sauce ingredients until very smooth. Serve with the shredded meat.

RABBIT WITH
MUSTARD

Understand

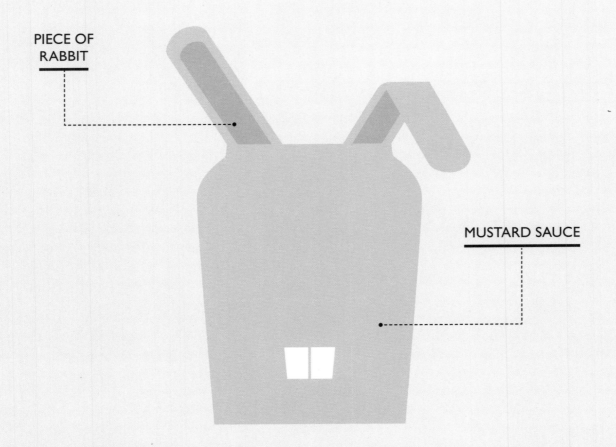

PIECE OF
RABBIT

MUSTARD SAUCE

WHAT IS IT?

Brown rabbit stew: browned pieces of rabbit, covered and cooked in a mustard sauce then coated in the reduced cooking liquid mixed with cream.

TIME TO MAKE

Preparation: 25 minutes
Cooking: 40 minutes

SPECIAL EQUIPMENT

Sieve
Large sautoir pan (deep straight-sided sauté pan)

TRICKY ASPECT

Browning the rabbit meat without burning it

TECHNIQUES TO MASTER

Mincing (page 280)
Slicing thinly (page 280)
Crushing garlic (page 280)
Decanting (page 282)
Deglazing (page 283)
Reducing a sauce (page 283)
Straining through a sieve (page 281)
Pushing through a sieve (page 281)
Browning (page 282)

ACCOMPANIMENT

Mashed potato (page 60)

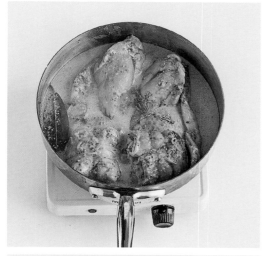

SERVES 4

2 garlic cloves
100 g French shallots
3 flat-leaf (Italian) parsley sprigs
1 rabbit, cut into 6 pieces (ribcage removed),
saddle cut in half and tied with kitchen string
1½ tablespoons olive oil
40 g strong mustard
40 g Meaux (wholegrain) mustard
150 ml dry white wine
1 thyme sprig
1 bay leaf
200 g crème fraîche
1½ teaspoons salt
freshly ground black pepper (6 grinds)

1 Preheat the oven to 180°C. Place a baking tray on the bottom shelf. Peel and crush the garlic. Peel and thinly slice the shallots. Wash, dry, pick and mince the parsley leaves. Remove any fatty bits or blood from the rabbit pieces, then season with 1 teaspoon of the salt.

2 Heat one tablespoon of the olive oil in a large saucepan over medium heat. Brown the rabbit pieces without burning them. Work in several batches to avoid overcrowding the pan.

3 Decant the rabbit pieces, add the remaining olive oil and sweat the shallot with ¼ teaspoon of the salt. Stir, then cook until soft. Add the garlic and cook until fragrant, about 30 seconds. Stir in the two mustards.

4 When the mustard starts to stick a little, deglaze the pan with the wine and let it reduce to almost nothing.

5 Return the rabbit to the pan, stir, then add enough water to cover two-thirds of the rabbit. Add the thyme and bay leaf, bring to the boil, then cover and simmer for 30 minutes, with a further 10 minutes to cook the thighs.

6 Decant the rabbit onto the hot baking tray. Strain the cooking liquid through a sieve without pushing then pour into a saucepan and reduce by half. Whisk in the crème fraîche and bring to a simmer. Reduce until it coats the back of a spoon. Adjust the seasoning.

7 Return the rabbit pieces to the pan, coat them in the sauce, then scatter over the parsley.

ROAST CHICKEN WITH
HERB BUTTER

Understand

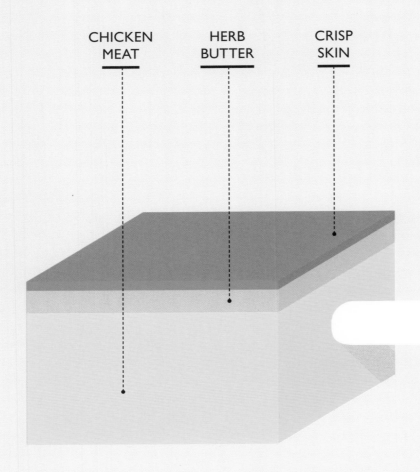

CHICKEN
MEAT

HERB
BUTTER

CRISP
SKIN

WHAT IS IT?

Chicken stuffed under the skin
with a herb butter, roasted with
potatoes and served with gravy.

TIME TO MAKE

Preparation: 45 minutes
Cooking: 40 minutes
Resting: 10 minutes

SPECIAL EQUIPMENT

Flameproof casserole dish
Fine-mesh sieve
Piping bag + plain 10 mm piping nozzle

TRICKY ASPECT
Stuffing under the skin

TECHNIQUES TO MASTER
Mincing (page 280)
Chopping finely (page 280)
Degreasing a frying pan (page 283)
Deglazing (page 283)
Scraping off stuck-on bits (page 283)
Reducing a sauce (page 283)
Straining through a sieve (page 281)

IT'S READY . . .
When the skin is well browned and the
juices run clear.

TIPS
To stuff without a piping bag: work quickly
with your fingers to avoid melting the butter.
Use a turkey baster to baste the chicken.

WHY COOK THE CHICKEN ON
ONE THIGH?

*To protect the breasts, which cook at
a lower temperature than the thighs.*

1

2

3

SERVES 4

1 CHICKEN

1 × 1.5 kg chicken (dressed weight)
2 teaspoons salt
freshly ground black pepper (8 grinds)
85 g butter

2 POTATOES

500 g firm-fleshed potatoes
1 garlic bulb
1 teaspoon salt
150 ml white poultry stock (page 10)

3 HERB BUTTER

1 French shallot
20 g flat-leaf (Italian) parsley
20 g chervil
1 tarragon sprig
5 g chives
200 g butter, softened
1 teaspoon salt
freshly ground black pepper (3 grinds)

continued on page 214

Making roast chicken with herb butter

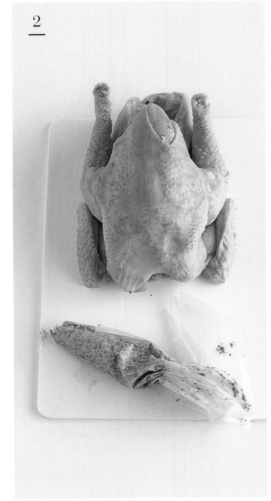

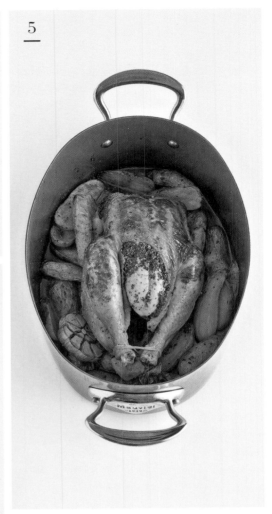

1 Preheat the oven to 220°C. To make the herb butter, peel and mince the shallot. Wash, dry, pick and finely chop the parsley, chervil and tarragon. Wash, dry and mince the chives. Incorporate the herbs into the butter, then add the shallot. Season with the salt and pepper.

2 Separate the chicken skin from the flesh using two fingers and working from front to back. Insert the herb butter under the skin using a piping bag fitted with a plain 10 mm nozzle, then massage to distribute the butter over the breast and thighs. Cover well with the skin to ensure that the flesh doesn't dry out during cooking. Season the cavity and the outside of the chicken with the salt and pepper.

3 Wash the potatoes and cut in half lengthways. Cut the garlic bulb in half crossways.

4 Grease a casserole dish with 15 g of the butter then put the chicken in, resting on one thigh. Spread around the potatoes and the halved garlic bulb. Dot the potatoes with the remaining butter cut into pieces. Roast for 15 minutes.

5 Baste the chicken with the cooking butter and turn it onto its other thigh. Roast for another 15 minutes. Baste again. When the potatoes start to turn golden, season them with salt and turn them over. Turn the chicken onto its back and roast for another 10 minutes. Check if it is cooked by lifting and letting the juices in the cavity run out: they should be clear. Rest the chicken, covered, on a wire rack for 10 minutes.

6 Remove the potatoes and garlic using a slotted spoon. Degrease the casserole dish. Deglaze with the poultry stock. Bring to the boil, scraping any stuck-on bits off the bottom. Reduce to the desired consistency. Strain through a fine-mesh sieve and check the seasoning.

7 Break the chicken into pieces and serve with the potatoes, cloves of roasted garlic and the sauce.

POACHED
CHICKEN

Understand

CHICKEN   LEEK

TURNIP

CARROT

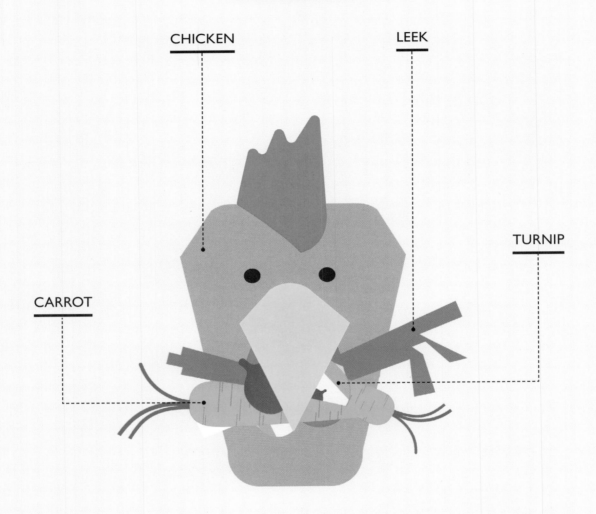

WHAT IS IT?
Chicken poached over very low heat in an aromatic cooking liquid, served with the vegetables it is cooked with.

TIME TO MAKE
Preparation: 20 minutes
Cooking: 3 hours

SPECIAL EQUIPMENT
Large flameproof casserole dish

VARIATION
Pot-au-feu (page 186)

TECHNIQUES TO MASTER
Making a bouquet garni (page 34)
Turning vegetables (page 38)
Skimming (page 283)

DEGREASING THE BOUILLON
Let it rest for 5 minutes then remove the grease that has risen to the surface. Refrigerate overnight then remove the fat that has congealed on the surface.

STORAGE
2 days in the refrigerator (meat and vegetables submerged in the bouillon). Reheat by bringing to the boil then simmering for at least 15 minutes.

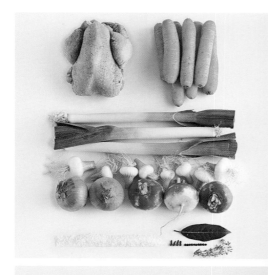

SERVES 4

2 onions
4 whole cloves
6 baby leeks
1 bay leaf
1 thyme sprig
10 peppercorns
1 × 1.9 kg chicken (dressed weight)
8 carrots
6 turnips
300 g bulb spring onions (scallion)
30 g coarse salt

1 Peel the onions and stud them with the cloves. Discard the outer leaf from each leek. Separate the white and green parts of the leeks, retaining the white parts and one green leaf. Make a bouquet garni by wrapping the green leek leaf around the bay leaf, thyme and peppercorns. Insert the bouquet garni into the cavity of the chicken.

2 Peel and wash the carrots and turnips. Cut the turnips into quarters and the carrots into 6 cm lengths, then turn the carrot and the turnip pieces. Discard the green leaves from the spring onions, cut off the roots and wash.

3 Place the chicken and studded onions in a large flameproof casserole dish. Pour in about 4 litres (16 cups) water, to nearly cover the chicken. Bring to the boil on the stovetop, then add the salt and simmer for 2 hours, skimming regularly. If necessary, cover any part of the chicken sticking out of the water with a piece of baking paper.

4 Add the remaining vegetables and cook for a further 1 hour, skimming regularly. Drain the chicken and cut it into pieces. Transfer the vegetables to a serving dish with the cooking liquid.

5 Serve in bowls with a piece of chicken and the vegetables from the pot and a little of the cooking liquid.

STUFFED CHICKEN

Understand

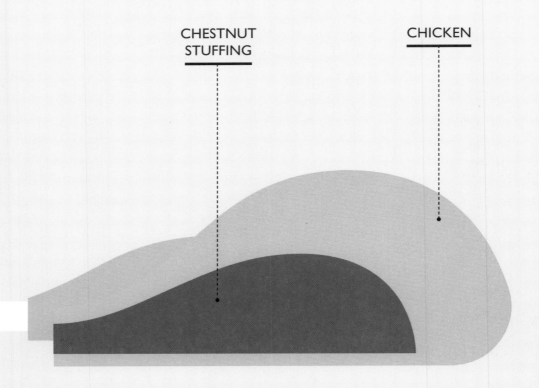

CHESTNUT
STUFFING

CHICKEN

WHAT IS IT?

Chicken stuffed with a poultry mousseline sauce with chestnuts, browned in a frying pan then cooked with steam in a casserole dish in the oven.

TIME TO MAKE

Preparation: 55 minutes
Cooking: 1 hour 20 minutes

SPECIAL EQUIPMENT

Ovenproof frying pan
Food processor with a blade attachment
Trussing needle and kitchen string

VARIATION
Turkey stuffed with chestnuts

TRICKY ASPECT
The mousseline stuffing

TECHNIQUES TO MASTER
Trussing (page 278)
Degreasing a frying pan (page 283)
Deglazing (page 283)
Scraping off stuck-on bits (page 283)
Browning (page 282)
Basting (page 283)
Straining through a sieve (page 281)
Scraping out (page 281)

WHAT HAPPENS DURING
COOKING?

The stuffing is protected from overcooking and drying out by the ribcage of the chicken; the flesh captures the flavours of the stuffing.

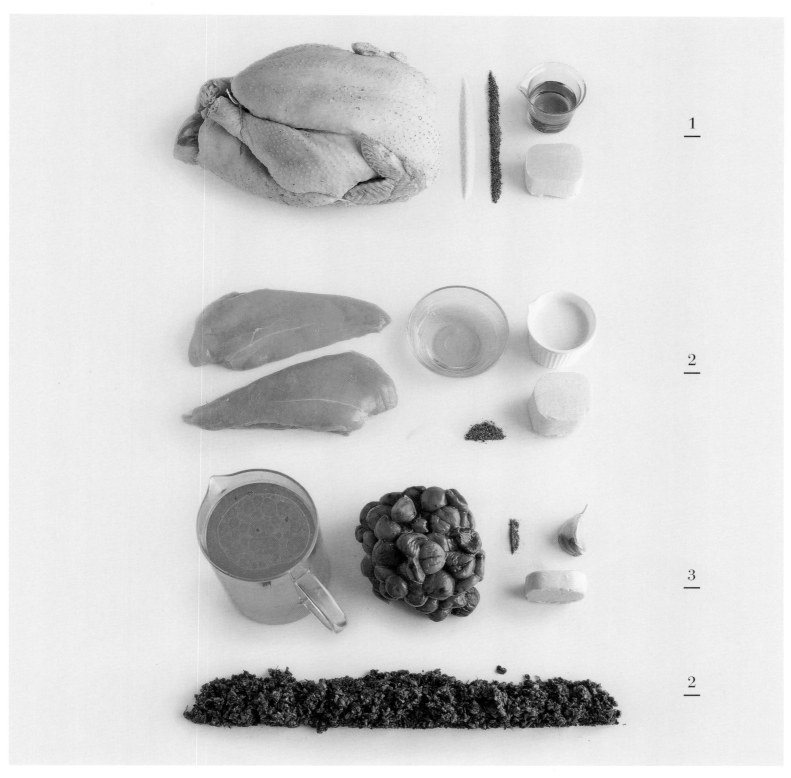

SERVES 4

1 MEAT

1 × 1.5 kg chicken (dressed weight)
2 teaspoons salt
freshly ground black pepper (6 grinds)
1½ tablespoons olive oil
50 g butter

2 STUFFING

Poultry mousseline sauce
75 ml pouring (single) cream
200 g chicken breast fillets
75 g butter
1 egg white
½ teaspoon salt
freshly ground black pepper (3 grinds)
pinch of cayenne pepper

Flavouring
220 g roasted chestnuts
150 g mushroom duxelles (page 42)

3 CHESTNUT PURÉE

2 garlic cloves
750 ml (3 cups) white poultry stock (page 10)
680 g roasted chestnuts
50 g butter

continued on page 220

Making stuffed chicken

1   To make the poultry mousseline sauce, refrigerate the bowl of your food processor and the measured-out cream. Remove any fat and sinew from the chicken breasts if necessary. Cut them lengthways into strips then into 2 cm cubes. Cut the butter into 2 cm cubes.

2   Process the chicken with the egg white, salt, black pepper and cayenne pepper. Gradually add the butter and cream, alternating between the two, then process for about 3 minutes, until the mixture is smooth. Using a silicone spatula, transfer to a bowl, scraping the side of the processor bowl and smoothing over the top of the stuffing. Cover with plastic wrap, with the plastic touching the surface, and refrigerate.

3   To make the chestnut purée, peel the garlic. Bring the stock to the boil and add the chestnuts, garlic and 20 g of the butter. Bring to the boil again, then simmer for 20 minutes. Remove from the heat and set aside, covered.

4   Roughly chop the chestnuts for the stuffing. Mix them with the duxelles and the poultry mousseline sauce, then set aside in the refrigerator.

5   Massage the skin of the chicken with half the salt. Season the cavity with the remaining salt and the pepper. Using a spoon (or a piping bag), stuff the chicken with the chestnut and mousseline mixture, pushing it in well.

6   Truss the chicken. Cut the string and secure the two ends with a double knot.

7   Preheat the oven to 200°C. Heat the olive oil in an ovenproof frying pan and brown the chicken on all sides, starting with the thighs, then the breast, then the back.

8   Turn the chicken onto its belly. Add the butter, let it foam up then spoon it over the chicken. Cover and transfer to the oven for 75–80 minutes, turning the chicken over and basting halfway through cooking.

9   Drain the chestnuts for the purée and retain the cooking liquid. Process the chestnuts with 2–3 ladlefuls of the cooking liquid, until you have a smooth, creamy purée. Add the remaining butter and process again. Cover and set aside.

10   Remove the chicken from the pan and set aside to rest, covered. Degrease the frying pan (retaining the grease). Deglaze with the remaining chestnut cooking liquid. Bring to the boil, scraping any stuck-on bits off the bottom. Reduce by half. Strain through a fine-mesh sieve, add 1½ tablespoons of the reserved grease, then stir and adjust the seasoning. Serve the chicken with the sauce and the chestnut purée.

CHICKEN
BALLOTTINES

Understand

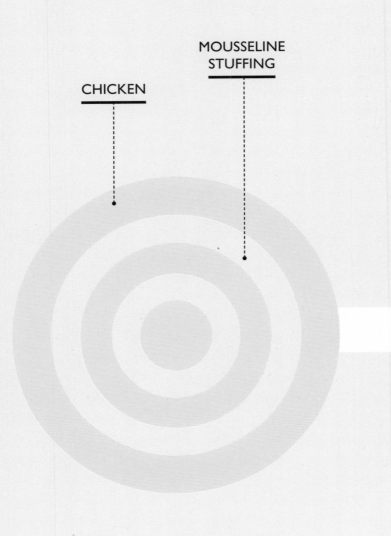

MOUSSELINE STUFFING

CHICKEN

WHAT IS IT?

Boned chicken thighs, rolled and stuffed with a poultry mousseline sauce, then poached and served with a morel sauce.

TIME TO MAKE

Preparation: 55 minutes
Cooking: 1 hour

SPECIAL EQUIPMENT

Food processor with a blade attachment
Kitchen string
Non-stick frying pan

VARIATIONS

Mousseline stuffing made with veal (*noix*: topside, or *sous-noix*: chump), fish (whiting, hake, pike, etc.) or crustaceans (langoustines, crayfish, prawns (shrimp) or lobsters).

TECHNIQUES TO MASTER

Mincing (page 280)
Scraping out (page 281)
Deglazing (page 283)
Scraping off stuck-on bits (page 283)
Poaching in hot water (page 84)
Degreasing a frying pan (page 283)

IT'S READY . . .

When the ballottines are browned on the outside and soft in the middle.

TIP

Ask your butcher to bone the thighs.

SUBSTITUTE DRIED MORELS

Rehydrate 40 g dried morels in hot water for 30 minutes. Squeeze to remove the water. Add 2½ tablespoons of the soaking liquid with the shallots.

WHY COOK AS BALLOTTINES?

To ensure well-cooked thighs (the proteins of which coagulate at higher temperatures thans those of the breasts) while maintaining tenderness in the breast.

Learn

SERVES 4

1 MEAT

4 chicken thighs (about 800 g)
1 teaspoon salt
freshly ground black pepper (8 grinds)
3 tablespoons olive oil

2 POULTRY MOUSSELINE STUFFING

110 ml pouring (single) cream
300 g chicken breast fillets
1 egg white
½ teaspoon salt
freshly ground black pepper (4 grinds)
pinch of cayenne pepper
110 g butter

3 MOREL CREAM SAUCE

300 g fresh morels
2 French shallots
30 g butter
½ teaspoon salt
2 tablespoons white wine
200 ml pouring (single) cream

continued on page 224

Making chicken ballottines

1   To make the mousseline stuffing, refrigerate the bowl of your food processor and the measured-out cream. Trim the chicken breast if necessary. Cut into strips lengthways then into 2 cm cubes. Process the chicken, egg white, salt, black pepper and cayenne pepper. Gradually add the butter and cream, alternating between the two, then process for 3–4 minutes, until the mixture is smooth. Using a silicone spatula, transfer to a bowl, scraping the side of the processor bowl and smoothing over the top of the stuffing. Cover with plastic wrap, with the plastic touching the surface, and refrigerate.

2   To bone the chicken thighs, stick the knife into the joint between the two bones (tibia at the bottom and femur at the top). Cut the length of the upper thigh to the femur then scrape the bone to remove the flesh. Lift the bone and scrape off the remaining flesh. Continue scraping until you reach the joint. Twist at

the joint and cut through the nerves and tendons to separate the bone. Repeat for the tibia.

3   Lay the thighs skin side down on a large cutting board. Season with the salt and pepper. Spread the mousseline stuffing over the thighs. Roll the flesh into a cylinder around the stuffing. Tightly roll each ballottine in several layers of heatproof plastic wrap. Tie up the ends with kitchen string.

4   Poach the ballottines in simmering water for 40 minutes.

5   Cut the morels in half lengthways. Wash under a trickle of water using a pastry brush. Gently squeeze them all at once, then dry with paper towel. Peel and mince the shallots, then sweat them in the butter in a medium saucepan over medium heat. Add the morels and the salt, then cover and cook for 20 minutes.

6   Remove the plastic wrap from the ballottines and brown them a little with the olive oil in a frying pan over high heat. Remove from the pan, then degrease the pan and deglaze with the white wine.

7   Scrape any stuck-on bits off the bottom, then stir in the cream. Add the shallot and morel mixture. Bring to the boil and reduce until the sauce is thick enough to coat the back of a spoon.

8   Trim the ends of the ballottines, then cut them into thick slices. Serve with the morel cream sauce to one side.

VENISON IN
WINE SAUCE

Understand

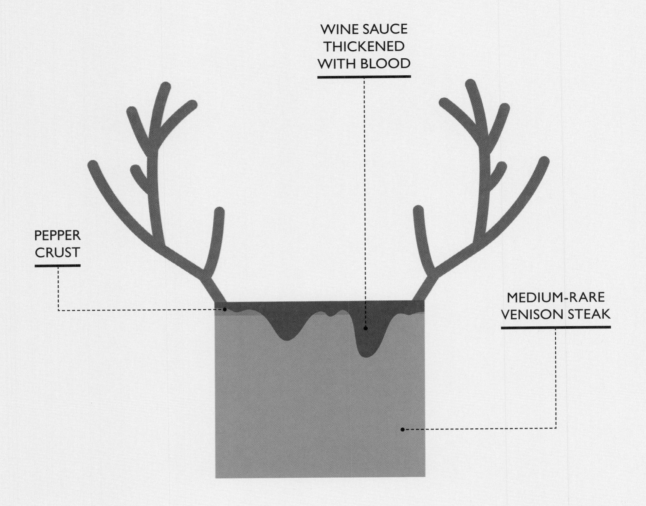

WINE SAUCE
THICKENED
WITH BLOOD

PEPPER
CRUST

MEDIUM-RARE
VENISON STEAK

WHAT IS IT?

Pan-fried venison steak served with
a red wine sauce made by deglazing
the pan and thickened with blood.

TIME TO MAKE

Preparation: 35 minutes
Cooking: 1 hour 50 minutes

SPECIAL EQUIPMENT

Large sauteuse pan (deep-sided
sauté pan with flared sides)
Fine-mesh sieve

VARIATION

Grand veneur sauce: red wine and redcurrant
jelly sauce thickened with blood

TRICKY ASPECT
Thickening with blood

TECHNIQUES TO MASTER
Crushing spices (page 280)
Degreasing a frying pan (page 283)
Mincing (page 280)
Cutting in brunoise (page 36)
Reducing a sauce (page 283)
Deglazing (page 283)
Scraping off stuck-on bits (page 283)
Whisking in butter (page 282)
Straining through a sieve (page 281)

Skimming (page 283)
Flambéing (page 282)
Basting (page 283)
Making foaming butter (page 283)

STORAGE
Keep unthickened sauce in the refrigerator
(24 hours maximum) and thicken it at the
last moment.

WHY USE MODERATE HEAT FOR
THICKENING WITH BLOOD?

*Above 75°C, the blood proteins
coagulate and create a grainy texture.*

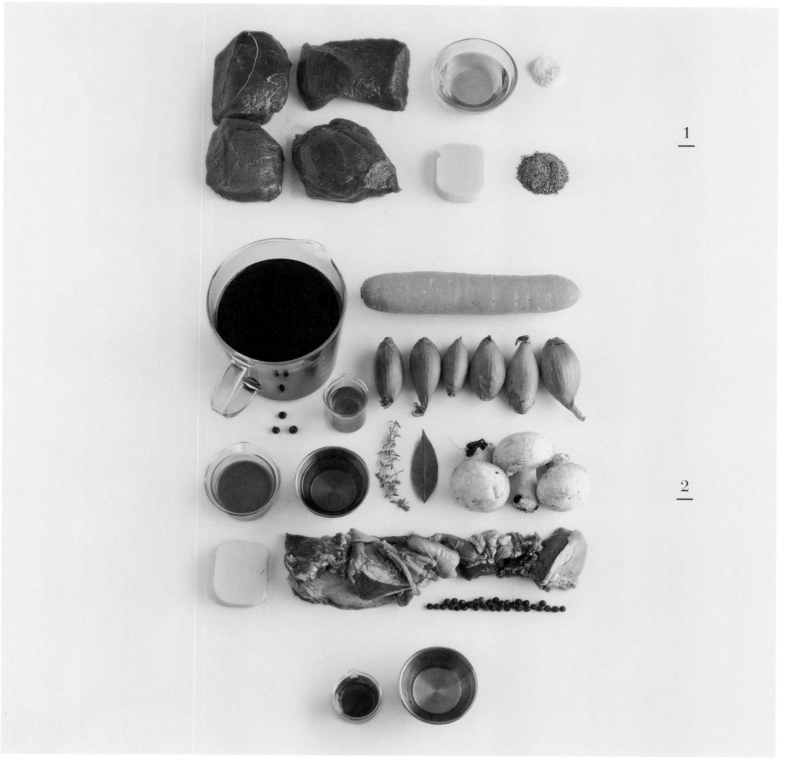

1

2

SERVES 4

1 MEAT

4 × 150 g venison steaks, with trimmings
½ teaspoon freshly ground black pepper
1 tablespoon olive oil
15 g butter
1 teaspoon salt

2 WINE SAUCE

70 g carrots
35 g button mushrooms
70 g French shallots
½ teaspoon peppercorns
1½ tablespoons olive oil
20 g butter
1 tablespoon cognac
1 thyme sprig
1 small bay leaf
1 tablespoon wine vinegar

500 ml (2 cups) red wine
2 teaspoons aged wine vinegar
3 juniper berries
½ teaspoon fleur de sel
1½ tablespoons game blood
(or, if unavailable, pig's blood)

continued on page 228

Making venison in wine sauce

1 To make the sauce, peel and wash the carrots. Remove the stalks from the mushrooms and peel the caps. Peel and mince the shallots. Cut the vegetables in brunoise. Crush the peppercorns.

2 Heat the olive oil in a saucepan and brown the trimmings briefly over very high heat, then over low heat for 2–3 minutes.

3 Degrease the pan, then melt 10 g of the butter and sweat the vegetable brunoise with the crushed pepper for 2–3 minutes. Flambé with the cognac. Add the thyme and the bay leaf, then reduce the liquid completely. Deglaze with the wine vinegar. Reduce the liquid to nothing, using a spatula to scrape off any stuck-on bits.

4 Add the red wine and reduce by half over medium heat, skimming regularly. Pour in 700 ml water, then simmer for 1 hour 30 minutes, skimming occasionally. At the end of cooking, the sauce should have reduced by one-third. If not, bring to the boil over medium heat and let it reduce.

5 Push through a fine-mesh sieve and set aside.

6 To prepare the meat, lightly coat the venison steaks with the pepper.

7 Heat the olive oil in a saucepan over high heat. Reduce the heat to medium and seal the venison steaks for 2 minutes on each side. Add the 15 g of butter, then let the steaks brown for 3 minutes more on each side, regularly spooning the foaming butter over the top. Drain the steaks on a wire rack, and cover them with foil to keep them hot.

8 Discard the cooking fat and deglaze the saucepan with the aged wine vinegar and 2 tablespoons water. Add 200 ml of the wine sauce. Bring to the boil, skim, then cook over low heat for 5–10 minutes. Adjust the seasoning then whisk in the remaining 10 g of butter to make the sauce shiny and smooth. Crush the juniper berries, then sprinkle them into the sauce with the fleur de sel. Strain the sauce through a fine-mesh sieve.

9 Return the sauce to the saucepan, bring to a simmer, then remove from the heat. Gently whisk in the blood. Adjust the seasoning.

10 Serve a venison steak on each plate and coat with the sauce.

CALF'S LIVER
WITH RAISINS

Understand

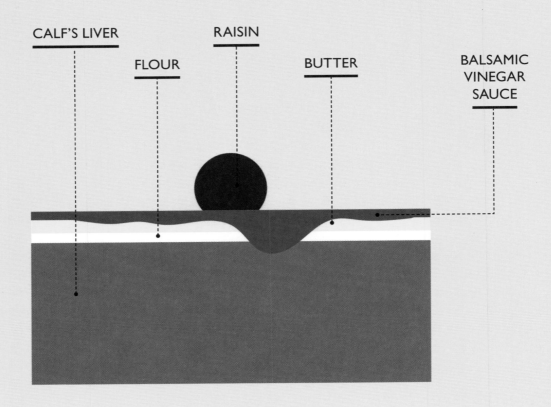

CALF'S LIVER   RAISIN

FLOUR   BUTTER   BALSAMIC VINEGAR SAUCE

WHAT IS IT?

Slices of calf's liver sautéed in butter and served with a vinegar and raisin sauce.

TIME TO MAKE

Preparation: 15 minutes
Cooking: 5 minutes

SPECIAL EQUIPMENT

Wire rack

VARIATION

Calf's liver à l'anglaise (sautéed calf's liver + bacon + beurre noisette)

TRICKY ASPECT

Cooking the liver: the centre must be pink

TECHNIQUES TO MASTER

Mincing (page 280)
Deglazing (page 283)
Scraping off stuck-on bits (page 283)
Reducing a sauce (page 283)
Whisking in butter (page 282)

ACCOMPANIMENT

Mashed potato (page 60)

WHY DUST THE LIVER SLICES WITH FLOUR?

The starch in the flour absorbs moisture from the liver, which improves the browning of the liver (Maillard reactions, page 282).

SERVES 4

60 g raisins
2 French shallots
2 × 300 g calf's liver slices
1 teaspoon salt
20 g plain (all-purpose) flour
60 g butter
60 ml (¼ cup) balsamic vinegar
freshly ground black pepper (4 grinds)
½ teaspoon fleur de sel

1 Bring 100 ml water to the boil, then remove from the heat and add the raisins. Peel and mince the shallots.

2 Cut the liver slices in half. Pat dry with paper towel, season with salt, then dust with flour. Tap gently to remove any excess flour.

3 Heat half the butter in a large frying pan until lightly golden. Add the liver pieces and brown for 3 minutes over medium heat. Turn them over, add another 10 g of butter and cook for 2–3 minutes, spooning the butter over the liver pieces constantly. Transfer to a wire rack, then season with the pepper and sprinkle with the fleur de sel.

4 Sweat the shallot for 1 minute in the same pan. Deglaze with the balsamic vinegar, scraping any stuck-on bits off the bottom. Add the raisins with their soaking water. Reduce the sauce until slightly thickened. Cut the remaining butter in dice and whisk into the sauce.

5 Return the liver pieces to the pan and coat with the sauce.

BOEUF EN CROÛTE
WITH FOIE GRAS

Understand

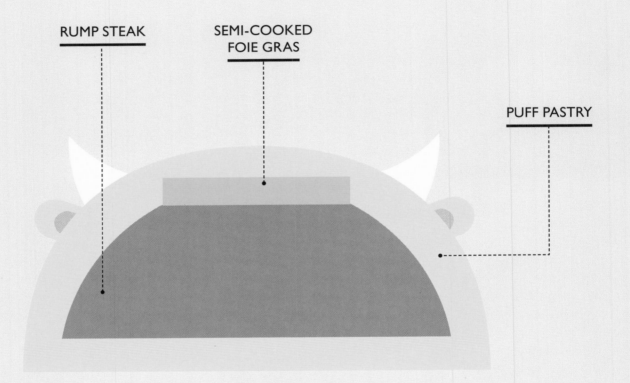

RUMP STEAK

SEMI-COOKED
FOIE GRAS

PUFF PASTRY

WHAT IS IT?

Roast beef in a puff pastry crust,
stuffed with foie gras.

TIME TO MAKE

Preparation: 35 minutes
Cooking: 25 minutes
Resting: 15 minutes

SPECIAL EQUIPMENT

Rolling pin
Pastry brush
Large pizza cutter with a thin blade

VARIATIONS

Crust made with shortcrust pastry
Beef wellington: boeuf en croûte stuffed with
mushroom duxelles

TRICKY ASPECT

Working with the puff pastry

TECHNIQUES TO MASTER

Browning (page 282)
Deglazing (page 283)
Scraping off stuck-on bits (page 283)
Degreasing a frying pan (page 283)
Straining through a sieve (page 281)

WHAT DOES THE PASTRY
CRUST DO?

*It protects the meat from overcooking
and allows the core temperature
to remain at 55°C, despite a very
high cooking temperature.*

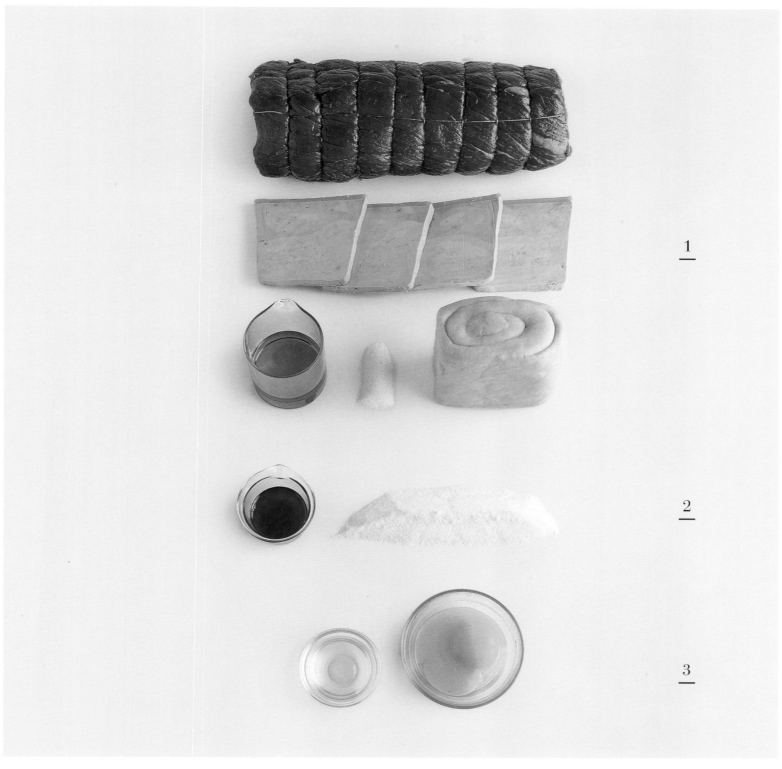

SERVES 4

1 MEAT

1.5 kg rolled and tied rump steak
1½ teaspoons salt
2 tablespoons olive oil
660 g puff pastry (page 46)
225–300 g semi-cooked foie gras
(page 112), cut into 3–4 × 75 g slices that
will cover the length of the rolled rump

2 GASTRIQUE SAUCE (PAGE 55)

60 g icing (confectioners') sugar
2½ tablespoons sherry vinegar

3 GLAZE

2 egg yolks beaten with 2 teaspoons water

continued on page 234

Making bœuf en croûte with foie gras

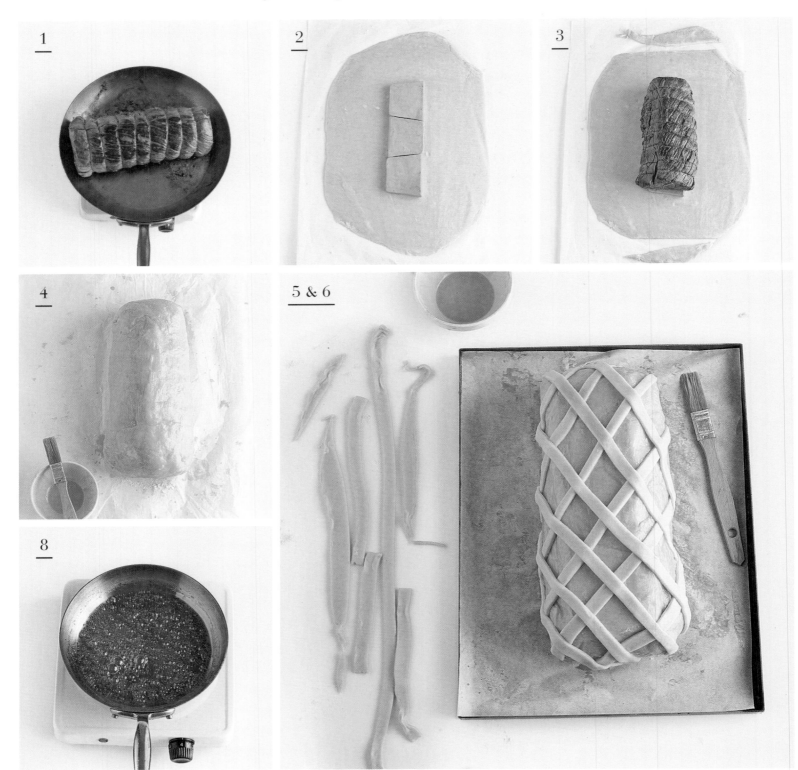

1 Pat the meat dry with paper towel. Season with the salt. Heat the olive oil in a frying pan over very high heat and brown the rump on all sides. Let it cool on a wire rack. Set aside the frying pan with its stuck-on bits for the sauce.

2 Preheat the oven to 240°C and place a shelf on the lowest rung. Line a baking tray with baking paper. Cut the pastry into one large 500 g piece and one small 160 g piece. Roll out the large piece with a rolling pin into a rectangle 3–4 mm thick and large enough to comfortably envelop the rump. Arrange the foie gras slices in a lengthways line down the centre of the pastry.

3 Remove the string from the rump and place the meat on top of the foie gras.

4 Wrap the pastry around the meat, taking care to push out any air bubbles. Using a pastry brush, glaze the pastry with the egg and water mixture. Transfer the bœuf en croûte to the prepared baking tray, with the join on the bottom. Set aside in the refrigerator.

5 Roll out the second piece of pastry into a rectangle the same length as the roast and 3–4 mm thick. Cut into strips 1–1.5 cm wide.

6 Remove the bœuf en croûte from the refrigerator and glaze the pastry again. Arrange the pastry strips in a criss-cross pattern over the bœuf en croûte. Glaze.

7 Reduce the oven temperature to 220°C and bake bœuf en croûte for 25 minutes. Remove from the oven and set aside to rest for 15 minutes before serving.

8 To make the sauce, heat the icing sugar in a small saucepan to make a dry caramel (page 55). Carefully pour in the vinegar; the sugar will crystallise. Cook over medium heat until the sugar has dissolved. Remove from the heat.

9 Degrease the pan you seared the beef in and heat over very high heat. Deglaze with 2–3 tablespoons water. Scrape the bottom of the pan to remove any stuck-on bits. Strain this liquid through a fine-mesh sieve and pour over the gastrique (sugar and vinegar), then reheat and stir. Cut thick slices of the roast and coat with the sauce.

COUSCOUS

Understand

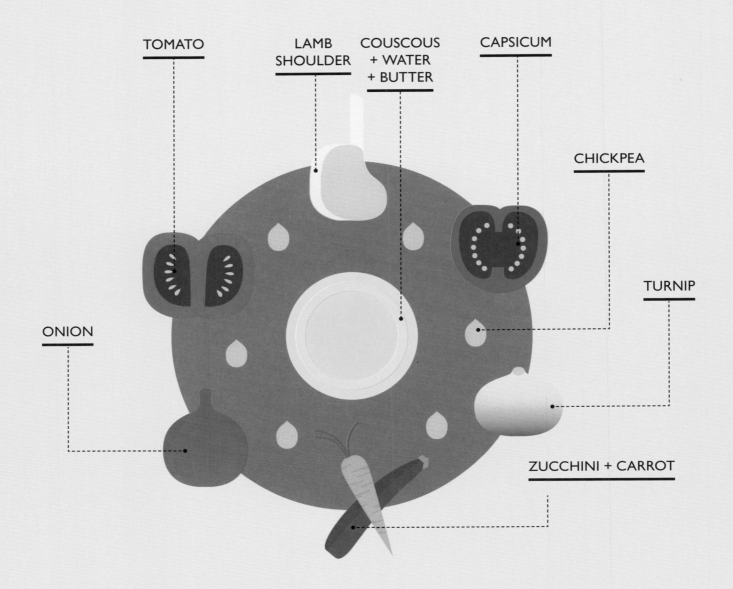

TOMATO

LAMB SHOULDER

COUSCOUS + WATER + BUTTER

CAPSICUM

CHICKPEA

TURNIP

ONION

ZUCCHINI + CARROT

WHAT IS IT?

Couscous cooked in water, served with a lamb stew with seven vegetables and a spiced bouillon.

TIME TO MAKE

Preparation: 40 minutes
Cooking: 1 hour 25 minutes
Resting: 5 minutes

SPECIAL EQUIPMENT

Couscous pan (or stockpot + steaming basket)

TRICKY ASPECTS

Not burning the bits stuck to the bottom
Cooking the vegetables
Preparing the couscous (cooking and separating the grains)

TECHNIQUES TO MASTER

Slicing thinly (page 280)
Browning (page 282)
Degreasing a bouillon (page 283)
Decanting (page 282)

IT'S READY . . .

When the zucchini and the lamb are tender.

STORAGE

In the refrigerator for up to 2 days.
Remove the fat solidified on the surface before reheating.

SUBSTITUTE DRIED CHICKPEAS

Soak 125 g dried chickpeas in a large volume of water for 12 hours with ½ teaspoon bicarbonate of soda (baking soda). Drain and rinse. Cover with water in a small saucepan, bring to the boil, then cook over low heat, covered, for 1 hour. Add 1 teaspoon salt 5 minutes before the end of cooking.

SERVES 4

1 MEAT AND BOUILLON

1 red onion
1.3 kg lamb shoulder, boned and cut into 15 pieces
1 teaspoon salt
3 tablespoons olive oil
1 teaspoon harissa
2 teaspoons tomato paste (concentrated purée)

2 VEGETABLES

2 carrots
3–6 turnips
1 green capsicum (pepper)
2 tomatoes
1 zucchini (courgette)
250 g tinned chickpeas

3 COUSCOUS

450 g fine-grained couscous
1½ teaspoons coarse salt
450 ml boiling water
60 g butter

continued on page 238

Making couscous

1   Peel and slice the onion. Pat the meat dry with paper towel, then season with half the salt.

2   Heat the olive oil in a large stockpot over high heat and brown the lamb pieces, working in several batches. Decant the lamb.

3   In the same pot, fry the onion over medium heat until golden, then add the remaining salt, the harissa and the tomato paste, stirring for 1–2 minutes.

4   Return the lamb to the pot. Pour in 500 ml (2 cups) water and bring to the boil. Reduce the heat, then simmer, covered, for 1 hour.

5   Peel the carrots and cut them in half lengthways, then slice on a slight angle into three pieces. Peel the turnips and cut into quarters. Remove the ends of the capsicum, remove the seeds and cut into rounds (not too thin), then cut each round in half. Wash the tomatoes and remove the stalks, then cut into quarters and deseed. Wash the zucchini, cut off each end, then cut in half or thirds lengthways (depending on its thickness), then on an angle into three slices.

6   Add the carrot, turnip, capsicum and chickpeas, along with the water from the tin to the pot. Bring to a simmer and cook, uncovered, for 15 minutes. Add the zucchini and tomatoes. Cook for 10 minutes. Degrease regularly.

7   Tip the couscous into a large baking dish. Add the salt to the boiling water, then pour over the couscous and stir immediately with a spoon. Smooth the surface and let it swell for 5 minutes. Cut the butter into pieces then add to the couscous. Rub the butter into the couscous to separate the grains.

8   Transfer the couscous to a steamer lined with baking paper and set over the stockpot until ready to serve.

HAMBURGERS

Understand

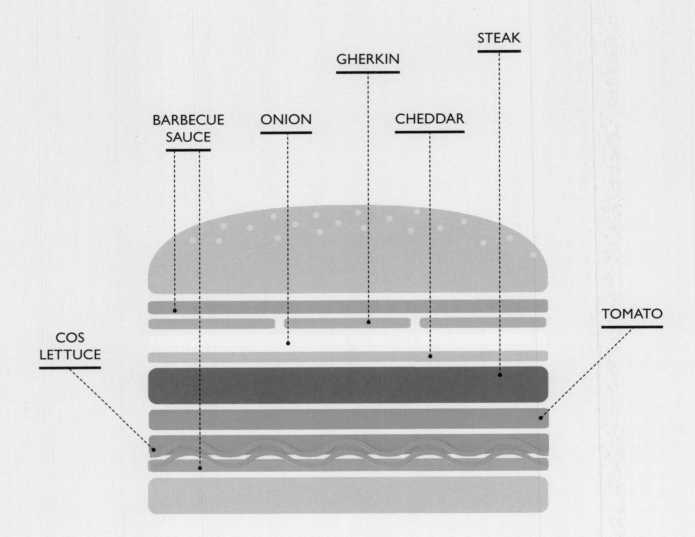

STEAK

GHERKIN

BARBECUE
SAUCE

ONION

CHEDDAR

TOMATO

COS
LETTUCE

WHAT IS IT?

Hot sandwich made with brioche-style bread, minced beef (brisket + sirloin), cheese, crisp salad vegetables and a lightly sweetened sauce.

TIME TO MAKE

Preparation: 35 minutes
Cooking: 13 minutes

SPECIAL EQUIPMENT

Large frying pan or barbecue grill
Thin spatula

TRICKY ASPECT

Cooking the meat: making a good crust on the outside without burning, and retaining a rare centre

TECHNIQUES TO MASTER

Straining through a sieve (page 281)
Pushing through a sieve (page 281)
Decanting (page 282)

TIP

If your butcher cannot mince the brisket, cut it into 2 cm dice and mince with a mincer or a food processor with a blade attachment (for a food processor, harden the meat in the freezer for 15 minutes then mince by pulsing several times).

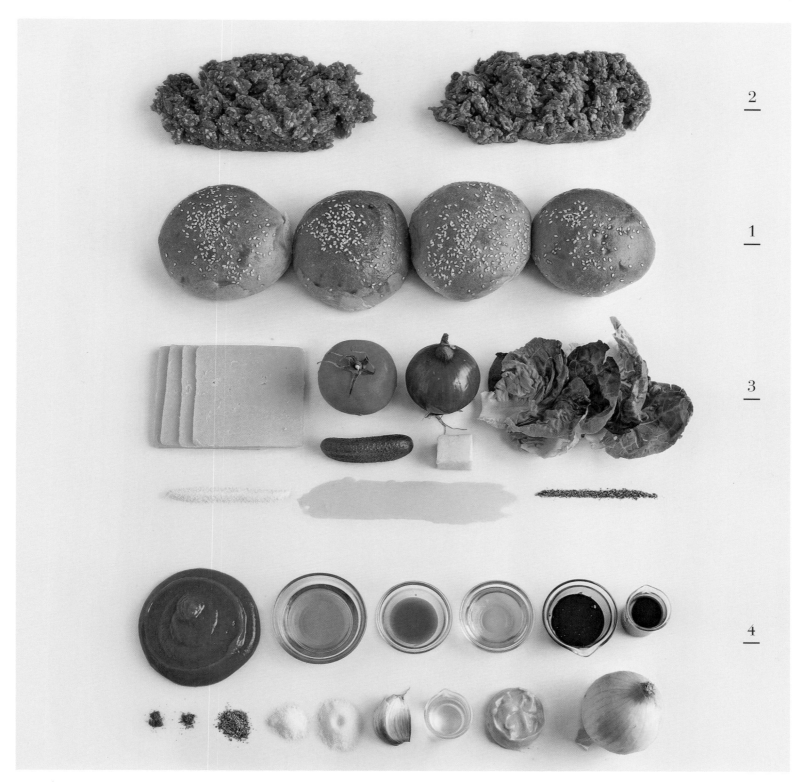

SERVES 4

1 BREAD

4 hamburger buns (9–10 cm diameter)

2 PATTIES

400 g freshly minced (not tightly packed)
beef: 200 g brisket and 200 g sirloin
1 teaspoon salt

3 FILLING

4 cos lettuce leaves
1 tomato
1 small red onion
1 gherkin
1 teaspoon olive oil
4 slices cheddar (maximum 2 mm thick)
10 g butter
1 teaspoon salt
freshly ground black pepper (8 grinds)

4 SAUCE

1 onion
250 ml (1 cup) bottled tomato sauce (ketchup)
40 g treacle
1½ tablespoons apple cider vinegar
1½ tablespoons Worcestershire sauce
1½ scant tablespoons dijon mustard
½ teaspoon Tabasco
1 teaspoon sugar
freshly ground black pepper (8 grinds)
1 garlic clove
1½ tablespoons olive oil
½ teaspoon espelette pepper
pinch of cayenne pepper

continued on page 242

Making hamburgers

1   To make the sauce, blend the onion with 70 ml water in a food processor until it forms a smooth cream (about 30 seconds). Push this through a fine-mesh sieve and retain 100 g of the strained purée. Mix this with the tomato sauce, treacle, vinegar, Worcestershire sauce, mustard, Tabasco, sugar and pepper.

2   Peel and finely chop the garlic. Heat the oil in a medium saucepan over medium heat. Add the garlic and the espelette and cayenne pepper. Cook for about 30 seconds, until fragrant. Add the tomato sauce mixture and bring to the boil. Simmer, uncovered, for about 25 minutes, until the sauce thickens.

3   To prepare the filling, wash the lettuce leaves and cut in half. Cut eight slices of tomato. Peel the red onion and cut into thin rings. Cut the gherkin lengthways into four slices about 5 mm thick. Cut each slice in half crossways.

4   To prepare the patties, on a chopping board, gently divide the mince into four equal piles. Without lifting them, form each pile into a round the diameter of the buns and 1–1.5 cm thick. Don't smooth the surface. Season the patties with half the salt, then turn them over using a spatula and season the other side with the remaining salt.

5   Heat the oil in a frying pan over the highest possible heat. When the oil starts to smoke, cook the patties, without touching them, for about 1 minute, so they form a nice dark crust. Turn them over with a spatula, reduce the heat to medium, place a slice of cheddar on each one and let it melt for 1 minute. Remove the patties to a wire rack.

6   Cut the buns in half crossways. Melt half the butter in a frying pan over medium heat until it turns golden. Add half the buns, cut side down, and brown. Repeat with the remaining butter and bun halves.

7   Spread 1 tablespoon of the sauce over each toasted side of the buns. On each bottom half, layer a half lettuce leaf, two slices of tomato, a patty with the cheese, several onion rings and two pieces of gherkin. Season with the salt and pepper and close with the top half of the bun.

DAUPHINE POTATOES

Understand

COOKED DAUPHINE
POTATO

RAW DAUPHINE
POTATO

PUFFED-UP DAUPHINE
POTATO

CRISP
SURFACE

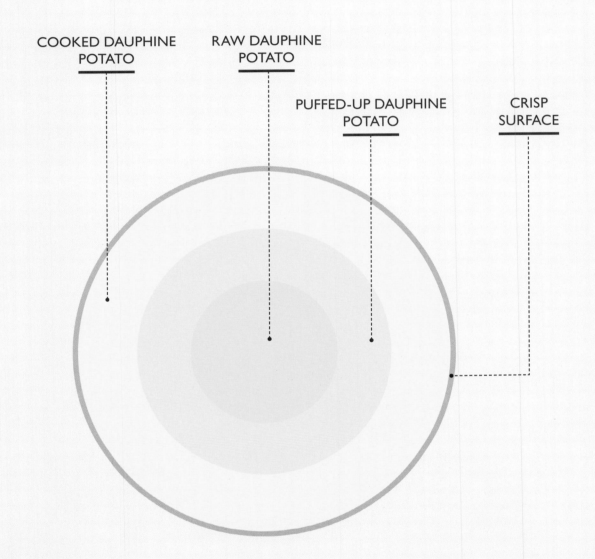

WHAT ARE THEY?

Mixture of mashed potato and choux
pastry, shaped into little balls, then fried.

TIME TO MAKE

Preparation: 45 minutes
Cooking: 40 minutes to 1 hour

SPECIAL EQUIPMENT

Wide flat-bottomed sieve + dough scraper
(or potato masher or food mill)
Piping bag and plain 20 mm piping nozzle
Thermometer, skimmer or slotted spoon

TRICKY ASPECT

The texture of the mashed potato, cooking

TECHNIQUE TO MASTER

Piping (page 281)

THEY'RE READY . . .

When they are golden and puffed up.

STORAGE

To reheat: 3 minutes in the oven at 200°C;
add salt after. To make in advance: freeze raw
then fry for an extra 3 minutes.

NOTE

You must have half as much choux pastry
as mash. Weigh each.

TO ACCOMPANY

Roast meats, roast poultry, lacquered
duckling (page 200), hamburgers (page 240)

HOW DO THE DAUPHINE
POTATOES PUFF UP?

*The water in the mixture evaporates
and makes them swell up.*

WHY DO THEY FLOAT TO
THE SURFACE?

*As the water evaporates, the balls become
less dense and rise to the surface.*

Learn

MAKES 40

1 MASHED POTATO

500 g potatoes (bintje or similar)
coarse salt

2 CHOUX PASTRY

50 g butter
½ teaspoon salt
70 g plain (all-purpose) flour
2 eggs, lightly beaten

3 SEASONING AND TO COOK

salt
freshly ground black pepper
pinch of freshly grated nutmeg
1 litre (4 cups) peanut oil

continued on page 246

Making dauphine potatoes

1   Wash the potatoes and place in a large saucepan with some coarse salt and cold water. Bring to the boil. Simmer for 20–40 minutes, depending on their size.

2   To make the choux pastry, melt the butter with 120 ml (½ cup) water and the salt in a saucepan over medium heat, stirring. Bring to the boil then boil for 2–3 seconds.

3   Remove from the heat, add the flour in one go and incorporate it, gently at first. When the pastry pulls together, mix vigorously.

4   Dry the pastry by stirring for 30 seconds to 1 minute over medium heat. Remove from the heat from time to time to prevent it burning on the bottom of the saucepan. Stop when the pastry no longer sticks.

5   Process the dried pastry for a few seconds in a food processor to cool it down (or stir it with a wooden spoon). Gradually add two-thirds of the egg. If the pastry sticks to the spoon then falls to form one (or several) peaks, it's ready; if not, add the remaining egg.

6   Drain the potatoes, then return them to the saucepan over the heat, moving them around so the skin is well dried. Leave to cool a little then peel.

7   Roughly mash the hot potatoes using a fork, then push through a wide flat-bottomed sieve using a dough scraper (or mash with a potato masher). Season with salt and pepper, and add the nutmeg.

8   Mix the choux pastry with the mashed potato using a spatula or a dough scraper. Fill a piping bag with the dauphine potato mixture (or use a spoon).

9   Pipe about 40 balls on a chopping board. Heat the peanut oil in a heavy-based saucepan or deep-fryer to 160°C or until a scrap of dough dropped into the oil browns in 20 seconds. Cook the pastry balls, eight at a time, in the oil, watching that they don't stick together. They will sink then rise to the surface again. Cook them for 4 minutes. Remove from the oil using a skimmer, then season with salt and drain on paper towel. Repeat with the remaining potato balls.

SOUFFLÉ POTATOES

Understand

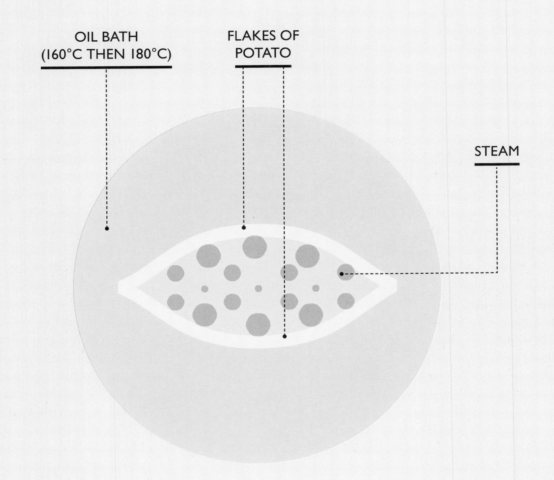

OIL BATH
(160°C THEN 180°C)

FLAKES OF
POTATO

STEAM

WHAT ARE THEY?

Thin rounds of fried potato, that 'soufflé' during cooking: they puff up and turn golden.

TIME TO MAKE

Preparation: 15 minutes
Cooking: 20 minutes

SPECIAL EQUIPMENT

Two small saucepans
Thermometer
Mandoline, small skimmer
Round biscuit cutter (5 cm diameter)

TRICKY ASPECTS

Synchronising the temperature of the two oil baths
Transferring the potatoes from one oil bath to the other

THEY'RE READY . . .

When the potato rounds are puffy and lightly browned.

TO ACCOMPANY

A leg of lamb, a duck breast (page 204) or a rack of lamb cooked at low temperature (page 83)

HOW DOES THE POTATO ROUND PUFF UP?

The heat turns the water in the potato into steam, which puffs up the round.

HOW DOES IT SPLIT IN TWO?

The water vapour lifts the two surfaces of the slices. Once dried by cooking, the two surfaces remain separated.

MAKES 30–40

peanut oil, for deep-frying
2 large floury potatoes (300 g each)
(such as desiree or similar)
1 teaspoon salt

1   In two heavy-based saucepans, prepare two oil baths: one at 160°C and the other at 180°C. Peel the potatoes, wash them under cold water, then dry them with a clean tea towel (dish towel). Using a mandoline, cut them into 2 mm thick slices.

2   Cut a disc out of the middle of each slice using a 5 cm biscuit cutter. Set aside in a bowl of cold water.

3   Wash and dry five to eight slices and immerse them in the 160°C oil bath. Remove the pan from the heat and stir with a spatula so that the slices are moving constantly.

4   As soon as one slice starts to form little blisters on the surface (after 2–4 minutes), remove it from the oil using a small skimmer and transfer it immediately to the 180°C oil bath. Stir with a spatula.

5   When the slice has puffed up, browned and dried (after a few seconds), remove using the skimmer, season with salt and drain on paper towel. Once the first batch is completed, reheat the first oil bath to 160°C and start again with five to eight new slices.

POTATO
MILLE-FEUILLES

Understand

THIN SLICES
OF POTATO

CREAM

WHAT IS IT?

Thin slices of potato, soaked in
cream, arranged in layers, baked in
the oven, then compressed.

TIME TO MAKE

Preparation: 40 minutes
Cooking: 1 hour
Resting: 6 hours

SPECIAL EQUIPMENT

Rectangular cake tin (about 8 cm × 25 cm)
Mandoline

VARIATION

Gratin dauphinois (potatoes + milk +
cream + garlic)

TRICKY ASPECT

Cutting the potatoes

TECHNIQUES TO MASTER

Using a mandoline (page 284)
Trimming (page 281)

IT'S READY . . .

When an inserted knife meets no resistance.

TO ACCOMPANY

Rolled lamb shoulder (page 192),
rack of lamb (page 183), salmon

HOW DO THE POTATOES BECOME TRANSLUCENT AND 'MELTING'?

*During cooking, the starch in the
potatoes swells up with water and
gelatinises, which modifies the texture.*

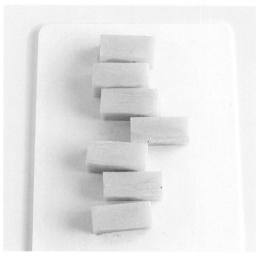

SERVES 4

150 ml thin (single) cream
2 teaspoons salt
freshly ground black pepper (12 grinds)
pinch of freshly grated nutmeg
1.2 kg very large floury and soft-fleshed potatoes
(350–400 g each) (such as bintje or similar)
1½ tablespoons olive oil
½ teaspoon fleur de sel

1 Preheat the oven to 170°C. Line a 25 cm × 8 cm loaf (bar) tin with baking paper, ensuring that some of the paper hangs over the edge of the tin. Mix the cream, half the salt, half the pepper and the nutmeg in a large flat-bottomed bowl.

2 Peel and wash the potatoes. Trim them to obtain rectangles the width of the tin (8 cm) then cut into 1.5–2 mm slices using a mandoline sitting over the bowl. Stir from time to time to soak the slices in the cream mixture.

3 Arrange the potato slices in the tin, in layers, side by side but overlapping if necessary to fill any gaps. Season with the remaining salt and pepper every two layers. Cover with the overhanging baking paper then with foil, and bake for 1 hour or until the potatoes meet no resistance when pierced with a knife.

4 Cut a rectangle of cardboard a little smaller than the tin and wrap in foil. When you take the tin out of the oven, place the cardboard on top of the mille-feuille, spread out weights on top (about three 500 g weights) and let it cool to room temperature. Remove the weights and the cardboard, cover the tin with plastic wrap and refrigerate for at least 6 hours.

5 Turn out the mille-feuille with the help of the overhanging baking paper, transfer to a tray, remove the paper, trim the edges and cut into thick slices.

6 Heat the olive oil in a non-stick frying pan over medium heat and brown the top and bottom of each mille-feuille. Serve sprinkled with the fleur de sel.

GLAZED VEGETABLES

Understand

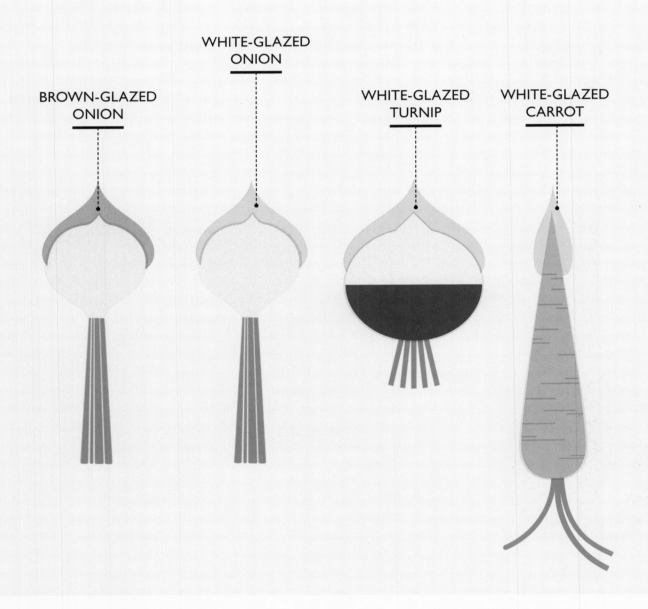

BROWN-GLAZED
ONION

WHITE-GLAZED
ONION

WHITE-GLAZED
TURNIP

WHITE-GLAZED
CARROT

WHAT IS IT?

Small vegetables browned in water,
butter and sugar to coat them in a
shiny clear syrup (white-glazed) or
caramelised syrup (brown-glazed).

TIME TO MAKE

Preparation: 20 minutes
Cooking: 10 minutes

SPECIAL EQUIPMENT

Large sauteuse pan (deep sauté
pan with flared sides)

TRICKY ASPECT

Cooking the vegetables through by the time
the liquid has reduced

TECHNIQUES TO MASTER

Cutting a baking paper disc (page 285)
Turning vegetables (page 38)

TIPS

If the vegetables aren't cooked at the end,
add boiling water.
If the vegetables are cooked but the water
hasn't evaporated, remove them from the
pan, reduce the liquid, then return them
to the syrup.

TO ACCOMPANY

Meats in sauce, game, white fish

HOW DO THE ONIONS BROWN?

*After the water has evaporated,
the temperature passes 100°C,
which triggers caramelisation
reactions: brown compounds form
and make the onions golden.*

WHAT IS THE PURPOSE OF THE

PAPER DISC?

*To slow down evaporation and retain
sufficient water to cook the vegetables.*

SERVES 4

VEGETABLES

180 g baby onions (about 25)
OR
250 g baby turnips
OR
250 g baby carrots

SYRUP

15 g butter
1 teaspoon sugar
¼ teaspoon salt

1   Peel and wash the vegetables. If using turnips, turn them.

2   Place the vegetables in a single layer in a frying pan. Cover to half their height with water (about 100 ml), then add the butter, sugar and salt.

3   Bring to the boil and cover the pan with a disc of baking paper. Simmer gently until the water has completely evaporated.

4   Remove the paper disc and cook for 1 minute more, watching the reduction: the butter and sugar should form a shiny syrup. To brown-glaze onions, continue to reduce the syrup until it caramelises.

5   Gently coat the vegetables in the syrup.

ROAST PUMPKIN

Understand

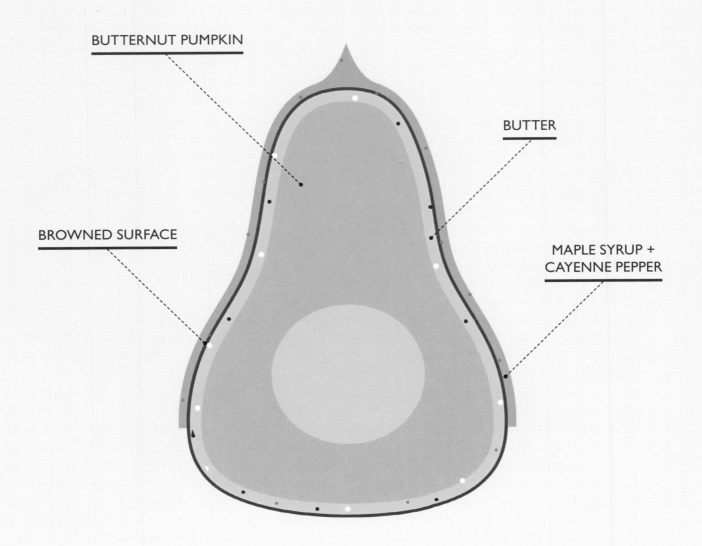

BUTTERNUT PUMPKIN

BUTTER

BROWNED SURFACE

MAPLE SYRUP +
CAYENNE PEPPER

WHAT IS IT?

Roast slices of butternut pumpkin,
served with spiced maple syrup,
goat's cheese and pecans.

TIME TO MAKE

Preparation: 25 minutes
Cooking: 35–40 minutes

SPECIAL EQUIPMENT

Very sharp vegetable peeler with a rigid blade
Baking tray

TECHNIQUE TO MASTER
Toasting nuts (page 281)

IT'S READY . . .
When the pumpkin is browned on both sides.

TO ACCOMPANY
Eggs, poultry

SERVES 4

1 × 800 g butternut pumpkin
35 g butter
½ teaspoon salt
freshly ground black pepper (10 grinds)
40 g pecans
60 g goat's cheese
3 tablespoons maple syrup
pinch of cayenne pepper
1 thyme sprig

1 Preheat the oven to 220°C and place a shelf on the lowest rung. Using a strong vegetable peeler, peel the pumpkin, also removing the white layer under the skin. Cut in half crossways, separating the thinner part from the rounded part, then cut in half lengthways. Use a spoon to remove the seeds.

2 Melt the butter in a small saucepan. With the cut side down, cut each piece of pumpkin into slices 1.5 cm thick. Put them in a large round-bottomed bowl, then add the melted butter, salt and pepper. Mix well.

3 Place the slices on a baking tray in a single layer. Roast for 25–30 minutes, until the underside is well browned. Turn each piece over using a spatula. Roast for a further 10 minutes: the other side should be browned and the flesh tender.

4 Toast the pecans in a dry frying pan then roughly chop. Cut the goat's cheese into dice.

5 Mix the maple syrup and cayenne pepper in a small bowl. Arrange the pumpkin on a platter then pour over the spiced maple syrup. Add the cheese and pecans, then sprinkle the dish with thyme leaves.

ROAST CAULIFLOWER

Understand

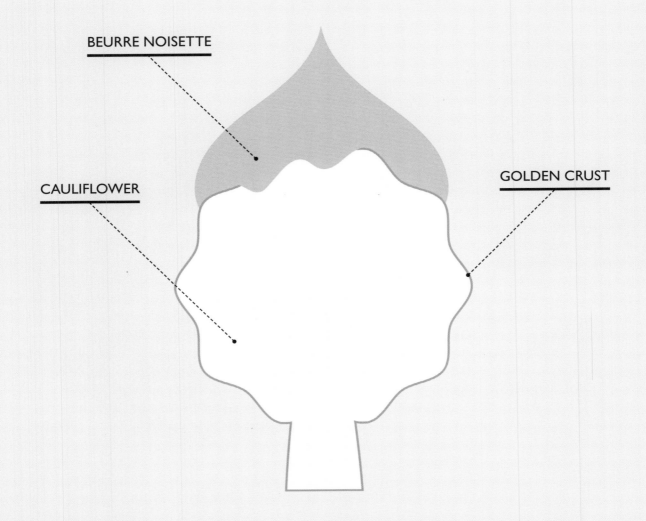

BEURRE NOISETTE

CAULIFLOWER

GOLDEN CRUST

WHAT IS IT?
Cauliflower cooked whole in the oven, regularly basted with melted butter during cooking.

TIME TO MAKE
Preparation: 10 minutes
Cooking: 60–75 minutes

TRICKY ASPECT
Browning: the cauliflower must not be burnt

IT'S READY . . .
When the cauliflower is very dark on the outside and tender in the middle.

TO ACCOMPANY
A leg of lamb, rabbit with mustard (page 210), koulibiac (page 176), crayfish à la nage (page 144), turbot bonne femme (page 156)

HOW DO PLANTS COOK?
The structure of plants is characterised by cell walls that provide rigidity. During cooking over 70°C, the cell wall breaks down and the vegetable softens.

SERVES 4

1 cauliflower (about 1 kg)
90 g butter, softened
1 teaspoon salt

1 Preheat the oven to 200°C. Cut the stalk off the cauliflower and remove the green leaves. It must sit flat. Clean by rubbing with moist paper towel.

2 Put the cauliflower in a small baking dish or an ovenproof frying pan. Cover the entire surface of the cauliflower with the butter. Season with salt.

3 Roast for 60–75 minutes until the cauliflower is tender, basting it with the butter every 10–15 minutes. Cut into pieces at the table.

GLAZED
BRUSSELS SPROUTS

Understand

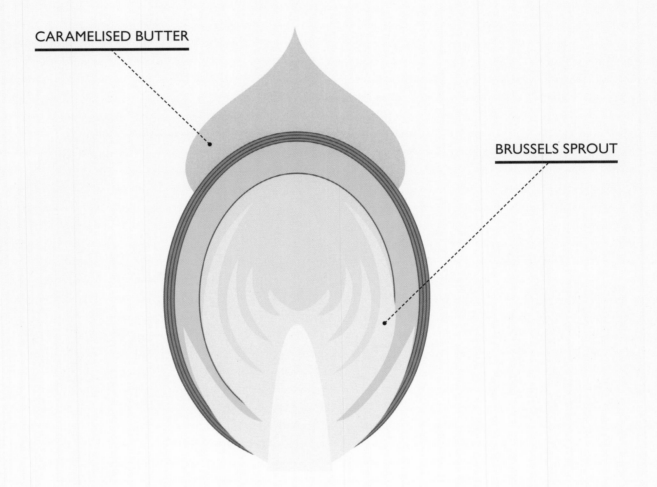

CARAMELISED BUTTER

BRUSSELS SPROUT

WHAT IS IT?

Brussels sprouts braised then browned in butter and sugar with hazelnuts.

TIME TO MAKE

Preparation: 25 minutes
Cooking: 25 minutes

VARIATION

With roasted and shelled chestnuts (don't toast them)

TRICKY ASPECT

Glazing the hazelnuts: they become bitter if cooked too long

TECHNIQUE TO MASTER

Toasting nuts (page 281)

IT'S READY . . .

When the sprouts are very shiny.

TO ACCOMPANY

Roast pork (page 75)

WHY DO WE USE THE TERM 'GLAZING'?

The sugar and the butter mix to form, little by little, a viscous base that coats the nuts and sprouts like a glaze.

Learn

SERVES 4

500 g small brussels sprouts
1 teaspoon salt
60 g hazelnuts
45 g butter
15 g sugar
salt (optional)
freshly ground black pepper (6 grinds)

1 Remove the outer leaves of the sprouts and cut off the stalks level with the bottom of the sprouts. Wash and drain.

2 Put the sprouts and the salt in a saucepan of boiling water. Reduce the heat and simmer, covered, for 10–15 minutes, until the sprouts are easily pierced with the point of a knife.

3 Toast the hazelnuts in a hot dry frying pan until browned in places. Chop them roughly with a knife. Drain the brussels sprouts.

4 Melt 30 g of the butter with the sugar in a frying pan over medium heat. Add the hazelnuts and stir to coat. Cook for about 3 minutes, stirring occasionally, until the nuts are shiny and have browned a little.

5 Add the brussels sprouts and the remaining 15 g butter. Stir until the sprouts are sizzling. Add salt if necessary, and season with the pepper.

ASPARAGUS IN SABAYON

Understand

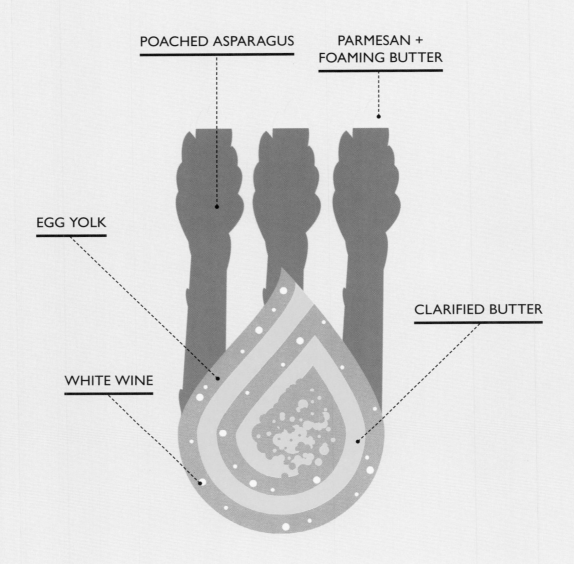

POACHED ASPARAGUS

PARMESAN + FOAMING BUTTER

EGG YOLK

CLARIFIED BUTTER

WHITE WINE

WHAT IS IT?

Poached asparagus, pan-fried in foaming butter and parmesan, served with a white wine and butter sauce based on egg yolks.

TIME TO MAKE

Preparation: 35 minutes
Cooking: 15 minutes

SPECIAL EQUIPMENT

Small sauteuse pan (sauté pan with flared sides) or small saucepan
Two large frying pans
Whisk

TERMS

Sabayon: technique of whisking egg yolks with a liquid over heat.
By extension: Italian dessert (thick custard with a wine base and sugar and egg yolk), sauce accompaniment (for asparagus, etc.).

DERIVATIVE OF SABAYON

Hollandaise sauce (page 30)

USES OF SABAYON

To accompany fish and crustaceans

TECHNIQUE TO MASTER

Making clarified butter (page 51)

TIP

Use a small saucepan to make whisking easier, otherwise the egg yolks will coagulate too quickly, without increasing in volume.

IT'S READY . . .

When the asparagus is soft and the sauce light.

HOW DOES THE EMULSION TRIPLE IN VOLUME?

By whisking, air is incorporated and the sabayon becomes foamy.

SERVES 4

1 ASPARAGUS

30 g parmesan
24 thick green asparagus spears (about 1.5 kg)
40 g coarse salt (20 g per litre/4 cups water)
50 g butter
freshly ground black pepper (2 grinds)

2 LEMON SABAYON

150 g clarified butter (page 51)
1 lemon
5 egg yolks
1 tablespoon white wine
1 teaspoon salt
pinch of cayenne pepper

continued on page 262

Making asparagus in sabayon

1   Keep the clarified butter warm (about 40°C) in a bain-marie of hot (not boiling) water over very low heat. Squeeze the lemon. Grate the parmesan. Cut 3–4 cm off the bottom of the asparagus spears and discard, then wash the spears.

2   Bring a saucepan of water to the boil and add the coarse salt. Poach the asparagus in the boiling water for 8–10 minutes, until tender. Drain.

3   In a small saucepan off the heat, whisk the egg yolks and gradually add the white wine to form an emulsion. Cook over low heat, whisking continuously, for 3–5 minutes to thicken the sabayon: it should be creamy and foamy.

4   Remove the pan from the heat and, still whisking, add the clarified butter to the sabayon in a thin trickle. Season with the salt and add the cayenne pepper, then stir. Cover and set aside at room temperature.

5   Melt the butter in two frying pans over high heat until it foams. Divide the asparagus between the pans, coat them with the butter and sprinkle over the parmesan.

6   Season with the pepper. Reheat the sabayon over very low heat, whisking constantly. Add the lemon juice and adjust the seasoning. Serve the asparagus with the sabayon.

CEP RISOTTO

Understand

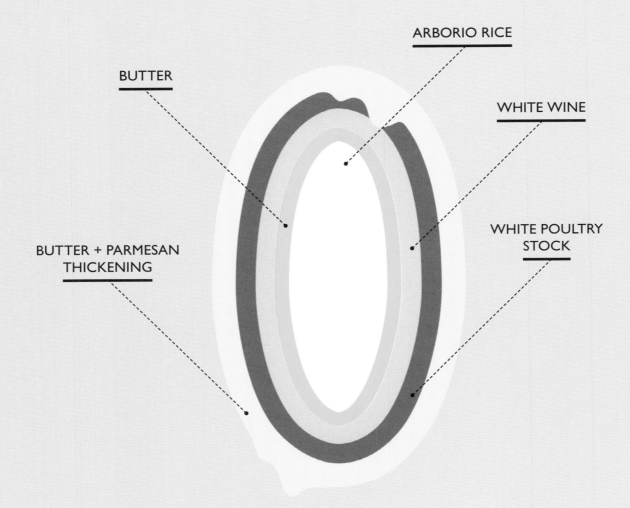

BUTTER

ARBORIO RICE

WHITE WINE

WHITE POULTRY STOCK

BUTTER + PARMESAN THICKENING

WHAT IS IT?

Short-grain rice fried until pearly in butter with onions, deglazed with white wine then cooked in stock, all flavoured with ceps and thickened with butter and parmesan.

TIME TO MAKE

Preparation: 50 minutes
Soaking: 15–30 minutes
Cooking: 25 minutes

SPECIAL EQUIPMENT

10 cm metal egg ring
Sauteuse pan (deep sauté pan with flared sides)

VARIATION

Risotto milanese: replace the ceps with 1 g saffron threads (soaked in a ladleful of the stock) added a few minutes before the end of cooking

TRICKY ASPECT

The end of cooking: the rice must be slightly al dente

TECHNIQUES TO MASTER

Making tuiles (page 276)
Crushing garlic (page 280)
Mincing (page 280)

TIP

The stock and the rice must simmer at the same intensity for the stock to be well absorbed by the rice.

IT'S READY . . .

When the risotto is creamy and the rice is still slightly al dente.

WHY NOT WASH THE RICE?

To avoid washing away the starch on the surface of the rice grains, which is necessary for the sauce to thicken.

SERVES 4

1 CEPS

1 garlic clove
20 g dried ceps or porcini mushrooms
200 ml hot water
10 g butter
¼ teaspoon salt
freshly ground black pepper (3 grinds)

2 RISOTTO

1 onion
250 g risotto rice (carnaroli or arborio)
20 g butter
1 litre (4 cups) white poultry stock (page 10)
100 ml white wine
salt, to taste
freshly ground black pepper, to taste

3 TO THICKEN

60 g parmesan
60 g butter

4 LACE TUILES

20 g parmesan

continued on page 266

Making cep risotto

1 Finely grate the parmesan for the thickening and the tuiles. Peel and crush the garlic. Peel and mince the onion. Soak the ceps in the hot water for 15–30 minutes, until they are soft. Squeeze them over the bowl. Strain the soaking water and mix with the poultry stock. Bring the stock to a low simmer. Rinse the ceps, then dry with paper towel.

2 To make the tuiles, heat a small non-stick saucepan over medium heat for 3 minutes. Remove from the heat, place a 10 cm egg ring in the middle and sprinkle 1½ tablespoons of parmesan inside it. Remove the ring, then return the pan to the heat until the parmesan is lightly golden, 1–2 minutes. Remove from the heat and carefully unstick the tuile using a thin spatula. Repeat three more times with the remaining parmesan (without preheating the pan).

3 To prepare the ceps, melt the butter in a saucepan over medium heat. Fry the ceps for a few minutes, stirring regularly. Stir in the garlic and cook for about 30 seconds until fragrant. Add the salt and pepper, and a ladleful of the stock, then cook for 2 minutes. Remove the pan from the heat.

4 Melt the butter for the risotto in a saucepan over medium heat. Fry the onion for 2 minutes, stirring, until translucent. Add the rice and stir frequently for 2 minutes. Pour in the white wine and reduce to nothing.

5 Add a ladleful of the simmering stock and stir constantly. Wait until it is absorbed, then add another ladleful. Repeat this process until all the stock has been incorporated. Add the mushrooms after 10 minutes.

6 Remove from the heat, then gently stir in the thickening butter and parmesan. Season with salt and pepper. Serve on plates, decorated with a parmesan tuile.

INK RISOTTO

Understand

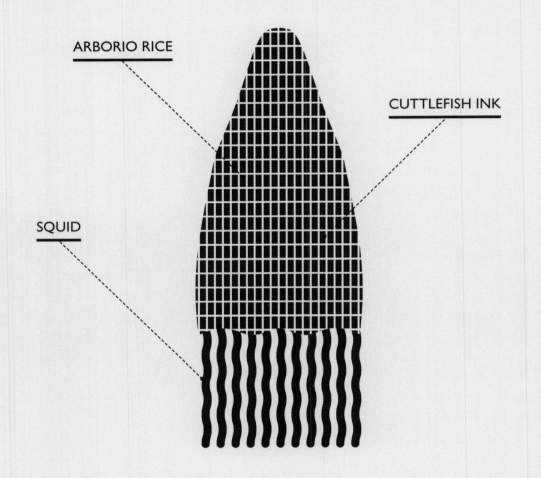

ARBORIO RICE

CUTTLEFISH INK

SQUID

WHAT IS IT?

Short-grain rice fried until pearly in butter with onions, deglazed with white wine then cooked in a cuttlefish ink bouillon.

TIME TO MAKE

Preparation: 40 minutes
Cooking: 15 minutes

SPECIAL EQUIPMENT

Sauteuse pan (deep sauté pan with flared sides)

VARIATION

Buy whole cuttlefish and set aside the ink sac when cleaning the cuttlefish. You'll need twice as many cuttlefish for this much ink. (The flesh of cuttlefish is less delicate than that of squid.)

TRICKY ASPECT

The end of cooking: the rice must be slightly al dente

TECHNIQUES TO MASTER

Crushing garlic (page 280)
Mincing (page 280)
Reducing a sauce (page 283)

TIP

The bouillon and the rice must simmer at the same intensity for the bouillon to be well absorbed by the rice.

IT'S READY . . .

When the risotto is creamy and the rice is still slightly al dente.

WHY ADD THE BOUILLON GRADUALLY?

To have control over the amount of liquid that is added to the dish and absorbed by the rice.

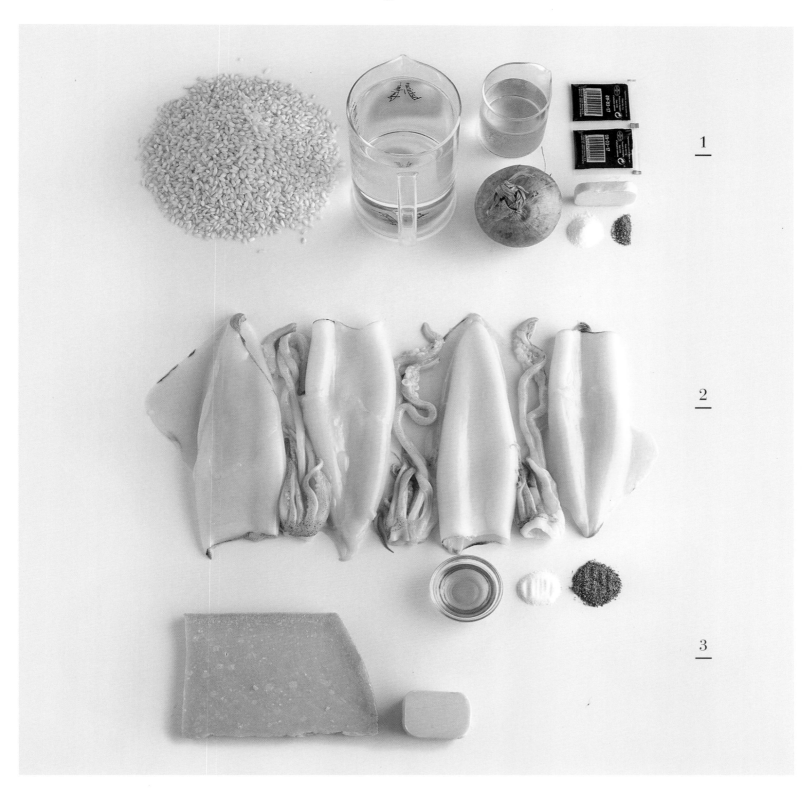

SERVES 4

1 RISOTTO

1 onion
20 g butter
250 g risotto rice (carnaroli or arborio)
100 ml white wine
10 g cuttlefish ink
½ teaspoon salt
freshly ground black pepper (3 grinds)

2 GARNISH

4 × 500 g squid (20 cm long), cleaned
2 teaspoons olive oil
½ teaspoon salt
freshly ground black pepper (6 grinds)

3 TO THICKEN

60 g parmesan
60 g butter

continued on page 270

Making ink risotto

1 Detach the squid hoods and set aside the tentacles. Put the hoods in a saucepan with 1.2 litres water and the salt, then bring to the boil and simmer until the water is fragrant. Remove the squid hoods but keep the bouillon simmering.

2 Finely grate the parmesan. Peel and mince the onion.

3 Rinse the squid hoods, cut down one side and then open out flat and dry them with paper towel. Cross-score both sides of the hoods with the point of a knife.

4 Cut the hoods into strips about 2 cm wide.

5 Melt the butter for the risotto in a saucepan over medium heat. Fry the onion with half the tentacles for 2 minutes, stirring, until the onion is translucent.

6 Add the rice and stir frequently for 2 minutes. Pour in the wine and reduce to nothing. Add a ladleful of simmering bouillon and stir constantly. Wait until it is absorbed, then add another ladleful. Repeat this procedure until the rice is cooked but still al dente.

7 Halfway through cooking, mix the cuttlefish ink into a ladleful of the bouillon and add to the risotto. Mix well.

8 Remove from the heat and gently stir in the thickening butter and parmesan. Season with salt and pepper.

9 Heat the olive oil in a frying pan over very high heat. Add the strips of squid hood and cook for 1 minute, until they curl slightly. Season with the salt and pepper.

10 Serve the risotto on a plate with the sautéed squid on top.

CHAPTER 3
ILLUSTRATED GLOSSARY

SERVING A SAUCE OR ACCOMPANIMENT

1 SERVING A SAUCE

A. IN A COMMA
With the spoon perpendicular to the plate, drop a dollop of sauce. Then, with the end of the spoon touching the plate, draw out the sauce to give it the shape of a slightly rounded comma.

B. IN A CIRCLE USING A FOOD RING
Pour the sauce in the middle of the ring, arrange the other elements of the recipe on top and remove the ring just before serving.

C. SIMPLE, USING A SPOON
Let the sauce run out as you move the spoon quickly across the plate. If the sauce is very runny, serve it in a small vessel on the side.

2 SERVING A PURÉE

A. USING A FOOD RING
Spread the purée in the middle of the ring, smooth the top with the back of a spoon and remove the ring.

B. IN QUENELLES
Soak two spoons in a bowl of hot water, take a little of the purée with one spoon, slide the bowl of the second spoon into the first, pushing the purée so that it ends up all on the second spoon. Repeat five to ten times, moving from spoon to spoon, to create a lovely quenelle. Moisten the spoons before starting each new quenelle.

C. SMEARED WITH A SPOON
Drop the purée from a spoon, then with the back of the spoon touching the plate, draw a line from the middle of the purée.

3 SERVING AN ACCOMPANIMENT

It must be visible but not dominate. Add the sauce, then the main dish, then the accompaniment.

A. IN A LINE
Arrange the accompaniment and the main element in two parallel lines.

B. IN A CURVE
Make the accompaniment follow the curve of the plate.

4 SERVING WITH A PIPING BAG

To sculpt soft elements and lend them elegance. Cut off the end of the piping bag and slide the nozzle inside. Crease the bag around it to hold it in place. Fill the bag with the mixture and twist the end of the bag closed, nozzle pointing upwards, until the mixture starts to come out. Hold the bag perpendicular to and above the plate, and push gently.

PLATING UP

THE PRINCIPLES OF COMPOSITION

Start by imagining the final plate. Perhaps draw it, to plan its composition better.

Use the whole plate without overloading it: plan for empty spaces.

Try to create combinations of textures, colours, heats, which will please the eye and the palate.

1 USING A FOOD RING

Traditional plate, clean and precise.

The ring allows soft preparations to be moulded (purées, thick sauces) giving them a clean form and height, or to serve recipes in a pile, sitting the different preparations that compose the dish on top of each other.

Fill the whole surface of the ring but not necessarily its whole volume. Pack it in using the back of a spoon, then remove the ring.

2 IN A LINE

Very modern plate, very white.

Draw a ribbon a few centimetres wide with the components of the dish, along the whole length of the plate, using a ruler or a piece of cardboard.

3 CREATING HEIGHT AND VOLUME

Generous and spectacular plate.

Pile up the differents elements of the dish. For example, a sauce moulded in a ring, a piece of fish and a crown of salad.

4 GRAPHIC

Geometric plate, refined.

Arrange the elements using the geometry of the plate. Compose clean forms and lines: half-moons (A), straight lines (B), a circle facing a straight line, and so on.

5 USING CONTRASTS

Contrast of colours: black olives on white fish.

Contrast of composition: an element with height (fish) versus an element spread out (brown prawns).

6 STRUCTURED OR UNSTRUCTURED

A. Structured: each element arranged on its own side.

B. Unstrucutured: disordered elements.

DECORATING

1 FLOWERS AND SPROUTS

Edible flowers (borage, pansy, nasturtium, etc.) or sprouts can be added to a dish to provide colour and freshness. To be used as small finishing touches, so as not to upset the balance of tastes in a plate. Arrange them carefully, using tweezers.

2 THIN FRIED FOOD

VITELOTTE POTATO CHIPS

Shave vitelottes or other blue–purple potatoes into thin slices 1 mm thick using a mandoline. Wash, dry and fry the slices for a few minutes in hot oil until dry, but not for too long (or they will brown). Season with salt.

LEEK CHIPS

Remove the overlapping leaves between the green and the white. Cut in fine julienne and fry for a few seconds in 2–3 cm of very hot oil. Season with salt.

FRIED PARSLEY

Fry flat (Italian) parsley leaves in 3 cm of very hot oil for a few seconds, until dry, but not too long (they darken quickly). Season with salt.

3 TUILES

PARMESAN

Heat a non-stick frying pan. Remove from the heat, place a food ring in the middle and sprinkle grated parmesan inside it. Remove the ring and return to the heat until the parmesan is melted and lightly golden. Remove from the heat, then carefully lift the tuile using a thin spatula.

BACON

Place thin slices of streaky bacon in a large frying pan. Sit a weight on top. Cook over medium heat for 3–4 minutes on each side.

BUCKWHEAT PANCAKES

Cut a circle from a pancake using a biscuit cutter. Brush with melted butter, then bake for 10 minutes at 180°C.

4 SALT AND PEPPER

Fleur de sel and freshly ground black pepper are the simplest ways to make a dish more appetising, and add texture and contrast to the composition of a plate.

5 ZESTS

Zester-grater: texture almost intangible in the mouth; light decorative element.

Zester: thicker and longer pieces of zest for more crunch and more obvious colour.

6 HERBS

Scattering aromatic minced herbs over a dish adds green tones.

DECORATING

THE PRINCIPLES OF DECORATION

The decorative elements should add elegance to a dish and give it depth and a note of sophistication. Moderation is the key; the dish itself must be respected and honoured.

1 DROPS

SYRUP

Reduce balsamic vinegar to a syrupy consistency. Let it cool. Arrange on a plate using a small spoon (let a drop run off without letting the spoon touch the plate) or a pipette.

PURÉE

Make a very smooth green bean or carrot purée and add using a piping bag with a small nozzle.

2 THINLY SLICED VEGETABLES

Cut very thin slices of vegetables using a mandoline then soak them for 10 minutes in an iced water bath to give them crunch and, depending on the vegetable, make them curl a little.

A. DECORATION USING HEIGHT

Gather the slices into a 'bouquet' between your hands then place on the plate.

B. FLAT DECORATION

Arrange the slices in a single plane, as for a carpaccio.

3 FOAM

Foam up a creamy cooking liquid (or another liquid containing a protein – egg white, gelatine or stock) in a high, narrow container using a hand-held blender. Place the foam on the dish (soup, nage, fish fillet, etc.) using a spoon.

PREPARING MEAT

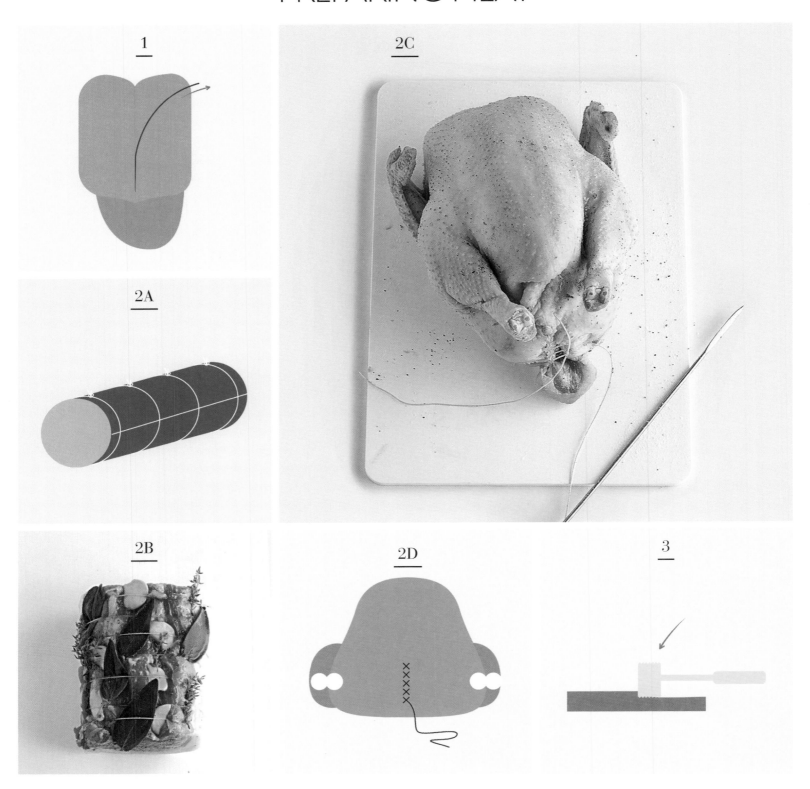

1 DEVEINING FOIE GRAS

Removing the veins from lobes of foie gras. Separate the large piece from the small and gently devein the liver with your fingers or with the rounded handle of a spoon. Open up each piece by cutting down the middle and separating the two cut edges. Remove the first vein at the surface. Remove the second, deeper vein, by carefully cutting the liver.

Deveining prevents the texture of the veins affecting the dish and allows removal of red filaments that will be visible even after cooking. It is not necessary to devein foie gras for pan-frying.

2 TYING AND TRUSSING

Holding the limbs of poultry in place (trussing) or tying up meat using a trussing needle and kitchen string allows neat presentation and uniform cooking.

Trussing poultry increases the cooking time by 25 per cent because the hot air penetrates the flesh more slowly. Stuffed poultry must be sewn up to prevent the stuffing falling out during cooking.

A. AND B. TYING A ROAST
Wind the string around every 2 cm. Wind the first piece of string under one end of the roast. Tie off the two ends securely with a double knot. Continue in this way the entire length of the roast.

C. AND D. TRUSSING STUFFED POULTRY
Thread a trussing needle with a length of kitchen string. Sew the opening shut tightly with crossed stitches. Tie off with a double knot.

3 FLATTENING MEAT

Using a meat tenderiser, a rolling pin or the bottom of a saucepan, hit the meat to flatten it uniformly and tenderise it by breaking some of the muscle fibres.

4 CATEGORIES OF MEAT

FIRST-CATEGORY MEATS

Tender pieces: scotch fillet or rib-eye steak, rump steak, eye fillet (fillet steak), ribs, skirt steak, hanger steak, sirloin steak, loin, topside and chump for veal; and chops and ribs for lamb.

Cooking style: short (pan-frying, grilling) so as not to dry out the meat.

SECOND- AND THIRD-CATEGORY MEATS

Firm pieces, rich in collagen (tendons): short ribs, brisket (thick rib), chuck tender, chuck roast, topside and chuck for beef; shoulder and chuck for veal; and shoulder for lamb.

Cooking style: long, to break down the collagen and tenderise the meat.

PREPARING FISH

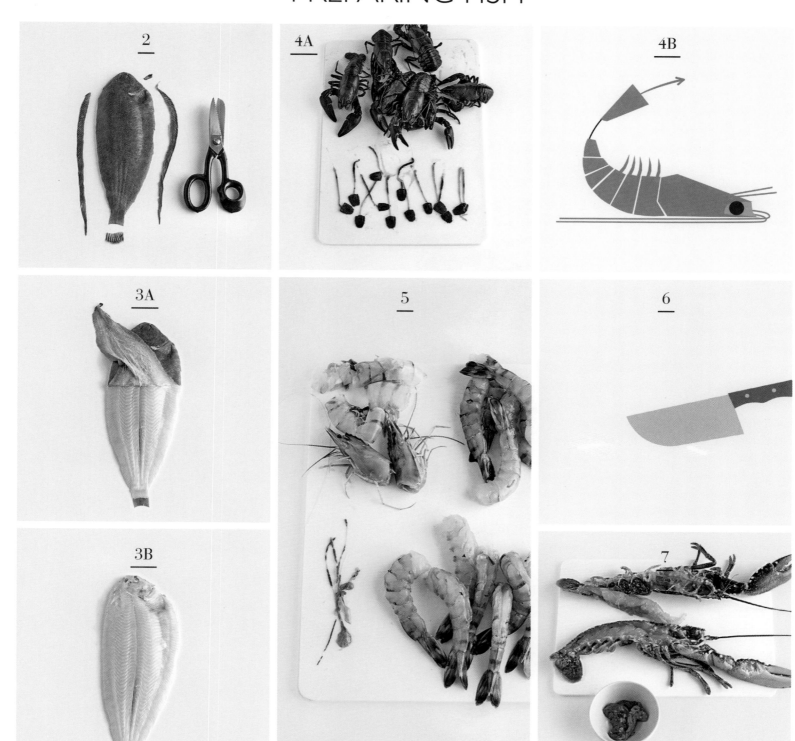

1 DRESSING

Preparing a fish (scaling, cutting off fins, gutting, etc.) or poultry (trimming, gutting, trussing, etc.) before cooking.

2 REMOVING FINS

Starting from the tail and working towards the head, remove all the fins using a strong pair of scissors.

3 SKINNING (MONKFISH, SOLE)

Tearing off the the skin. Using a knife, lift a sizeable piece of the skin by cutting between the skin and the flesh at the tail end. Hold the tail with one hand and pull the skin towards the head with the other. Discard the skin.

4 DEVEINING CRAYFISH

Removing the digestive tract of a crayfish.
A. and B. Place the crayfish on a work surface with one hand on the head and legs. Pull gently on the centre of the tail fin, twisting it left and right to pull out the digestive tract.

5 SHELLING

Remove the head of the prawn, remove the shell, then pull out the black digestive tract, cutting along the back with the point of a utility knife.

6 CRUSHING FISHBONES

Roughly chop the spine (and frame), cutting each bone into three or four pieces, depending on their size.

7 THE LOBSTER HEAD

This part of the lobster is also called the cephalothorax (the front part of a lobster). It contains the gravel pouch, the tomalley (liver) and a black digestive tract on each side. Perhaps reserve the tomally (creamy and greenish grey when raw, red when cooked), which can be used to thicken sauces.

CUTTING

1 MINCING

Herbs: make a pile of the leaves, roll them up tightly, then cut into thin strips.

French shallots: cut into very small dice.

2 CHOPPING FINELY (HERBS, GARLIC)

Chop into very small pieces using a chef's knife.

3 CRUSHING GARLIC

Crush a peeled garlic clove by pressing down firmly with the flat surface of a knife or a dough scraper.

4 SLICING THINLY

Cut a vegetable in thin slices.

5 PEELING CITRUS FOR SEGMENTS

Cut off the two ends of the citrus fruit to the flesh, which gives it a stable base. Peel the sides in an arc using a utility knife, starting from the top. Give the fruit a rounded shape, without leaving any trace of skin or pith.

6 CUTTING CITRUS SEGMENTS

Separate the segments from their dividing membranes using a very sharp utility knife.

7 PEELING TOMATOES

Remove the skin of tomatoes by plunging them into boiling water for a few seconds then refreshing them immediately in iced water. Or use a vegetable peeler made for soft fruits and vegetables.

8 ZESTING

Removing the fragrant peel of citrus fruits.

Zester-grater: zest almost intangible; light decoration.

Zester: thicker and longer pieces of zest for more crunch and more obvious colour.

9 CUTTING IN ESCALOPES

Cut slices diagonally.

10 CRUSHING SPICES

Place the seeds in a small frying pan and crush them with the bottom of a saucepan.

BASICS

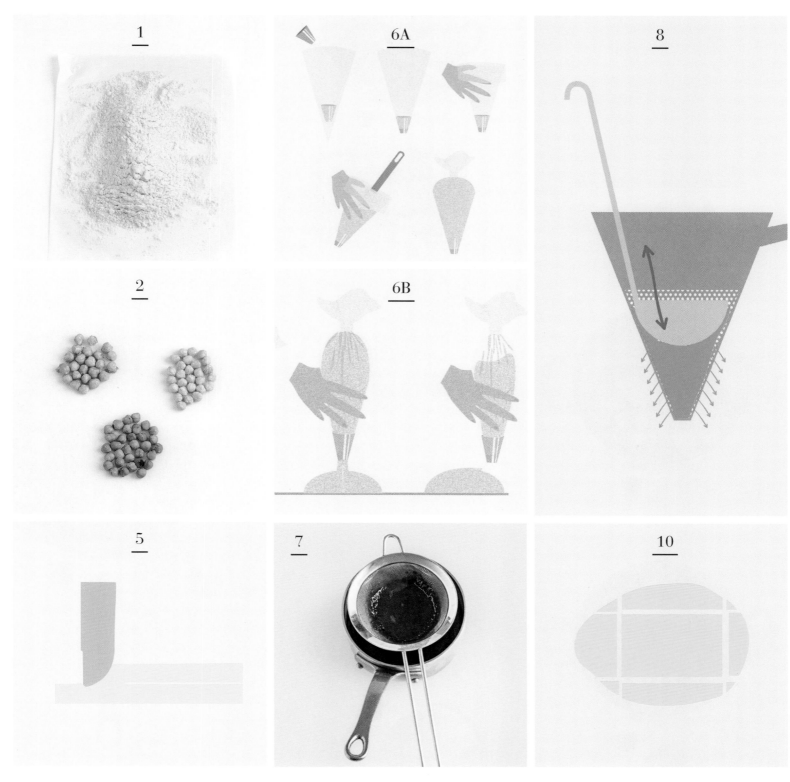

1 RUBBING IN BUTTER

Mix small pieces of butter into flour using the tips of your fingers. Coat each flour grain in butter until the colour is off-white and the texture is sandy.

2 TOASTING NUTS

Toast nuts in a dry frying pan over medium heat, stirring regularly, until they turn brown.

3 TOASTING FLOUR

Heat the flour in a dry frying pan over medium heat, stirring constantly.

Heat the flour sprinkled on top of a mixture with a sauce that you want to thicken, in a casserole dish, in a 180°C oven for 5–10 minutes, without stirring.

4 SCRAPING OUT

Carefully scrape the sides of the container using a dough scraper or silicone spatula to retrieve as much of the mixture as possible.

5 JOINING THE EDGES OF PASTRY

Brush the edges of the dough with water or glaze then press lightly between two fingers so that they stay together during cooking.

6 PIPING

Cut the end off the (disposable plastic) piping bag and slide in a nozzle. Crease the bag around it to hold it in place. Fill the bag with the mixture and twist the end of the bag closed, with the nozzle pointing upwards. Hold the bag perpendicular to the surface, 1 cm above it, and push. 'Cut' the mixture with a quarter-turn, staying as close to the plate as possible.

7 STRAINING THROUGH A SIEVE

Pour a mixture into a sieve to obtain the liquid and eliminate the inedible parts, or to make it smooth.

8 PUSHING THROUGH A SIEVE

Strain through a sieve while pushing hard with a ladle or spoon, to extract the maximum amount of liquid.

9 TOUCHING WITH PLASTIC WRAP

Place the plastic wrap so that it touches the surface of the mixture then press lightly to extract all the air. This preserves the food better.

10 TRIMMING

Give a regular shape to a food or mixture by removing the unpresentable or inedible parts.

COOKING

1

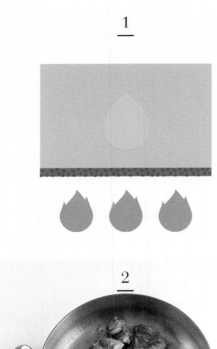

4

9

2

5

10

3

6

1 MAILLARD REACTIONS

Chemical reactions between the proteins and sugars in foods. These reactions occur as soon as there are no more water molecules at the surface (at 110–115°C). They manifest as browning and a powerful enrichment of the taste (aromatic roasted notes).

2 BROWNING

Gives colour to a food being cooked. Heat the chosen fat in the cooking vessel. Carefully pat the food dry with paper towel. Cook each side of the food until it browns. Work in several batches if necessary.

3 ADDING FLOUR TO STEWS

Sprinkle a stew with flour so that the sauce has thickened by the end of cooking.

4 DECANTING

Remove the pieces of food from the cooking vessel, leaving behind the sauce, using a skimmer or slotted spoon.

5 SWEATING

Extract water from a vegetable by heating it gently with a fat, avoiding any colouration.

6 STEAMING

Cook a vegetable slowly, covered, in its own water, with a little butter or water.

7 FLAMBÉING

Douse a boiling preparation with alcohol and, still over the heat, set it alight by bringing a flame close. Let the flame go out naturally.

8 USING A THERMOMETER

To watch the core temperature of a food during cooking, insert a thermometer, making sure it passes through the middle of the food and doesn't touch a bone.

9 THICKENING

Give body to a liquid by adding a thickening element (flour at the beginning of cooking, potato flour or egg yolk at the end).

10 WHISKING IN BUTTER

Incorporating butter into a sauce to increase its volume and creaminess. Cut cold butter in dice and add gradually over medium heat while whisking or swirling the saucepan. Wait for the first pieces to be incorporated before adding the next.

COOKING

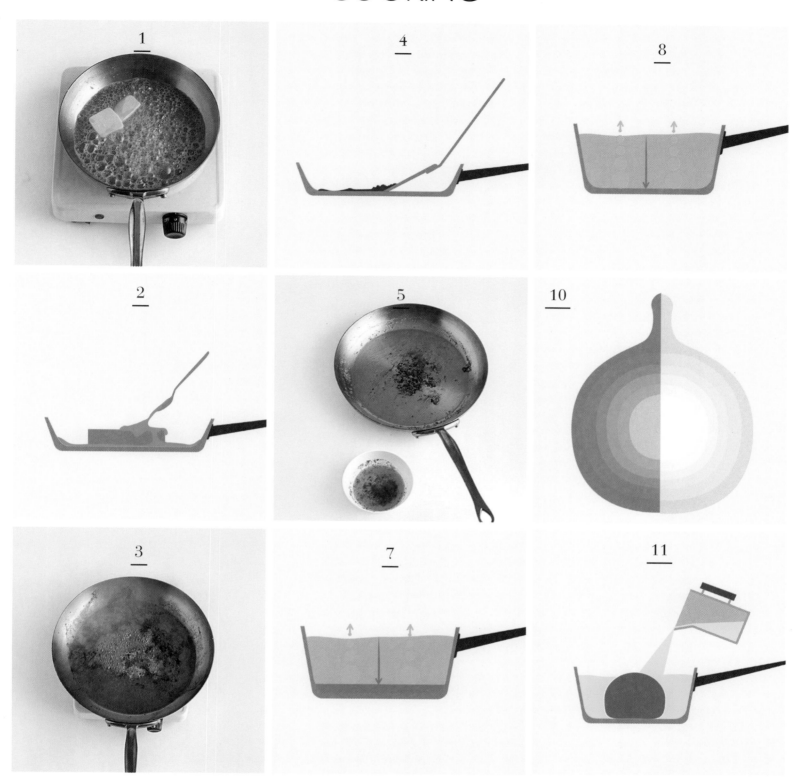

1 FOAMING BUTTER

Melted butter that, under the effect of the heat, releases foam: the micro-droplets of water dispersed in the fat transform into steam, which creates bubbles, and thus foam. It can baste a food during cooking and enrich it.

2 BASTING

Pouring a food's own grease or some melted butter over it to prevent it drying out. Use a spoon or a turkey baster. Baste as regularly as possible.

3 DEGLAZING

Liquefying caramelised pieces stuck to the bottom of a cooking vessel. If the vessel is hot, add a cold liquid (water, stock, wine), bring to the boil and scrape off the pieces with a spatula. If the vessel is cold, off the heat, pour in boiling water then scrape the bottom.

4 SCRAPING OFF STUCK-ON BITS

Gently scratch at the bottom of the cooking vessel with a flat spatula.

5 DEGREASING A FRYING PAN

Remove the excess grease by tipping the pan over a bowl so that it runs out.

6 DEGREASING A BOUILLON

Using a spoon, remove the fat that floats to the surface of a liquid preparation. If the preparation is cold, the grease will congeal and is thus easier to remove.

7 REDUCING A SAUCE

Concentrate a sauce by simmering to evaporate some of its water.

8 REDUCING TO NOTHING

Bring a liquid (water, wine, another type of alcohol) to the boil and let it evaporate completely (until dry).

9 SKIMMING

Using a skimmer, remove the foam or scum that forms on the surface of a liquid.

10 BROWN AND WHITE METHODS

The degree of colouration of a food being browned. *À blanc* (white): no colouration at all, just increased firmness. *À brun* (brown): the food turns brown.

11 COOKING LIQUID

Liquid (stock, wine, water) added to a preparation to allow it to cook.

UTENSILS

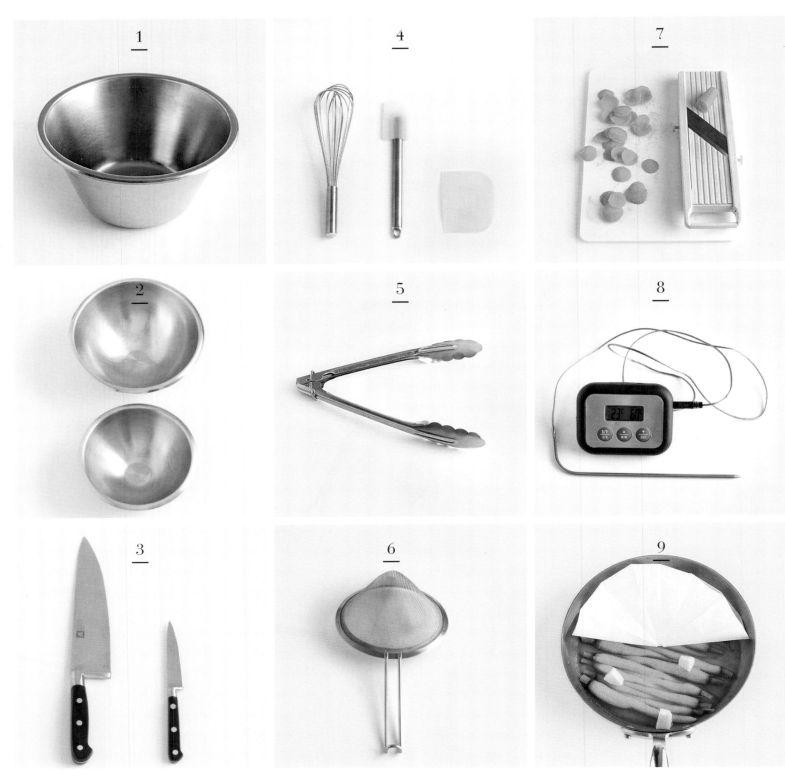

1 FLAT-BOTTOMED BOWL

Stainless-steel bowl with a flat, stable base. For discarding or reserving foods and washing vegetables.

2 ROUND-BOTTOMED BOWL

Half-spherical bowl for preparing mixtures. Often used for whisking egg whites to stiff peaks without any corners being missed.

3 CHEF'S AND UTILITY KNIVES

Chef's knife: thick blade 25–30 cm long, with a heel. The heel provides extra force for breaking up hard items (e.g. fishbones). Also used for cutting raw meats and chopping finely.

Utility knife: blade 7–11 cm long, thin tip. Multiple uses.

4 WHISK, SILICONE SPATULA, DOUGH SCRAPER

Dough scraper: half-moon-shaped, semi-flexible plastic utensil used for scraping cooking vessels and work surfaces.

Silicone spatula: flexible spatula. Whisk: stirring utensil.

5 TONGS

Allows delicate handling of foods during cooking.

6 SIEVE

Conical utensil used to filter preparations. Types include: the classic *chinois*, with rigid, small holes; and the *chinois étamine*, with very fine mesh that retains very small particles. It can sometimes be replaced with a fine-mesh sieve.

7 MANDOLINE

Cutting tool: for thin slices, julienne, gaufrettes (waffle chips), crisps, etc. Pass the food over the blade in a quick, clean movement, pushing down and using the protective guard or a cut-resistant glove.

8 THERMOMETER WITH PROBE

Tool that allows control of the temperature of an oven (thermometer and probe), a foodstuff (probe only) and frying oil (thermometer and probe), indispensable in the latter case, unless you use an electric deep-fryer. Watch that the thermometer or the probe never touches the bottom of the cooking vessel.

UTENSILS

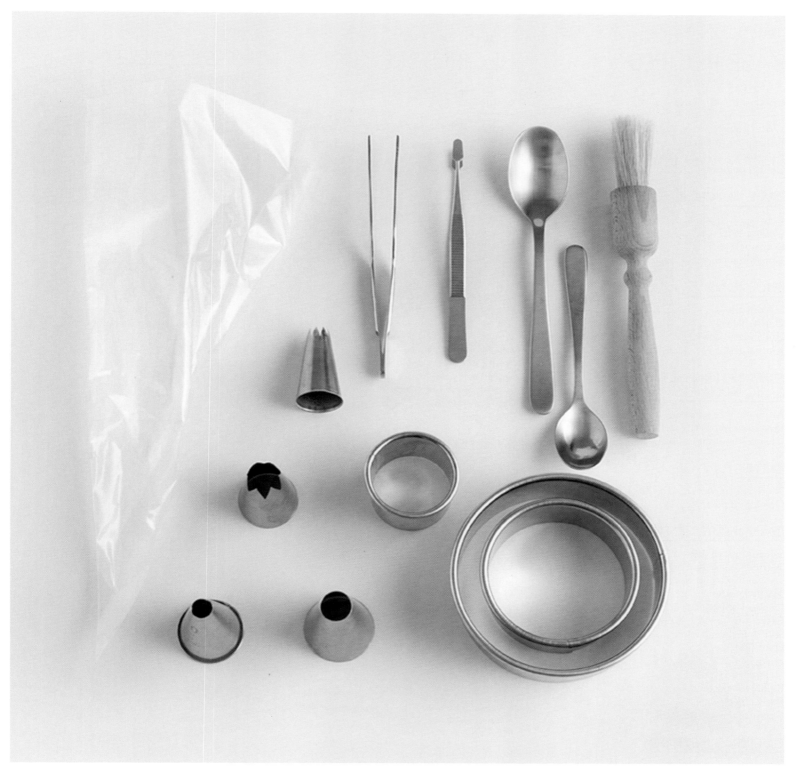

9 BAKING PAPER DISC

Prevents foods drying out or browning, while
also allowing evaporation, thanks to a vent cut
in the middle.

Cut a square of baking paper larger than the frying
pan. Fold the sheet in half, then in half again to get
a square. Fold on the diagonal, folding through the
twice-folded centre. You will have a right-angled
triangle. Keeping the thrice-folded corner as the tip
of your triangle, fold the right-angle side along the
longest side, then repeat twice more. You will have
a very thin triangle.

Place the point of the triangle at the centre of the pan
and cut off the overhang. Unfold the sheet and you
will have a disc.

To make a vent, cut a few millimetres off the tip of the
triangle before unfolding.

STOVETOP TEMPERATURES

The stovetop temperature indications in this book are
on a rising scale of strength: very low, low, medium,
high, very high.

These indications correspond to induction stovetops,
which often allow high and low temperatures above
and below those possible with a gas, electric or
ceramic stovetop. If you have a gas stovetop, perhaps
use a bain-marie for those recipes that require 'very
low', and plan for a longer cooking time for 'very
high' if you have an electric hotplate or a ceramic
stovetop. Also anticipate the reaction time of your
stovetop: hotplates don't change from hot to medium
instantaneously (unlike gas or induction stovetops)
so prepare two hotplates at different temperatures
if the recipe requires you to move from one to the
other quickly.

SERVING UTENSILS

Piping bag, nozzles, pastry brush for adding shine,
food rings of various sizes, spoons, tweezers to handle
elements carefully or remove unwanted items from
a plate.

POTS AND PANS

Saucepan or sauteuse pan:
Small: 14 cm; medium: 16–18 cm; large: 20–22 cm

Frying pan or sautoir pan:
Small: 20 cm; medium: 22 cm; large: 26 cm

Oval casserole dish:
Medium: 22 cm; large: 30 cm

Sauteuse pan: sauté pan with flared sides, which allows
simple stirring of the ingredients.

Sautoir pan: sauté pan with straight and low sides,
which allows sautéing of foods then cooking with a lid.

RECIPE INDEX

INGREDIENTS INDEX

MARIANNE'S ACKNOWLEDGEMENTS

Immense thanks to Emmanuel Vallois, Rosemarie di Domenico and
Pauline Labrousse for entrusting me with this project.
Thanks also to the passionate cooking team with whom I had the pleasure of writing this book.
More particularly, I would like to thank:
Pauline Labrousse for conceiving this immense project and organising it with her legendary gentleness.
Pierre Javelle for his wonderful photos and arrangements of
ingredients, always created with good humour.
Orathay Souksisavanh for her elegant styling but also because she is a walking encyclopaedia
of cooking and she generously shared her knowledge with me throughout the shoot.
Audrey Génin, who corrected my text while enriching it with her own knowledge of cooking.
Yannis Varoutsikos (illustrator) and Anne Cazor (food technologist),
who did me the honour of creating this book with me.
And thanks to Agathe's dad, 'Didier the Hunter', who found in his stores
what we needed to prepare venison steaks out of hunting season!

ANNE'S ACKNOWLEDGEMENTS

Thanks to the whole team who contributed to the creation of this work.

YANNIS'S ACKNOWLEDGEMENTS

I knew I should have listened to my grandmothers!
Luckily, my parents knew how to pass on a taste for good food
and good recipes accompanied with all their practical tips.
I hope my little Clémentine will also develop a taste for good food and good recipes.
For Granny Vonnette's delicious ravioli and pesto soup, and Granny Claude's incredible roasts.
And thanks to the team at Marabout for all their good advice.

Published in 2016 by Hardie Grant Books, an imprint of Hardie Grant Publishing
First published in French by Hachette Livre (Marabout) in 2015

Hardie Grant Books (Melbourne)
Ground Floor, Building 1
658 Church Street
Richmond, Victoria 3121
www.hardiegrant.com.au

Hardie Grant Books (London)
5th & 6th Floors
52-54 Southwark Street
London SE1 1UN
www.hardiegrant.co.uk

A Cataloguing-in-Publication entry is available from the catalogue
of the National Library of Australia at www.nla.gov.au

The Ultimate Cook's Manual
ISBN 978 1 74379 251 3

Designer: Yannis Varoutsikos
Styling: Orathay Souksisavanh
French editors: Audrey Genin, Émilie Collet and Veronique Dussidour
Translator: Nicola Young
English editors: Anna Collett, Lucy Heaver, Pamela Dunne

Colour reproduction by Splitting Image Colour Studio
Printed and bound in China by 1010 Printing International Limited